Inchicore, Kilmainham and District

Seosamh Ó Broin

Cois Camóige Publications
1999

Published by Cois Camóige Publications
46 Tyrconnell Park, Inchicore, Dublin 8.

A catalogue record for this title is available from the British Library.

ISBN 0-9535929-0-1

Typeset by Carole Lynch and cover design by Identikit.
Printed in Ireland by ColourBooks, Dublin.

Dedicated to my parents, John and Margaret Byrne,
who helped to pass on traditions of Community and Country

CONTENTS

Chapter One

From Earliest Times

The Dawn of History

The district of Inchicore/Kilmainham, bounded by the river Liffey and the Grand Canal and which also has the little Camac flowing through it, lies about three miles west of the city centre. Being largely a built-up area by now, it does not have any visible pre-historic monuments but is encircled by an outer ring of such reminders of earliest times.

Firstly, it is overlooked as indeed is much of west Dublin by the Dublin hills, on the crests of which are many pre-historic burial cairns. On a clear day, looking towards the south-west from the 3rd Lock Bridge, can be seen the bare outline of one of these cairns dating to at least 3000 BC on the top of Seefin mountain. Then, nearer to hand, numerous bronze-age vessels have been discovered in the districts of Greenhills and Crumlin.

Closer still, just off the Long Mile Road and not too far from Drimnagh Castle, was situated the mound known to generations of people as "The Grand Parlour". This tumulus was a prominent landmark from the top of which a magnificent view of the surrounding countryside could be obtained. It had remained unmolested over the centuries because of the old Irish belief that a place such as this was under the care of the "Good People". In local folklore a story was told up to the early part of this century of a farmer, on whose land the tumulus stood, who contemplated its removal at one time. However, his employees refused to touch it and when he himself undertook the task the horses he was using broke their legs.

The cairn on Seefin Mountain

Such beliefs were on the wane in 1938 when the tumulus was in

The 3500 BC pottery bowl found at this tumulus off the Long Mile road

imminent danger of being swept away during extensive sand and gravel quarrying nearby. However, the Clondalkin historian and member of the clerical staff of the Inchicore Railway Works, Liam Ua Broin, succeeded in persuading the appropriate authorities to have it scientifically excavated before its demise. The investigations disclosed that it was a mound within a mound having been used as a cremation burial place at two separate periods of time in both the Neolithic and early Bronze Ages. Among the contents discovered were a burial urn, food vessel, animal bones, flint scraper and a highly decorated pottery bowl. The latter, which relates to the earlier use of the tumulus is dated to 3500 BC and is on public display at the National Museum.

Today there is nothing whatsoever to indicate the site of this mound which is in a public park. Let us hope that it will be possible at some stage to provide a suitable memorial and information plaque to mark what is one of the most important pre-historic sites within the city bounds.

A comparatively short distance away from the site of this double tumulus, there is still in existence at Ballymount a further large mound. Limited archaeological investigation, including aerial photography, has taken place nearby and shows evidence of early habitation. When further work takes place on the mound itself it will add immensely to our knowledge of those early times. Again in the same direction several raths or ring forts at Belgard and Kilbride, opposite Baldonnel Aerodrome, are dated to the early Christian period.

The pre-historic mound at Ballymount

Further west of our own area, three fine burial urns were discovered at Palmerstown while the antiquarian Austin Cooper noted the presence of a rath or mound at Lower Ballyfermot in 1781. This mound was only a short distance beyond Ballyfermot Castle on the Chapelizod/Fox and Geese Road and is remembered as late as 1946 just before road and housing developments took place in the area. There being nobody to point out its significance it was swept away and its unmarked site, like the Drimnagh tumulus, is also part of a large public park. Possibly future excavation here might still yield some results.

Again, like its Drimnagh counterpart, this Ballyfermot rath had its own folklore as Benny Connolly told me very recently. Benny, who was born in Ballyfermot Lane near the graveyard, is one of the very few original inhabitants still living in the area. He remembered the feature in question and, perhaps more importantly, the field known as "The Lawn" near where it was situated. He told me that the older people used to be in awe of this field because of the belief that if you were not careful you could go astray in it and not be able to find your way out. He himself often walked across it in a straight line and never had any trouble. However, his mother lost her way in it nearly losing her mind and when she did get out she passed by her own house and finally only recognised it by its chimney. It is remarkable that a story such as this with its roots in our pre-Christian past should survive to within living memory almost on the threshold of the city.

Immediately across the Liffey, near Saint Mary's Hospital in the Phoenix Park, can still be seen the Knockmary Cromlech. Excavation here disclosed a central stone chamber containing early bronze-age burial artefacts.

It is hard not to imagine that those earliest Irish inhabitants who have left so many such reminders of their presence nearby did not also have settlements in our own district as well, particularly with the attraction of the two rivers. One possible location exists on the site of Inchicore House where the first map of the area indicated a small tower-like building in 1655. It was customary for the Anglo-Norman colonists to build their castles such as Drimnagh, Ballymount, Belgard and Ballyfermot near some of the pre-historic sites we have mentioned, suggesting a continuity of use by different sets of inhabitants over many thousands of years. For this reason the small building shown in 1655 may possibly have been preceded by a much earlier habitation and there is also the consideration that it occupied a very commanding position overlooking the river Liffey. The site in question is preserved by the Office of Public Works.

SAINT MAIGHNEANN

The earliest historical reference to the district occurs in the *Leabhar Breac,* which tells us that Saint Maighneann was visited at Kilmainham by Saint Fursa, who was making an itinerary of Irish Monasteries between 627 and 637. Kilmainham is next mentioned in 782, when the death occurred there of Feargus Ua Fidhchain, described as a "wise man of Kilmainham".

Our knowledge of the area is limited to the fact that within the province of Leinster it formed part of the sub-kingdom of Ua Dunchada, whose seat was at Lyons near Newcastle, County Dublin, and whose territory extended as far as the Liffey. This name was also associated with Carnan Cloch Ui Dhunchada which was close to Dolphin's Barn. The ruling family of the sept was the MacGiolla Mocholmog.

As the monastery at Kilmainham bears his name, we must assume that it was founded by Maighneann, of whom we only know that he was the son of Aedh, a Prince of Oriel in County Louth. The next reference to our local saint occurs in the Calendar of Aengus, which was compiled in the Monastery of Tallaght in the ninth century. In this ancient calendar of the saints of Ireland, two lines in rhyme are given for each day of the year and in these lines is the name of the saint commemorated on that particular day. December 18th was designated as the feast day of Saint Maighneann, who was honoured in the calendar with the lines:

Morgrian inna clandsa,	The great sun of these clans
Magniu maith am mindsa	Maigniu good his treasure

There is no contemporary life of the saint, but an Irish manuscript of the thirteenth century contains an extensive account of the many legends associated with him. This manuscript conveys a life of prayer and austerity and tells us that "From Shannon to Beann Eadair Maighneann was a tower of piety and in his own time a vessel of sanctity". It then goes on to relate in detail the numerous legends attributed to him and his many journeys throughout the length and breadth of Ireland, visiting his fellow abbots. One of the legends in this manuscript is later repeated in the *Annals of the Four Masters,* as follows:

> (December 18.) Maighnenn, Bishop and Abbot, of Cil-Maighnenn, near Áth-Cliath. He was of the race of Colla-da-crioch. He had a ram which used to carry his psalter and his prayer-book. There came a certain robber and thief, and stole the ram. Maighnenn, with his thrice nine clerics, went after the robber to his house. The robber denied having stolen the ram by oath on the relics, and on the hand of Maighnenn himself. The ram was cut up in quarters in a hole in the ground, after the robber had eaten some of it. The ram spoke below in the hole. Maighnenn and his thrice nine persons looked up to heaven and gave thanks to God for this miracle. But the robber was

deprived of his eyesight, and their strength left his feet and his hands, and he said in a loud voice "For God's sake, Maighnenn, do not deprive me of the light of heaven for the future." When Maighnenn heard the repentance of the sinner, he prayed fervently to God for him, and he recovered his eyesight again, and he was eminent in religion as long as he lived.

That the Saint's name and reputation were remembered in this manuscript nearly 600 years after his lifetime is an indication of his importance and influence in the early Irish church. His name also survived through the later Anglo-Norman period to enter English public records in 1611. In that year the *Patent Rolls of King James I* refer to "Mainhames Bush" as a land boundary in what is now the Phoenix Park, something which also suggests that the monastic lands stretched across to the other side of the River Liffey.

The Monastry of Kilmainham

Kilmainham was one of a cluster of important monasteries in west Dublin such as Tallaght, Clondalkin and Kilnamanagh, with possibly smaller churches at Bluebell/Killeen and Ballyfermot. Also across the river in the Phoenix Park was another small church known as Cell-Mo-Shamhog, but what its connection, if any, with Kilmainham was we do not know. However, it was important enough to give its name in an anglicised form to that vital crossing of the Liffey near Islandbridge which was known as the Ford of Kilmohavoc.

The monastery of Kilmainham itself was situated at a choice location on the high ground between the Liffey and the Camac with the Dublin/Wicklow mountains on the southern horizon and the Hill of Howth in the distance to the north east.

This monastery, like so many others of its kind, did not leave any visible trace of its presence over several centuries. In the early Christian period a monastic settlement was usually a large circular enclosure bounded by another bank or ditch. Within the inner enclosure was the oratory made from oak beams with a cemetery nearby and then the scattered wattle huts of the monks. The outer space was reserved for the everyday activities of the community which was self-supporting and included food production, bee-keeping, craftsmanship and metalwork. Fish weirs were established on the Liffey while a corn mill was powered by the fast-flowing waters of the Camac. Other features were An Prointeach (Refectory), an Teach Mór and Guest House.

These monasteries were the nearest approach to a town in what was otherwise a pastoral/wooded landscape and it was from such early beginnings that the later village of Old Kilmainham evolved. Of significance also was the fact that the monastery was alongside An tSlí Mhór, one of the ancient roads of Ireland over which monks, warriors and itinerant bards travelled either on foot, on horseback or by chariot. This road connected the early Irish settlement of Baile Átha Cliath with

The granite shaft in Bully's Acre

The Kilmainham brooch

the west coast and passed along James's Street, Inchicore Road and Sarsfield Road. The other ancient road to the south at that time, Slí Dala, did not pass through Kilmainham but rather through Dolphins Barn and the Crumlin Road.

The only surviving ancient monument in the entire Inchicore/Kilmainham district is the decorated granite shaft in the burial ground known as Bully's Acre. This was the original monastic cemetery near which the monastic settlement itself was situated. In popular tradition the shaft was associated with the grave of Brian Ború, but there is no foundation for this. Dating from the ninth century, its origin and that of its decorations are unknown, but it was probably the upright of a cross. It was customary to mark the grave of the founder of a monastery with a cross or pillar and, although later than Maighneann's period of office, this may have been its origin. Another possibility, for which there are precedents elsewhere, is that it marked the entrance to the monastery.

The only artifact to survive from the early Christian period is the beautiful little Kilmainham Brooch. Nothing is known of its origin except that it was found in the Kilmainham area when the first railway line was being excavated in 1845. It dates from AD 800 and is now one of the treasures of Ireland in the National Museum. Also discovered during the railway excavations was a bronze bell twelve-and-a-half inches in height. It too is on view at the museum, while a replica by the Kilmainham Art Foundry can be seen in Saint Michael's Church. The bell is dated to between the ninth and twelfth centuries and is more likely to relate to the pre Anglo-Norman period.

> "The Irish monastery of the 6th or 7th century as described was not greatly imposing in appearance. Yet this was the milieu which produced that most remarkable spiritual, intellectual and artistic movement of Dark Age Europe, the Celtic Church."

It is a source of pride that Maighneann's monastery which was an integral part of that great era of saints and scholars is an important element in our local heritage.

The Kilmainham bell

Chapter Two

The Viking Connection

Burial Place

Inchicore, Kilmainham and Islandbridge have a unique historical association with the Viking era. These pirate/traders first appeared off the Irish coast in 795 and continued to raid sporadically up to 830. From then on they succeeded in establishing several temporary bases on the east coast from where they could prey inland on the country and it was during this period that they plundered local monasteries such as Kilmainham. By 841 they were able to set up a more permanent base and settlement in the Dublin area at a location which is still the subject of debate. It was referred to as "Longphort Duibhlinn" in the Irish annals, a longphort being a defended enclosure to protect ships.

This first wave of Vikings buried their dead in ceremonial fashion, complete with weapons or household goods, in the area on the south side of the Liffey between Heuston Station and the western boundary of the Memorial Park at Inchicore. This is of more than parochial interest, being the largest Viking burial place outside Scandinavia, and it was here that the greatest quantity of their weapons was found.

The extensive and scattered burial area dates from 850 and indicates that these hardy men from Northern Europe had by then obtained control of a large portion of Dublin, including our own district.

The first hint of a Viking association comes with the discovery of Viking coins and a sword at Bully's Acre when the granite shaft there was being re-erected about 1800 following its collapse. However, it was in 1836 during gravel quarrying to the rear of Islandbridge Barracks that a Viking burial was first recognised. This part of Dublin, being well outside the built up area of the city, lay undisturbed for centuries until the construction of the Great Southern Railway in 1846. It was then that a large number of discoveries, mainly swords and iron tools, were made adjacent to Heuston Station, then known as the Cashel Terminus, and in the cuttings between there and Inchicore. For the laying of the railway tracks a huge quantity of earth had to be removed over a distance of one mile and unfortunately many other items were lost at that time. What was recovered was not scientifically excavated and neither were any of the precise locations recorded.

These discoveries attracted the attention of the Danish scholar Jens Worsaae, who visited Dublin a year later and confirmed that the items found were indeed of Scandinavian origin.

Sir William Wilde

However, it was in 1866 that the greatest bulk of Viking material was discovered in a newly-opened sand-pit from which road building material for the city was being drawn. It was the antiquarian, Sir William Wilde, father of Oscar Wilde, who drew the attention of the Royal Society of Antiquaries of Ireland to this historic find. Subsequently in a paper to that body he gave an account of "The antiquaries of Scandinavian origin lately found in the fields sloping down from the ridge of Inchicore to the Liffey and to the South West of the village of Islandbridge outside the boundary of the City of Dublin".

The ridge in question follows the line of Inchicore Road while the then city boundary followed the line of the South Circular Road to Islandbridge. It is believed that the sand-pit mentioned was located below the railway line near the site of the present Saint John of God's Day Centre and only a short distance across the road from that still more ancient burial place known as Bully's Acre.

In addition to skeletons, about seventy-eight items in all were found in the sand-pit, including five swords, a decorated sword-handle, six spear heads, four shield bosses, metal helmet crest, miniature battle axe, knife blades, as well as many household effects. The latter included two pairs of scales with richly decorated weights, knives, sickles, hammers and sharpening stones. We do not know whether these items were part of a funeral rite or an indication of a local habitation. Also discovered were personal items such as mantle pins, jewelled studs, glass beads and four pairs of bronze tortoise-shaped brooches of exquisite workmanship, the latter finds indicating female burials.

As a major Irish/Viking engagement had taken place not far away at Islandbridge, it was believed at the time these were battle-field burials, but this was later ruled out.

War Memorial Park

These important discoveries of 1866 were by no means the end of the story, for further dramatic finds came to light in

Viking sword hilt found 1866 in sand pit near the Saint John of God Centre

Viking sword hilt found 1866 in sand pit near the Saint John of God Centre

1933 and 1934 when the 1914 War Memorial Park, since known locally as the New Park, was being excavated. It is indeed ironic that the place selected for a war memorial should in fact have been the site of warrior burials many centuries earlier. Here, workmen digging out the sunken gardens in the Inchicore end of the park and only a few hundred yards from the Liffey, unearthed five separate grave sites.

In one of these, a double-edged sword carried the inscription ULFBHRT on its blade. In a further grave a sword with bronze plaiting on its pommel, a spearhead and axe were found in addition to four nails and two iron handles.

However, perhaps the most interesting site was that which contained a complete double-edged sword ritually broken in three parts, two iron daggers and a skeleton lying from south to north. It was found possible to remove the latter with the accompanying

Two bronze tortoise brooches found 1866 in sand pit near the Saint John of God Centre

weapons to the National Museum where they have been on public exhibition ever since. This was a most delicate engineering feat involving Museum staff with the assistance of Ordnance Survey Officer Capt. Nolan and UCD's Dr MacLoughlin.

Apart from the finds mentioned, an examination of the sites showed that some of them had also been used as burial places in the pre-Viking era. All five sites were in the townland of Inchicore North rather than Islandbridge as sometimes stated.

In 1989 during an archaeological excavation prior to the widening of the Con Colbert Road, a small but significant number of Viking artefacts was found in one of four ancient refuse pits by that veteran of many a "dig", Mr Paddy Healy. This site is only a short distance inside the Memorial Park and parallel to the Con Colbert Road, the Railway Line and Inchicore Road. The items found were a decorated bronze mount, a bone pin and cut antler, and gave rise to the possibility of further discoveries in the future.

A Local Viking Settlement?

As the Irish annals had consistently associated the longphort with Áth Cliath and Dubhlinn, which were the earlier Gaelic settlements near Christ Church, it was always assumed that it was situated at that location. However, when some years ago the excavations at nearby Wood Quay did not reveal any trace of the longphort there, the view was put forward that it might have been located elsewhere. As nearly all the finds at the burial places in Islandbridge, Kilmainham and Inchicore are contemporary with the longphort era, it has been suggested that the longphort settlement itself was also situated somewhere in this area.

The previous settlement here had been the monastery of Saint Maighneann and it was between that and the Liffey that the burials were made. It is argued that following their practice elsewhere of taking over plundered monasteries for their own occupation, the Vikings may have done likewise at Kilmainham. Also the confluence of the Camac and the Liffey nearby made a beaching point for their ships, while the fact that the monastery was on the route of the Slí Mhór to the west would have been an added advantage.

Some miles outside Stockholm on an inlet of the sea, an excavated Viking longphort took the form of an earthen bank on a ridge surrounded by a wooden stockade and with a burial mound not too far away. The Kilmainham terrain would meet this criterion but as already stated the Irish annals never mentioned Longphort Chill Mhaigneann and instead referred to Longphort, Átha Cliath or Dubhlinn.

However, it would not seem unreasonable to speculate that there was at least a subsidiary Viking habitation in the area. Perhaps this could be inferred also from the remarks of Mr Liam Gogan of the National Museum shortly after the 1934 Memorial Park excavations in which he had taken part. He was of the view that the main Viking citadel was situated on the prominence occupied by Christ Church and that

Viking weapons from Memorial Park, 1933

their garths (homesteads) and villages extended along the same ridge by Kilmainham, Inchicore and Islandbridge to Chapelizod and even to Clondalkin where they had a further base known to the Irish as Dún Amhlaoibh. He added that it was along this line that the major number of objects were discovered.

Another pointer to a local Viking presence may be the Irish-Viking place name Baile Formaid, originally Baile Thormaid and later anglicised as Ballyfermot. Perhaps it would be too fanciful to suggest further that this referred to the Viking pagan god, Thor.

For a definitive answer to the matter, we must await the results of further scholarship and archaeological investigation.

The longphort settlement lasted until 902, when the Irish drove out the Vikings. However, they returned fifteen years later in 917 and were able to establish themselves permanently. On this occasion, there was no doubt as to the location of their principal stronghold, which was on the site of Christ Church and Dublin Castle. Under their stewardship, this was to develop into a real town and major trading centre which later on would become the City of Dublin. Our own area was once more within the Viking sphere of influence and became part of their "Kingdom of Dyflinnarskiri", which on the west side extended out to Leixlip.

Death of a High King

The district has a further association with the era in question. In 919, a determined effort was made to prevent a Viking resurgence in Ireland. In that year the Árd-Rí, Niall Glún Dubh, raised a national force and engaged the foreigners under their leader Sitric at the Ford of Kilmahanok on the Liffey near Islandbridge. Not only were the Irish decisively defeated in this critical battle, but the High King himself was killed there as well.

For many decades constant conflict was to ensue involving not only Gael against Gall, but varying alliances of Gael and foreigners against other Gaelic factions. Our district was to witness the passing of the fighting men of many of these elements through its woods and meadows and along the Liffey and An tSlí Mhór.

In the meantime, the Vikings had begun to espouse Christianity and a process of assimilation with the Irish had commenced.

Towards the end of the century, Malachy of Meath was able to besiege Dublin successfully on three occasions and to exact heavy tributes from the inhabitants.

Then in 1012, the *Annals of the Four Masters* tell us that Murchadh, son of BrianBorú, plundered the country as far as Glendalough and Kilmainham, burning the whole country and carrying off many prisoners. This scorched earth campaign was directed as much against the province of Leinster as against the Vikings.

We again saw an invading force in the area with the arrival of the High King, BrianBorú, at Kilmainham in the autumn of 1013. From here he laid siege to Dublin town, but with the advent of winter was forced to return home. However, he returned to the fray in April 1014 and on the battle-eve of Clontarf, encamped once more with his Dalcassin army at Kilmainham. Following their famous victory over both Vikings and Leinster men on Good Friday, this army which had borne the brunt of the fighting passed back through Kilmainham – this time without their fallen chieftain Brian – on their way home to Kincora.

Tradition has it that his son, Murchadh, and grandson, Turlough, both of whom were also killed at Clontarf, were laid to rest under the granite shaft in Bully's Acre.

Chapter Three

When the Anglo-Normans Came

Knights Hospitallers

Less than 200 years after the cessation of Irish-Viking hostilities, our district was to see the arrival of a new set of invaders. These were the Anglo-Normans who, having landed in Wexford, went on to capture Dublin in 1170. In turn they were besieged by the last High King, Ruairi O'Connor, together with his other Irish allies. One of these, Ua Briain of Thomond, in the tradition of Brian Ború took up position with his army as part of the besieging force at Kilmainham. The siege went on for two months while peace negotiations were conducted by the Archbishop of Dublin, Saint Lorcán Ó Tuathail. However when these failed the Anglo-Norman knights in a surprise move broke through the Irish lines on the other side of the city and put them to flight in what proved to be one of the decisive battles of Irish history.

The new invaders now had full control of Dublin and the surrounding areas. Within four years, in 1174, they built near the site of Saint Maighnean's old monastery the fortified Priory of Kilmainham and it was here that Strongbow established the Knights Hospitallers of Saint John of Jerusalem. These were an order of clerics and soldiers, veterans of the Crusades, who had accompanied the Norman leader on his Irish adventure. In addition he bestowed on them a large tract of land stretching for about three miles from Heuston Station to Palmerstown and including much of the lands of Inchicore and Ballyfermot. A short time later they were also given the lands on the opposite bank of the Liffey, which is now the Phoenix Park, by Hugh Tyrrell, Baron of Castleknock. The Anglo-Normans did not seek to exterminate the Irish but allowed some to remain as workers while the rest they moved on to the poorer and more marginal land.

The site for the combined priory and fortress at Kilmainham was carefully chosen from a military point of view. It occupied an elevated position on the sandy ridge between the Liffey and Camac, both of which run parallel to each other for about a mile before they meet near Heuston Station. There was also the consideration that Dublin Castle was to be the centre of English rule in Ireland and Kilmainham was strategically placed to protect the south western approaches to the city. Indeed a later English King, Edward III, was able to justifiably claim that: "The Knights hold a good position for the repulse of our Irish enemies who daily make war upon my liege people."

This formidable group of buildings, of which no vestige remains today, was not on the site of the Royal Hospital but immediately to the west of it in what are now the extensive hospital grounds stretching towards Inchicore Road. The order had many establishments in Ireland but Kilmainham Priory was their headquarters and it was here that the Grand Prior resided. For the next 365 years this great house, operating in sophisticated feudal fashion, was to dominate the whole life of the area while the coming and going of the heavily armoured knights mounted on their war horses was to be a common sight.

The principal building was a square castle surrounded by a strong inner wall with towers at the four corners. Inside this wall were a number of detached buildings which included the Prior's residence, lodgings for permanent guests, a chapel and a prison.

This inner wall was completely surrounded by a much more extensive outer wall bounded by Kilmainham Lane, the High Road, on the south side and by the Liffey on the north side. At the river crossing at Islandbridge, formerly the Ford of Kilmohaloc and later Tyrrell's Ford, the Normans built a six arch bridge protected by a tower. The main entrance in the outer wall was on the south side and took the form of a heavily fortified tower gate several storeys high. It was stated to have faced the "Common Green of Kilmainham" on which today stands Kilmainham Courthouse and Jail. From this we can conclude that it stood near enough to the present Richmond Tower entrance to the Royal Hospital. The latter, however, had no connection with the area, having been originally sited at the bottom of Watling Street. As it was interfering with the tram traffic on the quays serving the recently opened Kingsbridge Station, the Great Southern and Western Railway Company had it dismantled at their own expense and rebuilt at its present location. What an example for some of our present-day developers!

The large area of ground between the inner and outer walls was known as the Manor Close. Here was situated numerous buildings such as guest houses, haybarns, granaries, stables, forge, dairy and brew house as well as gardens, orchards, shrubberies and acres of arable land. Some of these buildings would have been close to the present Garda Station.

Below the outer wall on both sides of the Camac was the Norman village of Kylmaynan, now known as Old Kilmainham and Rowserstown. The Church of Saint John of Kilmainham, serving both the Priory and local parish, was built near the High Cross at Bully's Acre. Tiles from the floor of this church were uncovered in 1850 and were similar to flooring found in ecclesiastical buildings in other parts of the country.

Further down the road near the wall of Clancy Barracks was the original site of the famous Saint John's Well, where devotions and pilgrimages were to be held for centuries to come. Then on the Liffey itself, was a watermill as well as a weir and pools for salmon fishing, the latter forming an important part of the economic life of Dublin in those centuries. Even down to this day, salmon fishing has been carried on at this Islandbridge location.

Meanwhile, back on the Camac and nearer to the village, the waters of that little river were used to turn a fulling mill, which was a mill in which cloth was pressed and scoured.

From the foregoing it can be seen that Kilmainham Priory was an elaborate and self-supporting institution, but where today only green pastures mark its passing.

The Knights Hospitallers in their capacity as a charitable order also established a leper hospital dedicated to Saint Laurence, Deacon and Martyr, on the western extremity of their lands not many hundred yards from the ford of Chapelizod on the highway to Palmerstown and which today would be in the vicinity of the West County Hotel. The eighty-four acres of land attached to the hospital were known up to the present time as Saint Laurence's land and stretched across through Ballyfermot to the present mainline railway bridge where they built a small church, also dedicated to Saint Laurence. This was referred to as the "Ecclesia De Villa Thurmot Alias Ballyfermote."

Castles

To further protect their newly-won territories against the incursions of the dispossessed Irish, the Anglo-Normans constructed a ring of castles such as Drimnagh, Ballymount, Belgard, Clondalkin, Ballyfermot, Gallonstown, Neilstown, Esker, Ballyowen and Castleknock, some of which still exist in varying states of preservation. In between the castles they dotted the countryside with lesser tower houses and fortified mansions. Drimnagh, the seat of the Barnwall family, having weathered the centuries in remarkable fashion, is the most complete and has been refurbished by a local committee.

Ballymount, on the banks of the tiny Coolfan stream, was a very extensive castle with massive walls, towers and outworks, but only a mound and tower-gate remain. The latter, which was hardly noticeable over the years in the fields behind the Red Cow Inn, now finds itself on the side of a major highway – the new Western Road Link.

The remaining square tower of Belgard Castle, once the home of the Talbot family, has been incorporated into the head office of Cement Roadstone Holdings. Across the road from it, there also stood the fortified residence of Kilnamanagh, in an area which had earlier associations with Saint Kevin, but all traces of this has vanished. Thus we can see that the invaders had constructed a very formidable chain of defence works along the southern side of the Naas Road, being keenly aware no doubt of the ever present threat from those Irish clans, notably the O'Byrnes and the O'Tooles, who had taken to the higher ground of County Wicklow.

On the other side was Ballyfermot Castle, near the railway bridge in the now built-up area known as Clover Hill. Here indeed we had a Norman enclave which included nearby the already-mentioned Church of Saint Laurence and not too far away a fortified building at Gallonstown near the 7th Lock.

D'Alton, in his 1830 history of County Dublin, mentioned that the walls of Ballyfermot Castle still remained and that it had adjoining to it a garden surrounded

The medieval oratory in Bluebell cemetery

by a curious brick wall built in a series of curves. Nearby he noted the "very perfect remains of the old church thickly covered with ivy" as well as a graveyard.

Only the graveyard and the curved walls were to survive to modern times but alas over the last twenty years they have fallen prey to our own domestic vandals. Today there is no trace whatsoever of this ancient burial place which withstood even the macabre attention of the body snatchers of an earlier age and in which interments took place up to the late 1920s. A former Lord Mayor of Dublin, Richard White of Chapelizod, was buried there in 1770.

In a direct line between Ballyfermot and Drimnagh Castles, but nearer to the latter, we still have, thankfully, in Bluebell Cemetery the ruins of an oratory dating from late Norman times and then known as the Parish Church of Drimna.

Esker is gone, while the ruins of the old church remain, as does a castle gate way at Neilstown. Very little of Ballyowen, just off the Lucan Road, is to be seen, but across the river Liffey the remaining fine tower of Castleknock is still a notable landmark. Only a few years ago a tower house known as Ashtown "Castle" was discovered in the Phoenix Park, having been concealed for decades within a large private mansion. It is in excellent repair and can be visited.

Chapter Four

Life at the Priory

Medieval Manuscripts

Notwithstanding their lengthy stay at Kilmainham, the amount of documentary evidence regarding the Knights Hospitallers is relatively small. We are fortunate, however, that at least two important manuscripts are still available. The first of these, preserved at the Bodleian Library in Oxford, is known as *Registrum de Kilmainham (1326–1339) – The Register of Kilmainham* – and is one of the oldest documents relating to our district. It gives valuable insights into the day-to-day activities of the Priory and is beautifully written on parchment, consisting of 117 quarto size folios, the text being entirely in Latin.

The second manuscript, preserved at the Public Records Office, London, written in Latin also, is known as *The Extent of Kilmainham 1542* and we shall be referring to same later on.

The Register was translated into English by Charles McNeill, on which he based his paper *The Knights Hospitallers of Kilmainham and their Guests* from which in turn we derive much of the following information as well as much of that contained in the previous chapter.

The Priory was the official residence of the Grand Prior of Ireland with his staff of knights, squires, chaplains, clerks and inferior attendants in great number and variety. There was also a local superior known as the Preceptor of Kilmainham who was responsible for the good order and discipline of the house, for the discharge of their charitable obligations and for the maintenance of the buildings. Under him was the local community of brethren, knights and a retinue of officials as well as craftsmen, labourers and servants.

Reminder of the Knights

The largest building inside the castle was the great hall in which all the residents, members of the order, guests and servants took their meals. In this hall were five separate tables divided by rank. The first was presided over by the Grand Prior who entertained the most distinguished guests. At the second table the prior of the church presided over the brethren and guests of some rank. The third table was for squires and ordinary guests, the fourth for higher attendants and craftsmen and the fifth for grooms and horse boys.

Guests

Apart from their military role, the primary purpose of the knights was to provide hospitality for pilgrims, the care of the poor and the distribution of alms. One of the most celebrated pilgrimages then was to the shrine of Saint James at Compostella in Spain. The members of the order also observed the long fasts at certain set times throughout the year.

A distinguishing feature of this priory, however, was the provision of lodgings not only to passing pilgrims, but also to more permanent guests. The latter made the Priory their home by virtue of explicit contracts, many of which are recorded in the *Register*. The extent of the accommodation granted was in proportion to the services or donations received. One such guest was John de Grauntsete, who in 1338 "for good and praiseworthy service" was granted maintenance and quarters equal to the Prior's for himself and proportionate allowances for his squire, attendant, groom and two horses.

At the time of the *Register* the Prior was Roger Utlaugh, who held many public offices including that of Lord Deputy and was particularly rewarded for service against Edward Bruce.

Another guest was Henry de Ston, who for his good services was granted maintenance for life in eating and drinking at the squires' table. Furthermore –

> "We grant to the said Henry that if he be detained by weakness, old age, sickness, mishap or other urgent cause so that if he cannot come to the aforesaid table for his meals, a competent delivery of victuals shall be served to him in his chamber."

The permanent guests were accommodated in separate dwellings known as "camerae" which were of various kinds. Some of them were a single chamber while others contained several rooms and might be houses with an upper and lower storey. It has to be assumed that these camerae were of wood like most of the ordinary dwelling houses of the period. Many of them were built by the occupants themselves at their own expense on sites marked out by the Priory authorities – an early form of "planning permission."

No information has been found on which to estimate the number of residents within the Priory in the fourteenth century, when it was at the height of its power and activity, but they were obviously considerable. From their names, we can see that they were of Anglo-Norman ancestry, but we do not know to what extent, if any, native Irish were employed.

The Liffey Fisheries

Under their Charter, the Hospitallers had many concessions and were almost a state within a state, something which led to serious tensions with the city authorities from time to time. Some of these arose from disputes regarding the much prized fishing rights on the river Liffey. When Hugh Tyrrell bestowed the lands of Kilmohavoc (Phoenix Park) on the Hospitallers, they now had domains on both sides of the Liffey, but were not granted full fishing rights on the river. The major rights were retained by the city as heretofore, from the Ford of Kilmohavoc (Islandbridge) to the sea, the Hospitallers being granted "a moiety of the water of the river Liffey as far as the watercourse near the Gibbet". The latter was one of the several places of public execution in Dublin and was situated in what is now Parkgate Street.

The earliest recorded dispute was that of October 1220:

> "The good men of the king's City of Dublin have informed the king that the city was always wont to have the Avenlith – the Liffey – in such a condition that any kind of victuals could be conveyed in boats up and down to the city and the citizens always had a fishery on that river. The Prior and Hospitallers of Kilmainham have lately made a pool whereby the citizens and city are much damnified; their fishery is totally destroyed because the pool prevents the fish from ascending and their boats can no longer pass up and down as they used to."

The location of this dam has not been positively identified; some historians holding that it was at Islandbridge, others that it was as far downstream as O'Connell Bridge. If the latter is correct, the Hospitallers were operating very much outside their own territory. However they were ordered "to rectify the pool so that ships and boats may have free passage and that fish may have free approach to the fisheries of the king and free return therefrom."

Following a further serious incident in 1261, an agreement was reached, part of which reads as follows:

> "Except for the Prior's right to one draught of fish, free boat and net, the Mayor and citizens are to have free fishing in the water of the river Liffey from the Bridge of Kilmainham to the sea. The passage of salmon, great or small, is not to be obstructed by nets, weirs, other engines or impediments. The nets of the Mayor and citizens as well as those of the Prior are to be emptied solely on the lands of the north side of the river between the Bridge of Kilmainham and the sea."

It is interesting to note that the above contains the first reference to a bridge at what is now Islandbridge – heretofore all the references had been to a ford.

At the time of the dissolution of the monasteries, the Hospitallers were said to have had a weir and four salmon pools and there was reference in the Register to an official who was in charge of the fisheries.

Riding the Franchise

The granting of Civic Liberties to the City of Dublin by Prince John in 1192 sets out the boundaries within which such liberties were to apply. These were not confined to the walled city, but took in a generous belt of territory from Blackrock-Merrion all the way around to the Tolka river at Ballybough. In the western part of Dublin, the boundary was loosely defined as being from "St Patrick's Cathedral by the valley (The Coombe) even to Karnaclone Gunnethe (which was near Dolphins Barn) and beyond the stream of Kilmainham (The Camac) even to the fords of Kylmehavoc and beyond the water of Avon Liffey to the north."

In order to assert their authority and to note any infringements, the Lord Mayor, his officials and sword bearer were enjoined by law to ride along the full length of the boundary at three yearly intervals. This perambulation, as it was known, usually took place in the autumn and in order to accomplish it in a single day, they had to set out at 4.00 a.m., an early start indeed for Dublin's first "City Marathon"!

The task was not undertaken with any great relish by the municipal officials because it also involved much expense as well as the difficulties of the terrain. However it was a custom which was to endure from the fourteenth to the eighteenth century, notwithstanding the many wars and turbulences.

There are several contemporary accounts in existence from which we learn that the Lord Mayor's party rode along from Dolphins Barn in the direction of Rialto and then crossed by a meadow known as the Iron Damme, which would be in the grounds of Saint James's Hospital. They then normally made their way down to Old Kilmainham possibly via Watery Lane (Brookfield Road) or perhaps nearer to Mount Brown. Here they crossed down by the "Forty Steps", officially "Cromwell's Quarters", to Bow Bridge, which was the traditional half-way stage of the journey.

They did not cross over the bridge, as they were near the mearing (boundary) of the lands of the Hospitallers over which they had no jurisdiction. Instead they "passed under an arch of the bridge through the water of Cammock." It was in this vicinity as time went on that it became customary for all to gather around to hear the Clerk in the presence of the Mayor, Recorder, Sheriffs and Aldermen, deliver an account of the previous Riding of the Franchise. Then having dismounted, they dined in the large pavilions and tents which had been erected on the banks of the Camac.

Thus fortified, the Mayor and his officials "took boat" and made their way up the Liffey to Islandbridge in which way they asserted their authority over that river. It is not at all clear, however, which route the main body of horse followed in order to rejoin the Lord Mayor's party who by now had landed on the north side of the Liffey near Islandbridge still known as Kilmainham Bridge or the Ford of Kilmahaloc. This seemed to have varied from one riding to another, perhaps taking into consideration the flow of water and tides in the Liffey. In one year they were stated to have gone towards the west "leaving the tilling lands of Kilmainham on their left." In another year it says that "they rode northwards through the water of the Liffey as far as the Ford of Kilmahaloc."

The full contingent together again on the Phoenix Park side were still in the Hospitallers demesne, but journeyed I believe, along a "right of way" parallel to the Liffey, now Conyngham Road, to Parkgate Street and so to continue their perambulation of the North City. The right of way had been guaranteed to the City under one of the fishery agreements previously mentioned.

Much later in the riding of 1692 all did not go well when an unpleasant incident occurred at Bow Bridge where for some unknown reason a mob had gathered. One of these hurled stones as the sword bearer rode underneath the archway of the bridge and a fracas developed. However the Lord Mayor, Sir Michael Mitchell, called upon a troop of horse soldiers who restored order.

There is still a lack of information on all the details of the ancient custom of Riding the Franchise. For instance, we still do not know why those making the journey deviated on some occasions from their usual itinerary and made instead for the "Cross of Kilmainham" before going to Bow Bridge.

In its later years, the event gradually developed into a pageant insofar as the centre of the City was concerned, with the participation of the trade and craft guilds of the City of Dublin.

Apart from Christmas, the local Anglo-Norman community also made merry at three principal festivals, the pattern at Saint John's Well on the 20th June, the fair and horse racing at Palmerstown on the 10th August, being the feast of Saint Lawrence, and at the fair in James's Street on the 10th November.

Chapter Five

WITHIN THE PALE

Right from the start Inchicore/Kilmainham was very much in the heart of what was later to be known as the English Pale. For the next four hundred years, until the decisive Battle of Kinsale in 1601 when the old Gaelic order came to an end, the territory of the Pale was to be the scene of intermittent and mainly guerrilla warfare between the Irish and the colonists. The former, being more lightly armed and seldom acting in unity, were unable to overrun the fortified castles but by means of forays and sporadic attacks made life very precarious for the colonists and their descendants during those centuries. Nearby places like Crumlin, Tallaght and Saggart were under frequent attack, their buildings being burned and their cattle driven off.

ACTION AT KILMAINHAM 1408

Locally, the most serious recorded encounter took place in August 1408 when an Irish force engaged the English near Kilmainham. The latter were led by the Prior and the Duke of Lancaster who had only recently come over as the King's Deputy in Ireland and had established himself at Kilmainham. In this encounter, the Duke was seriously wounded and according to English sources "scarcely escaped death."

This incident took place during that period when English power was at its lowest ebb and when that redoubtable Irish chieftain, Art McMurrough Kavanagh, held sway in Leinster. It was a time also when very often the Irish were strong enough to impose a black rent in return for immunity from attack – a tactic also employed against the Norse in earlier centuries.

In order to strengthen the English position in Dublin and the neighbouring countries, King Henry VI in 1429 encouraged his subjects by means of a building subsidy to erect more castles and tower houses of a minimum size.

> "It is agreed that every liege man of our Lord the King who builds a castle or tower sufficiently fortified shall receive a subsidy of 10 pounds from the Commons of the said counties."

A later edict of 1454 during the reign of King Edward IV ordered all men of the Pale, amongst other things, to own bows and arrows and to practice regularly at the butts on pain of a fine.

The decline of Anglo-Norman power in the fourteenth century had also, apart from attacks by the Irish, been aggravated by the Bruce invasion of 1317. Kilmainham Priory was on full alert as indeed was all Dublin when the Scottish King marched on the city in that year. However, having come as close as Castleknock he did not proceed further, but turned his attention to Munster instead. Further vicissitudes for the citizens of Dublin were to follow with the advent of the dreaded Black Death in 1348.

Action at Islandbridge 1534

As well as attacks from without, the Dublin colony had also, as the centuries passed by, to contend from time to time with rebellion from within. The most serious of these was the revolt of Silken Thomas, the Geraldine leader in County Kildare, who had become disenchanted with rule from London. It was during this period in 1534 that an incident involving Sir William Skeffington, the Lord Deputy of Ireland, who had been sent over from England with a large army to suppress the revolt, took place near Islandbridge, then known as Kilmainham Bridge.

In a letter to London he gives his version of the affair as follows:

> "At my coming homeward from Trim, which was the Sunday before St. Catherine's Day, there did fall such rain as hath not been seen in these parts, so that the footmen waded by the way to the middles in waters, which was pity to see, and that every man made a great haste to Dublin and left the footmen to come as they might. The Lords Chancellor, Bishop of Meath and Gormanstown, with other gentlemen, also Dacres and sixteen spears of his company tarried with me for the said footmen that could not have defended themselves with their bows, for their strings were so wet, and most of the feathers of their arrows fallen off. There came alarm that certain horsemen of Thomas Fitzgerald were laid at the wood end of Kilmainham, for to have distressed the footmen at a narrow bridge, where as no other passage was but at the same; and I hearing thereof sent in all haste that I could to stay the ordnance which, as chance was, were good pieces that day, and when I came at the bridge I passed over all the footmen and left not one behind. And that done I laid the said ordnances at the most advantage, and shot divers pieces among them, and drove them from their ground, and brought by that mean the said footmen safely to Dublin. And if I had not done this, there had been three or four hundred of them killed or taken prisoners.
>
> "And at my coming thither there was divers of the army in Dublin four hours before my coming. And that night my sickness took me, and I am sure there sickened one hundred more besides me, whereof at the least I think forty were dead. Assuring your mastership that I was never so nigh the jeopardy of death in my life, and thanks be to God now well recovered

thereof, and I trust past danger; and God willing, as soon as I shall be able to ride, I shall make that false traitor take as evil a rest as ever a wretch had."

It is interesting to note here that Skeffington's force were still using the older bow and arrow as well as the relatively new cannon gun.

During the course of this rebellion, Silken Thomas issued an edict that all "English by birth" were to leave the country. This threat was taken seriously by Rawson, the Prior of Kilmainham, who fled to England until the rebellion had been crushed. This would seem to indicate that by that stage the Hospitallers were not the force they once were.

Skeffington died at the Priory some months later in December 1535. It was also in 1534 that the O'Tooles, taking advantage of the government's difficulties with the Geraldines, succeeded in crossing over the Liffey at Kilmainham Bridge and proceeded to raid Fingal in North County Dublin. The citizens of the city got wind of this and, having armed themselves, decided to intercept the raiders on their return at the river crossing. However, for some reason they did not remain there but advanced to meet the O'Tooles at Salcock's Wood near Grangegorman. The result was a disaster for the citizens, who suffered many casualties while the O'Tooles made it back to their Wicklow base.

Chapter Six

THE EXTENT OF KILMAINHAM 1541

In 1541 King Henry VIII suppressed and confiscated the monasteries in Ireland and England. The Priory of Kilmainham was no exception and this meant the end of the road for the Knights Hospitallers. Before doing so, the King established a commission to carry out an inventory of all the lands and possessions of the Priory, this being known as the *Extent of Kilmainham*. This report, drawn up in Latin, is one of the very few ancient documents relating to the area. It provides a unique view of Kilmainham village, many aspects of contemporary life and is particularly useful in the matter of local place names.

The following is a résumé of the *Extent* insofar as it relates to Kilmainham and district:

HOSPITAL OF SAINT JOHN OF JERUSALEM IN IRELAND (KILMAINHAM)

Extent of the possessions in the Co. Dublin surrendered to the King by Sir John Rawson, late prior of the Hospital, made at Kylmaynan, 7 April, 1541, before Anthony Seyntleger, Thomas Walsshe, John Mynne and William Cavendysshe, on the oath of John Burnell de Castell Cnok, John Barnewall, of same, William Clynche of Newcastell, John Lyvet of Lucan, Richard Mason of Balydowde, William Braghall of Cromlyn, Patrick Neele, of same, Brian Taylor of Kylmaynan and John O'Quoyne, of same, true and lawful men of the neighbourhood.

They say that the house, mansions, and edifices now within the site of the manor of Kylmaynan, which manor was the chief hospital or manse of said prior and brethren, are very necessary and suitable for the manse and abode of the King's Deputy, but said house and buildings are now in great decay and require repairs to the extent of 100 marks. There are there 3 small gardens and 1 orchard with stone walls and 4 towers above said surrounding walls. One tower on the North with hanging bridge over the River Liffey running near said tower, at present broken down and which if rebuilt would be very useful in defence against invading enemies on that side.

Also a stone barn the roof of which was burned and thrown down by Thomas ffytz Gerald, rebel and traitor of the King, about 6 years ago, with all the grain then lying there. Also a church, very large, which is a parish church, of which a certain portion, namely the chapel on the south side may be thrown down without any harm, and of necessity should be thrown down as the parishioners of said church cannot otherwise support that church on account of their poverty, and the remainder of the church will suffice for the parishioners.

In fields adjoining Hospital, 260 acres, arable, of manor lands.

On the southside of Liffey a wood called **Inscore/Inchigore/Fustore** of 16 acres under wood and pasture reserved for Hospital's use.

[N.B. The writing here may have been indistinct as the place name has been variously interpreted as above by different historians.]

On the northside of Liffey a wood called Gretewood of 41 acres.

Also on both sides of Liffey, 260 acres pasture and heather of manor lands not valued as they lie within the farm of arable lands and it is not customary to set them to farm.

One water-mill on the Liffey with two pairs of mill stones under one roof.

On same river one weir with four pools for salmon fishing with boats and nets.

On southside of the house or manse one fulling mill between said house and le Cammocke river turning on said river.

One mill held by Richard Rawson of Bristoll by lease of Prior.

One parcel of land on southside of bridge called **le Gylden Bryge** on the banks of the Cammok towards Dromrathe called Walsshemanslandes, of 30 acres pasture held by James Bathe, Chief Baron of Exchequer, for life in place of his fee, by grant of Prior and Brethren, without rent.

One parcel of land called Droges, of 14 acres pasture and under wood held by Thomas Hyllock.

In **le Woodfeld**, 15 acres arable and pasture, held by Richard Savage at will of the King.

Extern lands of the Manor:

Twenty acres pasture called le Dammes and twenty acres called le Stryffe More held as commons by tenants of the village without rent.

An ancient stone bridge over Liffey, which runs through the manor, of six arches now broken down to the great harm of the manor and surrounding country, and requiring repairs valued about 100 marks.

In the manor a parcel of land called Melaghes Medowe (marshy meadow) about 1½ acres.

Village of Kylmaynan:

One messuage with appurtenances called Castlehouse and 1¼ acres called **le Barleyard.**

[NB A messuage was some form of dwelling house.]

Two acres of pasture at Quoytroltes Park on the West. Both held by John O'Quoyne.

Five acres arable on West of Village near the Liberty of Dublin City, held by Agnes Perpoyn and Katerine Rawson from the Prior and Brethren (19 April, 26 Henry VIII, 1535) for 95 years at 10 shillings per annum.

[N.B. One would have thought that the Dublin Liberty was on the East of the village.]

And three parcels of land, of one and three quarter acres on both sides of the Cammok to the south of the bridge called **le Bow-bryge**, held by Martin Kelly, Baker, at will of the King.

In said village a garden called le Kyngis Yardes on both sides of the Cammok, on the South called Sangwendeslandes, held by William Kerne of Dublin, baker, at will of the King.

One messuage, formerly held by Walter Whyte, tailer, now totally waste, held by Agnes Perpoyn, widow, with small brambly grove of pasture called Gyffordes Grove between Cromlyn and Kylmaynan.

Four gardens near land of Lady Anne Brymyngham on West held by Brian Taylor.

One garden near western gate of village on north side held by John O'Quoyne.

One garden held by Laghlyn O'Quoyne.

One garden on north of street of village, held by Thomas Lane.

In village fields three acres arable, held by James Rery at will of King.

Tenants for life in said village:

One house, and in the fields three and three quarter acres arable, held by James Whyte, organist, by grant of John Rawson, late prior, under the common seal, 16 March 16 Henry VIII, free of rent, except service of said James in the choir of Kylmaynan church at diverse times specified in writing, with an annuity of 53 shillings, food and drink during his life as specified in said writing and shown to the above jurors at the Inquisition.

Free Tenants:

One enclosed place and twenty-four acres arable in fields of village held by Master and wardens of St. Anne's Gild.

One messuage and garden and small enclosure, held by Nicholas Quoytrot, citizen and alderman of Dublin, who maintains the village ditch near his messuage.

One and a half burgage (a measure of land) called Quoytrotes Parke, in West of village, held by same.

Six acres arable at Barnegyll in said manor, held by heirs of Robert Barnewall of Drymnagh.

Forty acres arable in le Hyghfeld, do. near Thomas Woode, held by Patrick Chyllan. One meadow called Tyrelles Woode in village, held by Nicholas Scurlok.

In said village certain land called le Commen Gryne, i.e. three quarter burgage between the Towne Bryge and the mill called the Tokyngmyll (possibly the Tolling-Mill) the other side of the Cammok river, held by tenants of village in common.

Newtone de Kylmaynan:
In village of Newton near the forst called the Grete Woods are 160 acres, arable, 4 acres meadow, 37 acres pasture and thorn bushes which Arnold Ussher holds to farm by deed, with tithes of village, granted by late prior.

Perquisites of Manor Court with a custom called Mary Gallons contributed by tenants of manor and said villages.

[N.B. The custom of giving so many gallons of milk on certain feasts of the Blessed Virgin.]

Rectory of Chapelysold with Chapel of St. Laurence:
Tithes of grain of rectory beside said manor and chapel of St. Laurence.

The Village

Kilmainham was the first village, and a large one at that, on the road from Dublin to the south which no longer followed the old Slí Dala through Crumlin. In addition, the principal road to the west passed nearby via Bow Lane, Bow Bridge, Kilmainham Lane and on to Inchicore Road. The "Towne Bridge" across the Camac at Kearn's Place provided a link between these two principal roads. A village ditch with a gate on the western side was intended to keep out marauding animals.

It had been a very prosperous centre of population because of its close association with the Priory, its several mills and location beside the little Camac river. At the time of the inventory, the prosperity of the village had declined as had the fortunes of the Priory.

The name Rawson occurs frequently. These were relatives of the last Prior and it is possible that Rowserstown derives from same. It is interesting to note also that a small number of Irish names occur amongst the inhabitants.

The Commons

Another important matter to emerge from the document is the fact that there were two separate Kilmainham Commons, i.e. places where the villagers could graze their animals free of charge. The first of these, known as the Common Green, is mentioned both in the "Register" and the *Extent*. As we have seen from the former, it lay to the west of the village and later became the site of Kilmainham Courthouse and Jail. However, the second Commons, which is mentioned in the *Extent*, was called Stryffe More and later became known as the Upper Kilmainham Commons. It was situated on the higher ground to the south of the village and today the site is occupied by Cameron Square, some of the grounds of Saint James's Hospital and the district of Rialto. It was later to be the scene of race meetings and was finally enclosed by Act of Parliament in 1821.

The Woodlands

As well as the very extensive arable land, about 300 acres in all, the document also indicates the many woods in the area at that time, i.e.

Tyrell's Wood	Barnegyll (the top of the wood)
Thomas's Wood	Gyfforde's Grove
Inscore/Inchigore/Fustore Wood	

It is not possible to identify the location of these woodlands except in the case of the latter, which lay somewhere in the vicinity of present day Woodfield, that district opposite the Model School. This sixteen-acre wood which was reserved for the use of the Hospital gives some indication as to the situation of the original Inchicore.

Somewhat further afield was the Grettewood in the Phoenix Park and the celebrated oak wood near Drimnagh Castle.

The Place Names

If "Inscore" or "Inchigore" is the correct interpretation, and I believe it to be so, it is the earliest written reference to Inchicore in either the English or native records. In fact, there is no reference at all to the name in any of the Irish annals.

Many other local place names which are still in use are mentioned in the *Extent*. When the Anglo-Normans took over, they continued to use the existing Gaelic place names, albeit in a corrupted form. Where the place had not a Gaelic name or it may not have been known to them, they provided their own names, e.g. "Le Gylden Bryge," "Le Bow Bryge," "Le Woodfield." The use of the definite article "Le" indicates the Anglo-French background of the early colonists. Generally speaking, they do not appear to have used it in connection with the Gaelic place names and "Le Cammocke" seems to have been an exception.

The thirty acres known as Walsshemanslandes, south of Golden Bridge, probably covered some of the present Bulfin Housing Estate. It was stated to stretch towards "Dromrathe" (The Ridge of the Ring Fort) a Gaelic name which has not survived and could have been on the far side of the Grand Canal. It may well have been a continuation of the Drimnagh (The Sandyridges) area then lying more to the west than the modern Drimnagh. What is more important, however, is that the presence of a rath or ring-fort indicates an early settlement of people there long before the arrival of either Norse or Norman.

Stryffemore sounds like a Gaelic name also and as mentioned was used as a Commons. Near it was a twenty-acre pasture called Le Dammes mentioned in accounts of Riding the Franchise as the Iron Damme. It was along here that the ancient city watercourse flowed.

The fourteen acres of pasture and underwood known as "Droges" may have been near Woodfield, but we cannot hazard a guess as to its derivation.

Golden Bridge and Bow Bridge were both vital crossings of the Camac river for the roads to the south and west. The former no doubt was an ornate structure and has given its name to the district nearby ever since. With regard to the other bridge, it could well be that the word "Bow" refers to the shape of the bridge. We know from the accounts of the Riding of the Franchise that it was a three arch bridge and that it must have been pretty high when horsemen could pass under it. In any event, it was obviously the larger of the two bridges, as the Camac was wider here, being almost at the end of its course before joining the river Liffey.

With regard to Le Barleyard near the village, it has been suggested that it may have been the origin of Bully's Acre, but this is only conjecture.

Newtown De Kylmaynan was a small settlement on the other side of Islandbridge.

Chapter Seven

The Post Priory Period

The mid-sixteenth century was a period of traumatic events, with the suppression of the monasteries and the coming of the Reformation which introduced a religious element into the political conflict. The monasteries had contributed indirectly to the prosperity of the city and county and with their closure a long period of economic stagnation was to continue well into the next century.

The lands of Kilmainham, with the exception of those immediately surrounding the Priory were sold, this being the first great change of land ownership in the area for centuries. From then on there are numerous records of such transactions and we shall just refer to a couple of these here which, like the *Extent*, mention forgotten place names and shed some light on the geography of the area at that time.

In the first one a parcel of twelve acres of pasture and furze in the western part of Kilmainham Wood went to a John Brown.

The second one is an example of a major transfer of land and property to a Sir Robert Napper. He became the owner of 170 acres between the Liffey and the Camac, which would automatically have included all the lands of Inchicore. This large holding was stated to have been bounded at the Kilmainham end by a road called the "Mill-Bater" and at the other end by an area known as the "Drugges" which was also mentioned in the *Extent*. One wonders if the former is a corruption of the Irish word "Bothar."

Amongst various other items in this sale was an acre in the "High fields of Kilmainham known as Barrots Land" as well as the water called "The common water of Austen".

Finally Sir Robert acquired the income from the ancient custom of "Mary Gallons" which was a levy paid annually by the inhabitants and tenants of Kilmainham.

The Priory

The Priory itself was taken over as a Vice-Regal Court for the King's Deputy in Ireland and it was here in 1556 that the Northern Chieftain, Shane O'Neill, "Shane the Proud", escorted by "a company of glib-haired Gallowglasses wielding mighty battle axes" made his submission to the Crown.

As the building was falling into decay by then, the Viceroy moved residence to Dublin Castle in 1565 and it was put in the charge of an official called the Keeper. During the reign of Queen Elizabeth, we find the appointment of a new Keeper in 1597 recorded in the following terms:

> "Appointment of Andrew Greene to the Office of Keeper of the House of Kilmainham and Keeper of the gardens, woods and demesne lands. To hold during good behaviour with a fee of 12 pence per day.
>
> "Her Majesty also grants him the mansion house over the south gate of Kilmainham with the garden and orchard on the east side of the gate.
>
> "She further grants him the grazing of ten kine (cows), two horses and forty sheep on the demesne lands of the house".

The second half of the century marked the advent of Tudor/Elizabethan England. It was at this time that English power in Ireland was gaining strength again and they now contemplated bringing the whole country under their control. In the meantime, attacks on the Pale continued, notably by Clan O Byrne.

An Leabhar Branach

The *Book of the O Byrnes* is a collection of seventy-three Gaelic poems written in praise of the O'Byrne chieftains during this period. Early manuscript copies of these poems are today in the possession of Harvard University, Boston, as well as Trinity College. One of the most notable of the poems from a historical/topographical point of view is that dedicated to Aodh Mac Seain which extols the exploits of that chieftain at nearly two hundred places in Leinster. These include nearly twenty in the Dublin area and among those mentioned are Rathgar, Crumlin, Tallaght, Rathcoole, Newcastle and Ballyfermot. The lines relating to the latter are as follows:

"Fa mhadhm Bhaile Formont, Frioth clu le hAodh or fhud coigcrioch".	"By the Ballyfermot raid, Aodh gained fame among the strangers".

Aodh Mac Seain was chief of the clan from 1548 to 1579 when he was succeeded by his son, the better known Fiach Mac Aodh Ó Broin.

The poems also give us an insight into the conflict from the Irish point of view and illustrate their intimate knowledge of the thickly wooded countryside. There are frequent references to their temporary sleeping huts amongst the trees which were used before their early morning forays. Finally, they show the vitality of the bardic tradition and the importance which the Irish attached to it even in the midst of their struggle for survival.

The slaying of Fiach Mac Aodh in Glenmalure in 1597 was a severe blow to the Wicklow men. However, the sporadic raids were to continue for another four years as the English garrison in Dublin had to be reduced in order to deal with O Neill and O Donnell in Ulster and this left the outskirts of the city more vulnerable to attack. It was at this time that Kilmainham was raided. In the course of a letter dated the 8th January 1598 written by the Lord Justices Loftus and Gardiner, they stated that:

> "The mountain rebels yester night burnt all the town of Kilmainham and part of Cromlin. So it appears that the Pale is the only mark they now shoot at. For defence therefore, the force in it should be increased rather than diminished".

The attacks on the Pale only came to an end with the decisive Battle of Kinsale in 1601 and the subsequent dispersal of the Wicklow clans. As the royal writ now ran throughout the land the Pale became redundant and, for the first time since the coming of the Anglo-Normans, the citizens of Dublin could breathe a relative sigh of relief.

It was indeed the end of an era both locally and nationally.

Chapter Eight

The Seventeenth Century

It was in 1611 that the reference to "Mainhames Bush" occurred. In that year an Englishman, Sir Edmund Fisher, had acquired some of the former lands of the Hospitallers in the Phoenix Park and Mainhames Bush is mentioned as being one of the boundaries of his holding.

It was Sir Edmund who also built the manor house called "The Phoenix" on that elevated site overlooking the Liffey on which today the Magazine Fort stands. He also had "the sole liberty of fishing with boats and nets in all that river".

Inchicore in the Phoenix Park

By 1618 the Government decided that it required an official residence away from Dublin Castle for the King's Viceroy in Ireland and they bought the "Phoenix House" from Sir Edmund Fisher for this purpose. They also bought all the surrounding lands on the north side of the Liffey to form a demesne in conjunction with the old Priory lands on the south side at Kilmainham and part of Inchicore, which were already in the possession of the Crown. The whole lot was deemed to be the "Phoenix Park."

In a dispute in later years regarding the mills at Islandbridge which was referred to the King, the following occurs:

> "A letter acquainting his Majesty with the situation of these mills in the **middle** of the Park."

It was only the north side, however, which was developed as an extensive game reserve for the Viceroy and the gentry and this was the forerunner of the present day Phoenix Park. The south side continued to be used for arable purposes. The designation of both the north and south sides as the Phoenix Park continued until the establishment of the Royal Hospital at Kilmainham in 1680.

An enquiry of 1615 found that the mill beside Kilmainham Bridge, which had not yet been called Islandbridge, had been:

> "An ancient mill, time out of mind and there had been an ancient weir there closing the stream or river on the west side of the bridge."

By the time of the 1641 Rising, this mill and fishery was under the control of one Francis McEvoy. In the forfeitures which followed that rising, the said Francis

McEvoy was deemed to be "attainted" and he lost mill, fishery and adjoining three acres of land. One wonders how someone with such an Irish name came into possession of such a property in the first instance.

Later in the century these mills, which by then were in the possession of the Crown, had become very extensive. They were known as the Island Mills and were the principal suppliers of corn to the army.

Rory O Moore and the 1641 Rebellion

The Irish leader, Rory O Moore, while planning the 1641 Rebellion with colleagues in the inner city, escaped capture by the skin of his teeth. He made his way by boat up the Liffey and came ashore at Islandbridge. From here he succeeded in reaching safety with relatives in Lucan.

With the capture of his colleagues the rising, while it did take place in other parts of Ireland, failed to materialise in Dublin. There were, however, sporadic incidents near Dublin, particularly in the county, the most serious of these being at Rathcoole. Afterwards, people who alleged that they suffered damage to their property as a result of these incidents put in claims for compensation. They set out details of their losses in what is known as The Depositions and we find some of these of local interest.

Anthony Garton, Gentleman and Protestant, swore that at the beginning of the present rebellion, the rebels came to Kilmainham at night-time and burned his dwelling to the ground as well as the most part of a malt house.

Margaret Cooke of Kilmainham Bridge (Islandbridge) stated that she and her husband were robbed and despoiled of household goods and provisions and that their house was wasted and pulled down. Furthermore their young son was so barbarously treated that he languished and died.

Francis Allen, late of Fox and Geese, also described as a Gentleman and Protestant, swore that he had been robbed of a great part of his goods and estate. This is rather interesting because of such an early reference to the Fox and Geese area on the Naas Road, which took its name from a local tavern. This means that the tavern in question was in existence even prior to 1641 and makes it by far the oldest public house reference we have come across in our district.

Another local connection with the 1641 Rebellion was the Court of Outlaws set up at Kilmainham following that upheaval. Here scores of people mainly from North County Dublin were tried. The court may have been held in some part of the old Priory buildings which had survived up to then or perhaps in a new building which was the forerunner of the original Kilmainham Gaol/Courthouse.

Cromwellian Period

The 1640s were to be years of strife for Ireland with various factions, Old Irish, Old English, Planters, Parliamentarians and Royalists all in contention. Dublin did not escape the turbulence, being under siege at one stage and with its water supply cut off. However, matters came to a climax with the arrival at Ringsend in 1649 of Oliver Cromwell, who lost no time in bringing the country to heel, following a bloody and decisive campaign.

A feature of the 1641 Rebellion was the fact that those descendants of the original colonists who had remained loyal to the Catholic faith made common cause, however reluctantly, with the native Irish.

When the Cromwellians had brought their campaign to a successful conclusion, they carried out a Civil Survey in 1654 with a view to confiscating the lands of their opponents, whether Irish or Anglo-Irish. This was one of the first major surveys of Irish land and it was a massive undertaking at the time. The survey was carried out on the basis of baronies, parishes and townlands, Inchicore/Kilmainham being part of the Barony of Newcastle and Uppercross. It opens with a description of the barony boundaries and an assessment of the soil qualities. Here we find an interesting reference to the Camac river:

> "This Barony is most bountifully and conveniently watered in all places on the north with the river Liffey, which yields much fresh fish such as salmons and the like. The river Cammock descends from the mountains by many small rills dispensing its streams in many parts of the West of this Barony before emptying itself into the Liffey on the north east of Kilmainham."

Parish details include the following:

Kilmainham Parish

It contains the townlands of Kilmainham, Inchicore, Dolphins Barn, the Phoenix and Newtowne.

The quality of the land is arable, meadow and pasture.

On Kilmainham there stands the ruins of a large castle.

A street of good habitable houses.

Two double mills and a single mill in repair.

An arched stone bridge across the River Liffey.

At Inchicore the ruins of a brick house.

Part of Ballifermott Parish

It contains the townland of Gallanstown on which stands a castle-like house habitable and the ruins of a gate house.

In an accompanying table, it was stated that there were 492 "profitable" acres in the townland of Kilmainham and ninety-three in Inchicore. With regard to the village of Kilmainham, it would appear to have recovered from the decline of one hundred years earlier and to have escaped the ravages of the Cromwellian period.

West of the Shannon

Following the Civil Survey an inventory was made of those whose land had been confiscated and who were due to be transplanted to poorer holdings west of the Shannon. They were ordered to give the names of all members of their families as well as any tenants or others who wished to accompany them on a voluntary basis. Their ages, colour of hair, height and distinguishing marks were also listed by the Commissioners of Revenue, who had charge of the arrangements, before a Certificate of Transplantation was issued. The inventory appears to have been made on a parish or townland basis and in the case of Kilmainham, forty-seven names in all were listed which included seven heads of families of which the following are some examples:

Bourne, Charles	64 yrs, middle stature, grey hair
Bourne, John	24 yrs, slender stature, bright brown hair
Bourne, Mary	20 yrs, tall stature, black hair
Quinn, Turlagh	40 yrs, tall stature, brown hair
Quinn, Rose	30 yrs, middle stature, brown hair
Quinn, Ann	65 yrs, tall stature, brown grizzled hair
McGoolfinn, William	46 yrs, tall stature, brown hair
McGoolfinn, Honora	30 yrs, slender stature, flaxen hair
McGoolfinn, Joan	20 yrs, tall stature, yellow hair
Gampbell, Henry	34 yrs, middle stature, red hair
Gambell, Margaret	34 yrs, tall stature, brown hair

A much larger number of "Ballyfirmott inhabitants" were listed, of which the following are some examples:

Kavennagh, Brian	30 yrs, middle stature, brown hair
Kavennagh, Ursula	28 yrs, middle stature, black hair
Birne, Tady	30 yrs, low stature, brown hair
Birne, Catherine	20 yrs, low stature, brown hair

It does not follow however that all who were listed in these records had to transplant. Originally the Cromwellians had decided on a comprehensive clearance policy and in fact had set 20 October 1656 as a deadline for the removal of those affected who were living in Dublin south of the River Liffey. They later modified their plans when they realised the effect this would have on the economy and it is now accepted that the numbers who were forced to cross the Shannon were not as great as previously believed.

The Irish language was still to be heard in Dublin city and county much to the annoyance of the new colonists who petitioned the Municipal Council:

"Whereas by the law all persons ought to speak and use the English tongue and habit -- contrary to which and in open contempt thereof, there is Irish commonly and usually spoken and the Irish habit worn not only in the streets on market days but also by and in several families in this city to the scandalising of the inhabitants."

A committee was set up to consider "ways and means of bringing the Irish people to conform to the English nation in their apparel, speech and names."

The Down Survey 1659

The Civil Survey and Inventory was followed by an ambitious mapping of the whole country by Sir William Petty in 1659 which is known as the "Down Survey." Early copies of these maps were at a later stage captured at sea by pirates and are today in the French Government Archives in Paris.

Like the Civil Survey, the maps were based on the Barony unit. This is the earliest map reference to our district and the village of Kilmainham together with the townlands of Kilmainham and Inchicore are clearly shown. As we can see from the map illustration, the townland of Inchicore stretched from the Liffey to the site of the Railway Works and from approximately the Model School to the other end of Sarsfield Road, which traversed the full length of the townland. This indication of the then location of Inchicore more or less follows that of the *Extent of Kilmainham* one hundred years earlier.

The townland of Kilmainham was much more extensive than that of Inchicore, stretching from Islandbridge to Rialto and perhaps beyond. It also took in the southside of present day Inchicore as well as the Goldenbridge area. This remained the position until all the local townlands were revised following the first Ordnance Survey Maps of 1830. At that stage Kilmainham was reduced and Inchicore was deemed to stretch over to Tyrconnell Road but was sub-divided into Inchicore North and South. New townlands were created i.e. Goldenbridge North and South, Jamestown, Longmeadows near the Liffey and Butchers Arms between Inchicore and Ballyfermot.

The Parish of Kilmainham was very extensive indeed as it also embraced the Phoenix Park and Dolphins Barn as well as Inchicore and Kilmainham itself.

All of these surveys were followed by a general census in 1659:

Inchicore	3 English	5 Irish
Old Kilmainham	60 English	70 Irish
Islandbridge	10 English	16 Irish

Some doubt has been cast on the accuracy of this census but it does seem to indicate a greater number of Irish than English notwithstanding the transplantation policy and the previous centuries of colonisation.

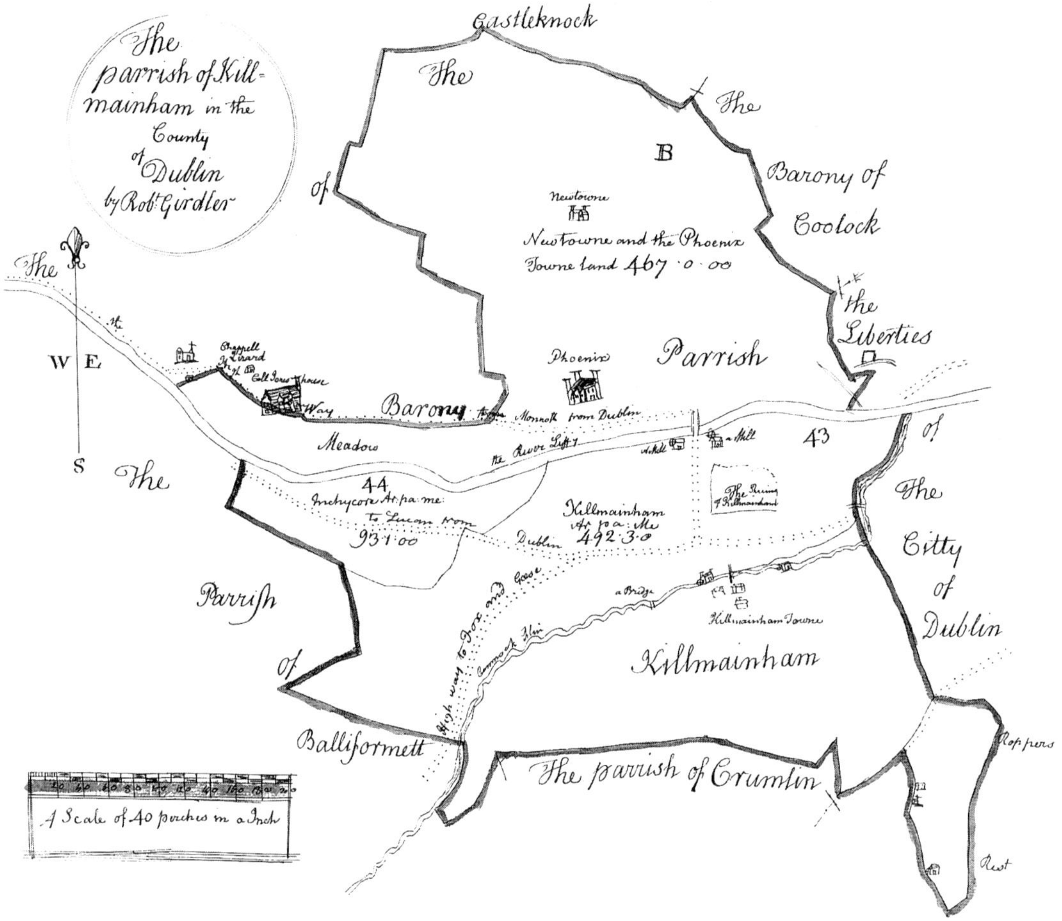

From the foregoing it is evident that Inchicore was still a rural townland with mostly arable land and sparse population but close to the progressive industrial pockets of Chapelizod, Islandbridge and Kilmainham. Also it was on the main road to the west of Ireland.

The one and only feature in Inchicore noted on the map appears to be the Brick House already mentioned in the Civil Survey and this occupies the site of "Inchicore House".

The Restoration of the Monarchy 1660

The Monarchy was restored in England in 1660 when Charles II came to the throne. He appointed James Butler, Duke of Ormond, as his Viceroy in Ireland. Dublin became more prosperous in these years, the laws against Catholics were relaxed and it was at this time that the Royal Hospital at Kilmainham was established.

It was at this time also that a property tax was introduced to provide additional revenue for the Crown. The Act imposed a tax on the owners or occupiers of houses at the rate of two shillings sterling for every hearth or fireplace in the house. This became known as "Hearth Money" and was payable twice a year on the Feast of Saint Michael, the Archangel and on the Feast of the Annunciation of the Virgin Mary. The tax was not to apply where the house had a low valuation or where the occupieris goods, lands or chattels did not exceed £10.

The names of the occupiers and the number of chimneys on each house were recorded in the Hearth Money Rolls. In the case of Inchicore, there was only one house (with one chimney) occupied by a Mr John Hill, which was liable for the tax.

With regard to Kilmainham, which probably included the townland as well as the village, forty-seven houses liable for tax are listed. The bulk of these had one or two chimneys, a small number had three or four while a Mr James Allen had the largest house with seven chimneys. A Mr Taylor is noted as having a house with two chimneys as well as a forge.

The Rolls also disclose that both locally and in the surrounding areas a sizeable minority of Irish names are mentioned. Also only a few miles away in Palmerstown Parish a townland called Irishtown is mentioned. All of this is further evidence that not all of the original Irish inhabitants were moved on subsequent to the coming of the Anglo-Normans or the Cromwellian clearances. Furthermore the mere presence of these names on the Rolls would seem to indicate that at that time some at least of the Irish were relatively comfortable.

Chapter Nine

The Royal Hospital

The Duke of Ormond, the newly appointed Viceroy, made representations to the King for the building of a large scale institution for old and disabled soldiers on the lines of the Hotel des Invalides in Paris. The King approved this application:

> "We direct a Hospital to be erected near our City of Dublin for the reception and entertainment of such ancient, maimed and infirm officers and soldiers as have faithfully served or hereafter shall serve us, our Heirs and Successors, in the strength and vigour of their youth, may in the weakness and disaster of their old age, wounds or other misfortunes may bring them into, find a comfortable retreat and competent maintenance therein".

The lands of the old Priory at Kilmainham were selected as a suitable site for the new hospital which was designed by William Robinson. A letter from Ormond to the latter commences:

> "To our trusty and well beloved William Robinson, Surveyor General".

The foundation stone was laid by Ormond on 29th April 1680 and the work got under way.

Transfer of Lands

As already mentioned, these lands were at that time part of the Phoenix Park and it was now necessary to put them under the control of the new hospital. In the course of a letter to Ormond, King Charles wrote:

> "Whereas we have directed the building of a hospital for the maintenance and convenience of such aged and maimed soldiers of our army in Ireland as are or shall be, become unserviceable.
>
> "And the said hospital is already begun to be erected upon part of lands now enclosed in our park called The Phoenix Park near the old ruinous building commonly called the Castle of Kilmainham, our will and pleasure is that the said lands whereupon the said hospital is now building together with such a quantity of land adjoining (not exceeding in the whole sixty four

The Royal Hospital Kilmainham

acres) as you shall think fit, is set apart and forever continued for the use of the said hospital.

"And for so doing these our letter shall be your sufficient warrant and so we bid you most heartily farewell".

As a result of this decision the old Priory lands between the new hospital and the Liffey were given to the Royal Hospital and the Phoenix Park boundaries became as they are today. Many years on, the hospital authorities were forced to cede portions of the lands for the new railway station at Kingsbridge as well as the main line to the south and for the building of Saint John's Road.

Fortunately at some stage the narrow strip of land on the south bank of the Liffey from Islandbridge to Chapelizod (on some of which the Memorial Park was built) was acquired by the Crown, thus enabling it to be used as a public amenity which complements the Phoenix Park on the other side of the river. Officially this has been known as the Phoenix Park extension.

An Artillery Depot

One of the clauses in the Charter granted to the Royal Hospital in 1684 brings to light the little known fact that a short time prior to that, an artillery depot with a practice firing range had been established on a small portion of the lands now being provided for the hospital. The Crown stipulated in the Charter that this area was to be retained for the army as follows:

> "The Master Gunner and other Officers of the Ordnance in our army may from time to time make use of the Gun Yard, House and Butt lately erected on the aforesaid sixty four acres, to exercise the gunners of our train of artillery there, in such manner as shall be thought fit".

The ground in question is indicated as being 2,500 feet in length and 100 feet in width but the exact location is not mentioned. However, as it was here that the old field pieces were being discharged, it had to be well away from the new hospital. For this and other reasons which we shall refer to later, it is most probable that this artillery depot and range was situated on the site of Clancy Barracks of which it was a very early fore-runner.

The Old Man's House

The Royal Hospital, situated on the city side of the old Priory or Castle, took four years to build and became known to generations of local people up to recently, as "The Old Man's House".

This extensive and beautiful building was designed in the form of a quadrangle and enclosed a spacious courtyard. The very old stained glass used in the east window of the Hospital Chapel may be the only survival from the old Priory Church. Some of the timbers for the Hospital came from the oak wood at Drimnagh. The main doorway to the Hospital leads to the Great Hall which was the show-piece of the whole building and brings back memories of that other great hall where once the Knights Hospitallers held court. High above the doorway rises the Clock Tower, a landmark for miles around, particularly when illuminated at night.

The Hospital had accommodation for three hundred men. For the next 240 years, right down to the early years of the new Irish State, successive generations of old soldiers were provided for here in comfortable surroundings, unaffected by the social deprivation outside. The only time they were seriously disturbed was during the few years of the Jacobite administration and to a lesser extent during Easter Week 1916.

From the Records

The Governors of the Royal Hospital over the centuries kept meticulous records and the following random selection illustrates something of the life of that institution:

Ordered – That it be an established rule that if any soldier of the Hospital shall presume to marry, he be immediately turned out of the house and the Hospital clothes taken from him.
Resolved – In order that they may have a decent appearance at the Hospital, each officer to be furnished with a scarlet coat, an Athlone hat with gold lace and a pair of blue worsted stockings, to be paid out of the pay of each officer.
Appointed – For the better preservation of the soldiers, many having been lost for want of a surgeon being at hand to bleed them or apply other remedies, Robert Curtis, Surgeon's mate, is appointed as Resident Surgeon of the Hospital.
Approved – Numbers of soldiers especially those who have come from abroad are violently afflicted with scorbutic disorders and are advised that Lucan Spa Water may be of great service to them. We are of opinion therefore that a car with proper vessels and a horse should be immediately provided and maintained at the Hospital for this sanitary purpose.
Ordered – That on Christmas Day, St Patrick's Day and the King's Birthday, each man should receive a double allowance of rations and two quarts of ale in lieu of beer.
Ordered – That no more than 180 men including Sergeants, Corporals and Drummers shall be sent to mount guard in town. (From time to time those who were fit were called upon for such duties).
Decided – Not to approve of the siting of two powder magazines in the grounds of the Hospital.
Our Opinion – In relation to the claim of the Archbishop (Protestant) of Dublin to visit the Chapel of the Institution, we are of opinion that the Chapel of Kilmainham, being a Royal Chapel, is not under the jurisdiction of the Archbishop and is not visitable by his Grace's Rural Dean.
Determined – The Master having informed the Governors that he had received a note from the Law Agent of the Dublin Corporation, claiming a right to fish in the river Liffey opposite the Hospital lands – The Governors declared their full determination to support the rights and privileges of the Hospital against the Dublin Corporation or any persons whatsoever who may attempt to injure such rights and privileges.
Granted – The Governors are pleased to sign a permission to John Green, fishmonger, for fishing in the river Liffey opposite the Hospital lands.

As we can see the Governors, very like their predecessors, the Knights Hospitallers, guarded their independent Charter jealously. Again the similarity persists when the age-old controversy regarding fishing rights in the Liffey raised its head once more.

Our Colonial Past

There are few places in Ireland apart from Dublin Castle which are more resonant of our colonial past than the Royal Hospital and its precincts. In the Great Hall full length portraits of those associated with the Hospital such as King Charles II, King William of Orange and the Duke of Ormond, hang on the walls while a brass plate which used to be on a Hospital doorway reads as follows:

> "This plate has been inscribed by the non-commissioned officers and privates of the Royal Hospital to record their deep sense of the condescension of Her Most Gracious Majesty, Queen Victoria, in having personally visited this room on the 7th August 1849, thereby evincing the kind interest taken by this Royal Personage in the veteran inmates of this noble institution".

All of this at a time when Ireland had just lost two million of its people due to the Great Famine!

The words "ADJUTANT GENERAL'S OFFICE" still loom large over another building nearby reminding us that for centuries up to 1913 British Military Headquarters in Ireland were also situated in these grounds. While in the officers' cemetery at the end of the long avenue headstone inscriptions record the world-wide campaigns of the far-flung British Empire.

Some typical inscriptions:
CAPTAIN KENNETH TOLNIE R.I.P. 24 MARCH 1809
Formerly of the Royal Highlanders in which distinguished corps he served in King George the Second's wars and was one of the few officers that survived the memorable attack on Ticonderoga in North America.

ROBERT COOK R.I.P. 8/6/1851
Formerly of the 29th Foot and Royal Newfoundland Fencibles who spent sixty-three years in the royal service at sea and on land.

CAPTAIN JAMES HAY R.I.P. 2/7/1854
He served in the West Indies under Abercrombie and in the Peninsula under Wellington as adjutant of the 7th Royal Fusiliers with which corps he was engaged in several sieges and battles.

CAPTAIN WILLIAM STRICKLAND McGILL R.I.P. 2/11/1886
Formerly of the 79th Cameron Highlanders with which regiment he served throughout the campaigns of the Crimea and the Indian Mutiny.

LT. COLONEL CHARLES BLACKBURNE D.S.O., R.I.P. 10/10/1918
Formerly of the 5th Dragoon Guards. Also his son, Peter, and daughter, Beatrice. All three lost their lives in the sinking of HMS Leinster by a German submarine.

The wheel of history has now come full circle with an Irish army providing contingents for United Nations peace-keeping operations in many of the trouble spots of the world.

The oldest legible headstone in this particular burial ground refers to Corporal William Proby R.I.P. 28 July 1700, an N.C.O. rather than an officer. It has been stated that Corporal Proby was a veteran of the Battle of the Boyne where he was wounded at Marshal Schomberg's side.

Closure

The Royal Hospital finally closed its doors in 1928 when the remaining pensioners were transferred to Chelsea. Part of the building was used as Garda Síochána Headquarters for some time, but then became unoccupied for many years. In 1980/84 with substantial E.E.C. funding, the building was comprehensively refurbished. Today it houses the Museum of Modern Art as well as being a centre for music recitals, while the grounds are open to the public.

The Jacobite Period 1687–1690

King James II came to the English throne in 1687 for a brief three year reign which saw a Catholic administration in Ireland including the Royal Hospital. Prior to that as James, Duke of York, he had a holding of one hundred and fifty acres at "Inchigore," which may account for the local name, Jamestown.

The Duke of Ormond was recalled and his last official function was at Kilmainham, where he proclaimed King James as King. The new king appointed "Fighting Dick" Talbot, a close relative of the Belgard Castle Talbots, as his Viceroy in Ireland. He was given the title of Earl of Tyrconnell from which we have locally, Tyrconnell Road, Tyrconnell Street, Tyrconnell Park and Tyrconnell Villas. It is likely that he held lands in the area and these may have previously been owned by his mentor at Jamestown. It was Talbot's wife, Lady Tyrconnell, who made the famous rejoinder to King James that "his Majesty had won the race" when he complained that his Irish troops had run away at the Battle of the Boyne.

Following the victory of King William of Orange at the Boyne in 1690, Dublin City and County was taken over without a struggle by the Williamites and their wounded were accommodated at the Royal Hospital.

In the Journal of John Stevens, a Jacobite officer, we find the following local reference:

> "With the remnants of what had been four regiments, having crossed over from the north side of the Liffey by Bloody Bridge (Watling Street), we halted in a field at Kilmainham, a hamlet adjoining the city. We intended to camp at Kilmainham Park but later decided to continue our retreat to Limerick".

It was during the Siege of Limerick that Talbot died.

The ensuing Treaty of Limerick and Flight of the Wild Geese were now to restore the Protestant/English ascendency in Ireland for centuries to come.

Richard Talbot, Earl of Tyconnel 1690

Chapter Ten

On to the Eighteenth Century

The eighteenth century was a period of significant expansion for the capital city, notwithstanding widespread deprivation, grinding poverty and overcrowding. With a population reaching 150,000 Dublin had become one of the larger cities of Europe. These decades could be said to mark the beginning of the city as we know it now with the development of the port, the laying out of the quays along the Liffey, the great squares and magnificent buildings such as the Custom House, the Four Courts, the Royal Exchange (now City Hall) and many others. For all of these improvements and beautiful buildings, it was an age of striking contrasts with splendour and squalor going side by side in Dublin.

Thomas Street was a bustling centre of business and country produce, while James's Street had its fair near the Fountain. In Fishamble Street, Handel had presented his Messiah. Not far away in South Earl Street in the Liberties the Gaelic poets, Tadhg and Sean O'Neachtain and their literary friends of the hidden Ireland were composing their verses.

The eighteenth century also witnessed the gradual relaxation of the Penal Laws, but full emancipation was many years away. In the earlier part of the century, trade and commerce had declined drastically in Dublin with terrible consequences for both the poor and the middle classes. This unhappy state was brought about by the imposition of crippling taxes on native manufacture by the English Government in order to protect their own industries. An improvement in trade and commerce was to come about in the last twenty years of the century under pressure from Grattan's Parliament and Volunteers before the Act of Union cast its dark shadow over the city and the country. The final years of the century were marked by the rise of the United Irishmen and the 1798 Rebellion.

Nearer to our own district, Saint Patrick's Hospital was built due to the generosity of Dean Swift and nearby Dr Steeven's Hospital opened its doors for the first time. The Poor House and Foundling Hospital where Saint James's Hospital now stands had already been established. Across the Liffey the Phoenix Park, under the dedicated Lord Chesterfield, was beginning to take shape as a public park. In our own district proper many important developments took place in this century also, with the opening of the turn-pike roads, the building of the South Circular Road and Sarah Bridge, the Grand Canal, the new Artillery Barracks at Islandbridge, the new Jail at Kilmainham and a paper mill at Golden Bridge. Less agreeable to the local residents was the transfer early in the century of the place of public execution from Parkgate Street to Kilmainham.

The centres of population were still at Kilmainham and Islandbridge, while Inchicore was still distinctly rural. In the early part of the century the only large buildings were Goldenbridge House and Inchicore House, but as the century progressed a number of gentlemen's residences with ornamental gardens began to appear.

The Annesley Case

The name of Inchicore came into prominence for the first time with the Annesley Case of 1743 which was the *cause célèbre* of the eighteenth century. One of the principals involved was an Englishman, Arthur Annesley, the 4th Lord Altham, who owned extensive estates in England and Ireland and who lived first in Wexford and later in Dublin City. He was what my father might describe as a "quare officer". He came out to live in Inchicore in 1720 having first, for reasons best known to himself, abandoned his young son, James Annesley, in the city. In the subsequent case a witness, Thomas Byrne, stated that he "advised James to go to Inchicore" while another witness testified that "the young boy came to my Lord's house at Inchicore, but was denied admittance".

It is believed that it was in Inchicore House that Lord Altham took up residence, there being few, if any, other large houses in Inchicore at that time. Also, while the reports of the long and complicated trial do not give the name of the house, it is described as "not being far from the Butcher's Arms Tavern". The latter was situated on Lower Ballyfermot Road on the site of the De La Salle Schools, less than half a mile from Inchicore House.

Lord Altham died about 1729 and his brother, Richard, equally unscrupulous, assumed the title and the estates. He took steps to have his nephew, James, sent off to the Colonies, but the latter after thirteen years made his way back and initiated proceedings in 1743, claiming that he was the rightful heir. The verdict was given in favour of the young man, but there were numerous delays and he died in 1759 before he could actually obtain possession of the estates. The uncle continued in possession until his own death two years later in 1761.

Races at Kilmainham Commons 1747

Notwithstanding the frequently disturbed state of the country, horse racing had continued for centuries in Ireland and was patronised by all classes of society, rich and poor, Catholic and Protestant. Local centres of the sport were at Crumlin, Palmerstown and Kilmainham Commons. Perhaps because of the sale of intoxicating liquor at the courses, the race meetings were often the scene of rioting and as a result were prohibited under an Act of 1739:

> "And whereas horse races are found greatly to promote and encourage idleness amongst the artisans, farmers and day-labourers of this Kingdom be it enacted etc."

However, a blind eye was generally turned to the Act and the races continued to be supported by both the gentry and the proletariat. In 1747 the races were due to be held as usual at Kilmainham Commons at the top of Brookfield Road or perhaps beyond Rialto Bridge and in fact took place on the first two days, Monday and Tuesday, the 2nd and 3rd of August. There appeared to be complaints from a neighbouring land owner, but for whatever reason the authorities decided not to allow racing on the third day. Their decision was to have tragic consequences, as we learn from a contemporary newspaper report:

> "On Wednesday last, the Sub-Sheriff of the County of Dublin, attended by a party of constables and a detachment of soldiers from the Poddle Guard under the command of a sergeant, went to the Commons of Kilmainham to prevent the assembly of people to see the races to be run there that afternoon as had been done the days preceding. To do this effectually orders were given to pull down the booths and break the barrels in which were strong liquors which was punctually executed. The populace, however, expressed their disapproval of such proceedings by crying out "Shame, shame", or as some say a stone having been thrown, the soldiers were commanded to fire which they did and killed one man on the spot and wounded three others who died soon after."

It appeared at the Coroner's Inquest that one Mr King whose lands were adjoining to the Commons and whose ditches had suffered by the spectators, "had been one great cause of this tragedy" and both inquests, viz. that held in the county on the body of the man killed on the spot and that held in the City on those who died of their wounds agreed in their verdicts of wilful murder.

A Local Windmill 1763

Water power as we have seen was being put to maximum use over the centuries on the Liffey and the Camac rivers, but wind power was not overlooked either. In the Dublin area at that time there were quite a few windmills in operation. We can still see the stump of one of these on the hill overlooking Rathcoole, while nearer at hand on the premises of Guinness's Brewery in James's Street is a massive windmill tower topped with a weather vane of Saint Patrick.

Rocque's map of County Dublin for 1756 indicates a windmill near the site of the present Kilmainham Jail to which there is an interesting reference in Sleaters Gazetteer of December 1763, as follows:

"In the storm of Thursday last, the windmill on Gallows Hill near Kilmainham was set a going with such velocity that the iron-work being greatly heated, set the mill on fire, by which it was entirely consumed".

Lead Ore at Kilmainham 1767

Dr Rutty in his *Natural History of Co Dublin 1772* states:

"At another quarry adjoining the Commons at Kilmainham called Flemings Quarry higher up the road than Jones's Quarry, there was raised in 1767 and 1768 in about eighteen months 50 to 70 tons of lead ore which yielded about 1,200 of lead from each ton of ore and about 24 ounces of silver from each ton of lead. There are two or three seams of lead in the quarry, all apparently making their course into the Commons".

At least one of these quarries seems to have been at the rear of Ardiffs, the printers. In a further reference to another find he says:

"The vein seems to take its course across the road to Andrews house near the wall of the court of the said house".

This is probably a reference to the "Ball Court" or hand-ball alley near Carrigan's Pub, formerly Muldowneys, which is shown on a later map of 1830.

South Circular Road and Sarah Bridge

Apart from the canal, the other most significant development of the local infrastructure was the building of the South Circular Road in 1775. This involved two new bridges at Kilmainham, the first one across the Camac and a second smaller one across the mill race nearby. The former was known at the time as Fortescue Bridge, but we do not know the origin of this name. The other small bridge became known as Drum's Bridge, as we shall see later on.

The new circular road contributed to the outward spread of the city and helped to open up our own area as well.

The completion of the circular road was culminated with the building of the impressive Sarah Bridge, which has a single stone arch measuring thirty-one metres. The foundation stone was laid by Sarah, the Countess of Westmoreland, in 1791 and hence the official name. However, it has been commonly known as Islandbridge over the years.

There had been several bridges near this historic crossing of the river Liffey, all of them known as Kilmainham Bridge. They were situated somewhat upstream from Sarah Bridge and nearer to the Ford of Kilmahanok. The last one being replaced by

*Sarah Bridge (Island Bridge), Kilmainham. From an engraving (*Sentimal & Masonic Magazine Vol. 1*)*

Sarah Bridge had suffered flood damage and was originally built in 1578 on the orders of Sir Henry Sidney, who was Queen Elizabeth's Lord Deputy in Ireland.

A New Artillery Barracks

A barracks for the Royal Irish Artillery had been located at Chapelizod since 1755. As this was not spacious enough for their needs, a new barracks was built in 1797 "on a piece of ground contiguous to the Royal Hospital at Kilmainham". This was also the time when the new Kilmainham Jail was nearing completion. As previously mentioned, there had been an artillery depot and range in the Hospital grounds prior to 1680 and we can assume that the new barracks was established on that same location. It became known as Islandbridge Barracks for generations, but was re-named as Clancy Barracks in 1942, Peadar Clancy having been Director of Ordnance during the War of Independence.

Over the years it had been greatly extended to provide for a Cavalry Barracks as well, alongside the Liffey and also an Ordnance Department and a Re-Mount Depot. At the latter, scores of horses were schooled and broken in for the many uses of the army and even of the Dublin Metropolitan Police.

Within the barrack walls, there was a Cambridge Square and one wonders if this had any connection with that tall old tenement building in Goldenbridge just outside Richmond Barracks, known as Cambridge House.

The notable Fenian and man of letters, John Boyle O'Reilly, as a young man served in Islandbridge with the 10th Hussars. Also employed there as a clerical worker prior to 1916 was Captain Robert Monteith, whose name will always be associated with Sir Roger Casement. He was dismissed from his position because of his connection with the Irish Volunteers.

The cavalry and the artillery have long gone from Islandbridge but since 1922 the barracks has been the Headquarters of the Ordnance Corps. However, it has recently been listed for closure which would bring to an end the 300 year old military tradition in the area.

Chapter Eleven

By Coach and Barge (1)

The Turn-Pike Roads

The first Turn-Pike road in Ireland, that between Dublin and Kilcullen in County Kildare, operated through Kilmainham and Inchicore as from 1729 under an Act of Parliament of that year. It commenced near the Fountain in James's Street and the second toll house and turn-pike gate known as "The Black Lyon Turn-Pike" was situated opposite Scoil Mhuire Gan Smál on present day Tyrconnell Road. At that time the old inn gave its name to some of the district nearby. A gate was erected across the road and passing traffic had to stop and pay a fee to a keeper at the toll-house before being allowed to go on. These gates were established at regular intervals, the next one being at the "Red Cow." The toll-house here was occupied as a dwelling up to modern times when it had to make way for road widening. Many will remember it as a squat little building somewhat below the level of the path and road. Although not used for such purposes for well over a hundred years it was known right up to the time of its demise as the Turn-Pike House.

Other taverns on the Naas Road were "The Blue Bell", "The Red Lion", "The Fox and Geese", "The Shoulder of Mutton" and later, near the Canal Bridge, "The Black Horse". Whatever other hardships travellers had to endure there was at least no danger of their going thirsty.

The road was administered by a Turn-Pike Trust known as the Kilcullen Road Company and consisted of well known people, mainly land owners. Their function was to develop and maintain the road in return for which they received the toll fees charged within a set scale. In the Directors' Journal of 1787, one of the few existing documents relating to this company and now in the possession of the National Library, we find some of the charges for the previous year as follows:

Coach with six horses	1/8 per horse
Coach with four horses	1/- per horse
Coach with two horses	6 pence per horse
Coach with one horse	3 pence per horse
Horse and cart	1 penny
Horse only	1 penny
Droves of cattle	1/8 per score
Droves of calves, hoggs or sheep	10 pence per score

From the same journal, we also learn of a meeting between the directors and local land owners at the house of a Mr James Wilson, near the Black Lyon Turnpike on the 27th June 1787 at which it was agreed to pay six guineas per acre for ground required to widen the road. Also under consideration at several of the directors' meetings was the question of widening Golden Bridge.

Hazards of the Road

The bad condition of the roads, particularly in the first half of the eighteenth century, which was liable to cause accidents, and the uncertainty of the weather made travelling by coach a rather hazardous affair. An additional menace was provided by the highwaymen and all coach drivers were accompanied by at least one armed guard. The directors also ordered that all disused quarries alongside the route, where these gentlemen of the roads were wont to gather, were to be filled in.

A newspaper reported in 1772 that there were three highwaymen well mounted operating on the Naas Road and that two travellers were very lucky to escape from them recently near Bluebell but not before one of them lost the contents of his saddle bag. In November 1793 a Myles Burke was hanged for highway robbery at Fox and Geese.

An inscription, which unfortunately is undated, on a silver teapot presented to a Rathcoole Inn Keeper reads as follows:

> "To Patrick Berry in testimony of his spirited conduct in apprehending a notorious highway robber".

Could this be a relative of another Patrick Berry, who at a later period was a vintner in Golden Bridge and after whom Berry's Lane, now Spa Road, was called?

It was not until 1820 that highway robbery was finally stamped out.

The Irish Post Office was established in 1784 and the mail coach service came into operation in 1789, bringing about a further increase in traffic. The southern mail coach left the centre of the city each night at 10.00 p.m. and under favourable conditions arrived in Cork thirty-one hours later, a time which was reduced to eighteen hours in the next century.

The Mullingar Road Company

Tyrconnell Road was not the only part of the district to have a turn-pike road. A second such road to the west was established in 1786 and was operated by the Mullingar Road Company, which lasted until 1854. It operated along Kilmainham Lane, Inchicore Road, passing the "Cow and Calf" and on to Palmerstown via Lower Ballyfermot, passing the "Butchers Arms" on the way. It also controlled a second road to the west, along Conyngham Road, through Chapelizod where we still have the "Mullingar House".

The Freemans Journal was rather apprehensive regarding the condition of Kilmainham Lane (The High Road) at that time as we learn from their report of October 1787:

> "An Act of Parliament passed last session empowering the trustees of the Mullingar turnpike to open the roads leading to Dublin on the south and north sides of the Liffey, but yet not the least steps have been taken to remove or remedy the desperate situation in which the passage leading from Bow Bridge to Gallows Hill is in. Numerous accidents happened last season and last night a dray returning to town was suspended in such a manner that the horse was very near being strangled. On the south side of this road near Kilmainham, there is a very great precipice and not the least wall or barrier to guide the eye or to protect the unfortunate horse of the still more unfortunate carrier, two of whom within the last twelve months have lost their means of livelihood by their horses tumbling down and were constrained to sell their miserable animals to the carrion butcher. Surely as they willingly pay turnpike, they have the right to have the road in proper repair and it is a doubt whether an action would not be against the Trustees for such damages as may accrue through their neglect."

Bow Bridge in the early years of this century

Up the Heights of Kilmainham

Presumably the above danger was subsequently rectified, but in any event we have by contrast the following delightful cameo of travel along here nearly fifty years later:

> "I left the Post Office in Her Majesty's Mail perched on the box-seat on a delightful evening in August. Our coachman was a jolly waggish fellow and – except in crossing over the Menai Bridge by moonlight – the four horses at full speed, I never beheld a prettier sight in the four-in-hand style than on emerging from Bow Bridge and Bow Lane.
>
> "He dashed up the heights of Kilmainham to the celebrated Widow Drum's, the horses at full speed, the guard's bugle sounding and the screaming of old women as the coachman twitted his lash and picked up cocks, hens and ducklings as we passed along, letting them fly back again. When we reached the widows, it was sublimely ridiculous and of course raised a chorus of laughter. On we passed in dashing style through Palmerstown, Lucan and so on to Athlone".

The above account is from *St Catherine's Bells*, the autobiography of Walter T. Meyler, the James's Street/Thomas Street business man and patriot, who was undertaking a trip to County Galway in 1836. It was the late Mr Tim Dawson, former President of the Old Dublin Society and one time resident of Jamestown Road, who first drew my attention to this book, which is a mine of information on the life and lore of old Dublin and, as we shall see, has several other references to our own district as well.

The Widow Drum's, her full name was Drummond, is now the "Patriots Inn". Old-timers in the area used to refer to the small bridge nearby spanning the mill-race as "Drum's Bridge", which was also a trysting place giving rise to the saying "See you at Drum's Bridge". Drums was also one of the local pubs where spades and other implements were provided for mourners who were burying their dead in Bully's Acre across the road.

The first toll gate on the Mullingar Road was situated a short distance beyond the entrance to Inchicore House nearly opposite the "Khyber Pass". The remains of the small stone toll-keeper's house was in existence up to about thirty years ago and formed part of the boundary wall of Inchicore House at the "Ranch" corner.

Widows Alms-House

A local man with the unusual name of John Loggins established a very successful coaching business in the eighteenth century near his home at Bow Bridge. He was to become very friendly with the Assize Judges whom he drove when on circuit. In these circumstances, he tended to wine and dine to excess and eventually became an alcoholic. However, he eventually reformed, lived a life of prayer and austerity and devoted himself to helping the less fortunate. One of the events which brought about this change of life-style was his brush with death when a bridge over which he had just driven collapsed behind him into a river below. Having sold his coaches and horses, he converted the unoccupied stables into an alms house for widows. Later he succeeded in extending this further and before his death in 1774 was able to afford a shelter to twenty widows.

The End of the Road

"Drimna Lodge", a large Georgian house situated near the junction of the Naas Road and Killeen Road and occupied up to about twenty-five years ago, when it was demolished, formed one of the last links with the Kilcullen Road Company. This house was built in 1820 by William Taylor, the Treasurer of the company, who resided there. All of his family, who were road engineers and mappers, were very much involved with the company for generations and at one stage virtually owned it. Mr Taylor was a very far-seeing man and even before the end of coach travel had already become involved with the proposed new railway company. Eventually he was to become Secretary of the Great Southern and Western Railway Company. It was surely a case of "If you can't beat 'em, join 'em".

While the Kilcullen Road Company had its ups and downs in the eighteenth century its financial position showed much improvement in the nineteenth century due to increased volume of traffic and better management. It was indeed a going concern until the establishment of the railways to the south of Ireland in 1846. This brought to an end long distance coach travel, and it was only a matter of some years before the company went out of existence for all time. As mentioned previously there is little surviving record, but in 1980 a volume labelled *Kilcullen Road Company* was discovered in a C.I.E. strong-room which provided much additional information on the latter years of the company including the financial statements for 1844/48. The following extract tells its own story:

> "The mails stopped running on the Naas Road on Wednesday, 30 September 1846 and commenced being taken by train on Thursday, 1 October 1846".

As the railway line to the west was not developed until some years later, the Mullingar Road Company was able to operate up to 1855 when the turn-pike gate at Sarsfield Road was taken down. In those intervening years, Inchicore was in the unique position of having coach, canal and rail services passing through the district.

Today the only reminder of a significant and colourful period in Irish transport history is the little milestone set against the school wall on Tyrconnell Road.

Chapter Twelve

By Coach and Barge (2)

The Grand Canal

The opening of the Grand Canal in 1779 which brought about the first great change in the landscape of the area was the most important local development of the century. It also provided competition for the coach and horse drawn road services, but as it turned out there was room for both forms of transport. The idea of linking Dublin with the river Shannon by an inland waterway had been mooted for decades and was only achieved after many disappointments and false starts, not to mention protracted construction works under various engineers. At the time it was, of course, a tremendous civil engineering achievement with the ground gradually rising to two hundred feet above James's Street Harbour at the highest point in County Kildare. The building of numerous locks and bridges along the route, as well as the supervision of hundreds of labourers of which there was no shortage in Ireland at that time, was no mean feat.

The actual work of digging out the canal commenced in 1756 but was not capable of receiving the water which was provided by the Morell river near Straffan until 1766. When it did so, Dublin Corporation entered into an agreement with the Canal Company to take their supply of water for the needs of the City from the canal and this arrangement lasted until 1868.

In 1769 it was necessary to build a bridge to take the newly constructed South Circular Road across the canal and although officially named as Harcourt Bridge, it soon became popularly known as Rialto Bridge because of a fancied resemblance to the more famous bridge in Venice. At the time it was described as both useful and ornamental. A further bridge was required at the top of Tyrconnell Road to take the Naas Road across the canal, and this became known as The Black Horse Bridge from the nearby inn of that name. It is also called The Third Lock Bridge.

In between these two bridges the little valley of the Camac river had also to be crossed and for this purpose a stone aqueduct was built, mentioned in contemporary records as:

> "The great arch or aqueduct built in the Glin near the high road at Golden Bridge".

Near the Fifth Lock a stream running from Blackditch and Gallanstown and which joins the Camac at Blue Bell was bridged also. Close by an old road which

The Black Horse Inn and Third Lock Bridge in the early years of this century

joined these areas from ancient times was severed by the new canal. Then near the Seventh Lock the narrow hump-backed bridge, which still survives, was built to take the Ballyfermot– Fox and Geese Road.

Cottage style houses for the lock keepers and their families were built at the First, Second, Third, Fifth, Sixth and Eighth Locks, all originally on the south side. The only house surviving today on that side is the one at the Fourth lock. From 1766, elm trees were planted all along the banks of the canal out as far as the Seventh Lock bridge. The Pipe-Water Committee of the Corporation "conceived that the canal would be a pleasing recreation as well as a salutory walk for the inhabitants of Dublin if trees were planted". However, they also had in mind that they would provide a supply of timber to renew the city water pipes, as they became decayed. Fortunately, however, this became unnecessary as wooden water pipes were shortly afterwards replaced by iron pipes and most of the trees survived until World War II. Today a few "veterans" are still to be seen.

Official Opening

On 15th April 1773 the foundation stone for the First Lock was laid with pomp and ceremony by the Lord Lieutenant, Earl Harcourt, but it was only in June 1779 that the first horse drawn commercial boat owned by one Thomas Digby Brooks "sailed" out from James's Street Harbour along the new canal for a twelve mile voyage to County Kildare. This was followed by passenger travel one year later.

In 1791 the canal was extended to Athy and finally in 1804 to the River Shannon. In the meantime in 1796 a further major development had taken place not far from the First Lock. Here a new branch was constructed to provide a connection with the Liffey and the port of Dublin near Ringsend. This locally involved a new bridge, Griffith Bridge, as well as seven other bridges all the way down to Ringsend. From 1804 only commercial traffic operated from James's Street Harbour while the passenger boats plied from the Canal Company's hotel at the Portobello Depot.

New Industries

The canal opened up the area to new industries. The most notable of these were the Harcourt Flour Mills, the Mount Shannon Flour Mills and the Goldenbridge Paper Mills (later Brassington's Saw Mills). The two flour mills were situated on the south bank near the first and second locks and were operated by the waters of the canal drawn off by a mill-race. Later on one of these mills became Parsons Paint factory to which up to sixty years ago canal barges brought the raw material in the form of sacks of resin. This substance was then ground down by the mill-wheels.

The paper mill was on the northside, close to where the canal crossed the Camac and was powered by the waters of that little river. This mill had a special relationship with the Canal Company, who issued notes from one to ten guineas with which they paid their employees. It was the Goldenbridge Paper Mill which provided the paper for these notes and when required the company's accountant went to the mill with the moulds and supervised the making of the notes. As soon as they were made, the moulds had to be taken away and locked securely at the offices of the Grand Canal Company at James's Street Harbour.

Nearly a hundred years later, when Brassington's took over this premises as a saw mill, they built a canal-side wharf where trees were unloaded by cranes and taken by bogey down to the mill. Indeed long after the closure of this mill, the rails for the bogeys were still in evidence on the side of the canal. On the opposite bank was the semi-circular lay-by where the boats having unloaded could turn about for their return journey. Nearby was Turrett House, the home of Mr Wayte, the canal chief engineer with its mini-nature reserve on the two ponds on each side of the avenue leading up to the house. Last occupant was the well-known business man, Mr Halpin.

Following the establishment of the Inchicore Railway Works in 1846, coal was brought by barge from the Port of Dublin to a jetty at the Fourth Lock. There it was transferred to side tipping wagons and brought over on a single track railway line to the coal bank in the Railway Works. This line, which was known to railway employees as the canal road, crossed over the top of the present Jamestown Road.

When in 1877 the tunnel under the Phoenix Park was opened to link the Great Southern Railways with the North Wall, the canal ceased to be used for the transport of coal to the railway works. The weighbridge and cottage (last occupied by the Perkins family) associated with the coal transfer is still remembered. Other industries near the canal were the two brick works, the more extensive one behind the Second Lock and a smaller one in later times at Jamestown Road.

James's Street Harbour itself was already close to an area long associated with the brewing industry and it was here in 1759 that a Mr Arthur Guinness went into business. His firm was to have an association with the canal which was to last for the whole lifetime of that waterway.

Apart from "Guinness", wheat, barley, coal, turf and general merchandise were transported. When turf was first brought to the harbour from the midlands, it caused a riot, as the locals complained that they were being overcharged. A further disturbance occurred shortly afterwards, when the boats and stores were forcibly searched by a mob who suspected that cotton was being sent down the country for processing. This proved not to be the case, but the harbour had for a time to be placed under a guard of constables and soldiers.

Canal barge 1933

The presence of the canal was also a factor which influenced the siting of Richmond Barracks in 1807 on its banks. The waterway had already been used during the 1798 Rebellion for the conveyance of large quantities of military stores to "different parts of the Kingdom" and when the French landed at Killala, the Marquess Cornwallis embarked a considerable number of troops at Dublin and Sallins and proceeded with them to Tullamore where they arrived fresh and fit for their march to Athlone. Subsequently the army made an agreement with the Canal Company whereby a certain number of boats were to be held in readiness for their use at an agreed sum of £900 per month.

The Passenger Boats

The passenger service was introduced by an advertisement in Faulkners Dublin Journal on 3rd August 1780, as follows:

> **GRAND CANAL**
>
> "The Publick are informed that a boat will set off henceforward to Osberstown near Naas on Mondays and Thursdays and from Osberstown to Dublin on Tuesdays and Fridays. The boat will set off precisely at six o'clock in the mornings. Passengers who choose to go in the covered Division of the boat to pay thirteen pence each and those who go in the open Division, sixpence halpenny. Each passenger to be allowed thirty pounds weight of luggage".

The passenger boats, fifty-two feet in length, were capable of taking a total of eighty travellers, forty-five as 1st Class and thirty-five as 2nd Class. A Sir John Carr travelling back to Dublin from Athy in 1805 has left us the following valuable description of the journey:

> "Upon the canal I found the boat nearly ready and precisely as the clock struck one the towing horses started and we slipped through the water in the most delightful manner imaginable, at the rate of four miles an hour. The boat had a raised cabin, its roof forming a deck to walk upon. The cabin was divided into a room for the principal passengers, having cushioned seats and windows on each side and a long table in the middle and another room for the servants of the vessel and pantry; the kitchen was in the steerage. From Athy to Dublin by water is 42 miles and the setting off and arrival of the boats are managed with great regularity. We had an excellent dinner on board consisting of a leg of boiled mutton, a turkey, ham, vegetables, porter and a pint of wine each at four shillings a head. We slept at Robertstown where there is a noble inn belonging to the Canal Company and before daylight set off for

> Dublin, where after descending a great number of locks and passing through a long avenue of fine elm trees, we arrived about 10 am".

Here it should be mentioned that the seating on the deck was only for 1st Class passengers. On passing a lock all had to go below and the hatches closed to prevent the entry of spray. The crew consisted of a captain, steerer, stopman, a boy and a barmaid, while the captain's wife supervised the catering arrangements. Blunderbusses, pistols and boarding pikes were on hand to repel marauders, but there is no record of crews being called upon to use these weapons.

The boats were drawn by two horses with postillions or mounted horsemen, who rode along the tow path and who were colourfully attired with jackets, leather breeches and hats with gold bands. Later, when a lighter and faster type of vessel known as a "Fly Boat" was put into service, the number of horses was increased to three.

From a Dr James Johnston, we have a further vivid cameo of canal travel, this time regarding an outward journey from Dublin:

> "The dress of the postillions, the measured canter or gallop of the horses, the vibrations of the ropes, the swell that precedes the boat and the dexterity with which the men and horses dive under the arches of the bridges without for a moment slackening their pace all produce a very curious and picturesque scene such as I have never seen equalled in Holland on any of its canals".

As they approached our area, leaving the city behind them, those early canal travellers had a beautiful view of the open countryside. Here they passed over the pretty winding glen of the Camac river with the distant back-drop of the Dublin hills and the nearer sandy ridges of Drimnagh and its castle.

Then as they headed for Clondalkin, there is no doubt that the main topic of conversation amongst passengers in April 1787 was the recent great explosion near that village at the Corkagh Gun Powder Mills. Extensive damage was caused over a wide area and contemporary records tell us that "the explosion was felt in the most distant parts of the County Dublin and even in the County Kildare for some miles near the banks of the Canal". Furthermore in the city it brought about the sudden fall of a chimney stack on Usher's Quay.

The passenger service traded successfully over the years, notwithstanding the competition of coach travel and built up the annual number of passengers to over 100,000. However, the age of steam was now at hand and like the coach, the passenger boat had also to give way to the newly established railways. Its career came to an end in December 1852, but the commercial boats continued right down to 1960, having been given a new lease of life during the Emergency years of World War II, particularly for the transport of turf. In 1911 the Grand Canal Company had commenced the motorisation of their fleet, but the horse was never totally eliminated, being used by a small number of independent operators to draw what was known as "hack boats".

The 27th of May 1960 was a sad day as the last barge, the "51M", passed through Inchicore on its four day journey to Limerick with a cargo of "Guinness". What had been the oldest public transport company in Ireland was now no more. The fascination of the regular coming and going of the boats with their varied cargo, the thud, thud of their engines and the sense of excitement as they passed through the locks was something to be savoured by the children of earlier generations.

For a long number of years the canal, bereft of its traffic, was allowed to deteriorate but, in 1986, was taken over by the Office of Public Works who made it navigable once more. Recently the newly formed local environment group in conjunction with F.Á.S. have initiated an ambitious scheme for the further improvement of this great amenity between Herberton Bridge and Bluebell.

Chapter Thirteen

Bully's Acre and Saint John's Well

Bully's Acre

Bully's Acre, also known as The Hospital Fields, was an ancient burial place near the old Church of Saint Maighneann and the later Church of Saint John the Baptist belonging to the Knights Hospitallers. The area was deemed to be part of Kilmainham Common and as such, a free burial ground for generations. It was accordingly much availed of by the poorer classes of Dublin. However, the more prosperous were also attracted here, as with its monastic associations it was considered to be holy ground. Furthermore, the tradition persisted amongst all classes that two of the heroes of the Battle of Clontarf, Brian Ború's son and grandson, were buried there in 1014. Some in fact clung to the mistaken belief that Brian himself was laid to rest there as well.

It was at Bully's Acre that Robert Emmet's body was temporarily laid following his execution.

In the mid-eighteenth century two local families, the Cullens and the Flanagans, controlled a lot of the activities in the vicinity of Bully's Acre and the nearby Saint John's Well. The Cullens were dairy farmers with an address at Gallows Hill, who had certain grazing rights in some of the hospital lands. In addition, they acted as unofficial caretakers at the burial ground and were able to obtain one to three pence per funeral according to the means of the relatives. The Flanagans were vintners with their premises not too far from the well and they also sold drinking glasses for use there. It has been said that the name of their pub was the Black Lion, but this may not be correct. However there was another house known as "The Sign of the Black Lion" in Islandbridge which sold garden mould in an area well known for market gardening.

Bully's Acre also became a well known centre for duelling and many an "affair of honour" between gentlemen was settled there. Judge "Bully" Egan was a noted duellist in his young days and while we have no evidence that he ever fought at this location, the possibility does exist and could suggest a further possible explanation for the origin of the name. On the other hand his nephew stated that the judge, who presided at the Old Kilmainham Courthouse, owned land at Bully's Acre which would indicate that he took his own name from the place.

As mentioned earlier, there is also the theory that it was a corruption of the "Barleyyard" referred to in the *Extent of Kilmainham*.

Over the years of the eighteenth century, those frequenting Bully's Acre became more unruly and the position was aggravated by the crowds who also came to the well. All of this created problems for the Royal Hospital who reported that "the whole situation is generally productive of riot and worse due to the vast crowds attending the well and the graveyard". On another occasion, they complained that "one of our fields is full of disorderly and idle people by day and night". Again: "Our grazing fields are rendered almost useless owing to the traffic through them to a well frequented by numbers of superstitious persons".

After many unsuccessful attempts to improve matters, the Governors in 1755 called upon the new Master of the Hospital, Major General Dilkes, to deal with the situation.

"He endeavoured", says Sir John Traill, the Hospital Surveyor, "to put a stop to the pernicious nocturnal revels. He applied to the magistrates, who frequently attended and dispersed them, and he completely enclosed the burial-ground by walls. He levelled the graves and removed the headstones. This had the desired effect. The frequent compliments to departed friends by decorating their graves with garlands and the worshipping of Brian's supposed monument ceased. These objects of respect and adoration being removed, St. John's Well lost much of its wonted powerful attraction and the burying-ground remained shut up for some years".

However, the last word had not been spoken yet.

Lord Galway's Walk

Encouraged by his success, General Dilkes then attempted also to obtain control of a passage known as Lord Galway's Walk. This pathway leading from Steevens' Lane across the hospital lands was originally created for the convenience of the Earl of Galway, a Lord Justice, who resided at Islandbridge. With the passing of time this came to be regarded as a right of way and provided an easy access for the crowds coming from the city to the well or the burial-ground. When Lord Galway died the General erected gates across the walk, but this move was opposed by other property owners and of course the proletariat still smarting over his previous victory were only waiting for an opportunity to strike back.

The County Dublin Grand Jury decided that it was illegal to close the right of way, but the Governors of the Royal Hospital appealed to the Courts who upheld the Grand Jury's decision. A large crowd had waited outside the court to hear the verdict and when this was announced, they immediately set off to take down the gates blocking the right of way. However, General Dilkes had anticipated this and removed the offending gates before they arrived.

The mob, not to be thwarted, then fell upon the walls of Bully's Acre and totally demolished them. The General lost heart at this stage and, as far as the burial ground was concerned, it was business as usual.

Nearly forty years were to elapse before it was possible to re-enclose the burial ground, as public opinion was strongly against doing so. However, by 1795 the place had fallen into such a dreadful condition that the Grand Jury were finally able to proceed without further opposition. In co-operation with the Royal Hospital, they erected a wall and gate but also gave a guarantee that the privilege of free burial would continue.

The Sack 'Em Ups

With or without walls, Bully's Acre like all of the Dublin cemeteries in the eighteenth century was constantly subjected to visits from the body snatchers or the "Sack 'Em Ups" as they were also known. These were people who dug up remains recently interred and sold them to doctors or medical students. They were particularly attracted to Bully's Acre because of the number of paupers buried there who had no one to protect their graves. A newspaper report of 1784 gives us some idea of those times:

> "A few nights ago returning from Island Bridge by the Circular Road I met four armed men coming out of the Burying Ground in the Royal Hospital fields. At first I was much alarmed thinking they were robbers but as I advanced I saw a coach and three dead bodies lying close by on the road. However I thought it prudent to set spurs to my horse without asking any questions."

One of the most notable incidents occurred when night watchmen surprised a Mr Peter Harkan of Crompton's Medical School and a party of students. They managed to escape, but not before Mr Harkan was seriously injured when the students had to drag him across the wall from the clutches of the watchmen. Another well known incident involved the body of Dan Donnelly, the prize fighter, and we shall come back to this later.

This practice only came to an end with the passing of the Anatomy Act of 1832, but by a coincidence Bully's Acre was by then about to be closed for good.

A cholera epidemic swept Ireland in 1832. During this outbreak thousands of burials took place at Bully's Acre, leading to overcrowded conditions. As a result, the authorities had no alternative but to close this ancient burial place for all time in 1833.

In the spring of 1849, two years after the famine, another wave of cholera swept over Ireland. As an emergency measure temporary huts were thrown up in the grounds of the Royal Hospital to accommodate some of the victims. One of these was the patriot poet, James Clarence Mangan, who arrived there in June 1849. He left after only three days however and made his way to a garret in Bride Street where he died some weeks later.

Headstones

Only a small proportion of people could afford headstones. On looking at the seventy or so which have survived, one would not suspect that vast numbers of people had been buried there. Some of the headstone inscriptions shed a little light on the social background of the times and the incidence of child mortality. Here are some short excerpts:

PHILIP REILLY R.I.P. 23/4/1786
Starch manufacturer of Pill Lane, age 33.

JUDITH HAYES R.I.P. 19/11/1797
Wife of Michael Hayes, Cotton Manufacturer, Rainsfort Street, Age 62.
Also her six children.

JANE MULLIGAN R.I.P. 16/7/1798
Wife of Thomas Mulligan, Shoemaker, James Street, age 36.
Also eight of her children who died young.

THOMAS MULLEN R.I.P. 15/8/1800
Publican, late of Thomas Street, age 40.
Also six of his children who died young.

LUCY ROURKE R.I.P. 28/3/1803
Wife of John Rourke, Usher's Court, age 36.
Also her seven children.

PATRICK BYRNE R.I.P. 28/7/1807
Silk Manufacturer, late of Skinner's Alley, age 40.
Also seven of his children who died young.

THOMAS NOWLAN R.I.P. 20/11/1807
Late of Spital Fields, age 53.
Also eleven of his children and four of his grandchildren who died young.

WILLIAM GREEN R.I.P. 21/4/1808
Bookseller, late of Anglesea Street, age 59.

LAWRENCE BYRNE R.I.P. 2/4/1816
Brogue Maker, late of New Row, Thomas Street, age 55.

The Oldest Headstone

Apart from Bully's Acre, there are two other cemeteries nearby, both of them primarily associated with the Royal Hospital. The first is known as the officers' graveyard, which originally was the burial place for all Royal Hospital residents, but at some later stage was confined to officers. (We have earlier given details of some of the headstones here). A separate burial place for privates and non-commissioned officers was then established and it is here that some of the British casualties during the 1916 Rising were buried.

However, it is within the confines of the officers' graveyard that the oldest headstone in any of the three cemeteries is located. This is in memory of Hugh and Elizabeth Hacket of whom we have no other details. It dates from 1652, well before the establishment of the Royal Hospital, and points to the area having been used for burials from much earlier times. As already mentioned, there was also the very strong tradition that it went back to the Battle of Clontarf.

Here a tribute must be paid to Mr Sean Murphy for his painstaking and invaluable work in having recorded and collated all the available information regarding the headstone inscriptions in these historic cemeteries.

Saint John's Well

One of Dublin's oldest customs was the annual pattern at Saint John's Well on the 25th June which was the feast day of Saint John the Baptist. This devotion was introduced by the early Anglo-Norman settlers and continued for nearly 700 years. As originally mentioned, the well was situated for most of that time near the wall of Clancy Barracks in what was then Priory lands. It can be taken that it was previously associated with the Church of Saint Maighneann but was re-dedicated by the newcomers to their own patron.

Here large crowds gathered annually over the centuries, but it gradually degenerated into something like a Donnybrook Fair, creating quite a nuisance for both city and hospital authorities. In 1710, the Irish House of Commons declared that these gatherings were a danger to the peace of the kingdom and ordered fines, whippings and imprisonment for those dangerous tumults and unlawful assemblies. In 1787 a strong letter from the Archbishop was read in all the Catholic churches:

> "Instead of gaining indulgences or reaping any benefit, they generally scandalised their holy religion and disturbed the public peace by their criminal excesses".

None of these strictures brought the pattern to an end, such was the attachment of the populace for this annual outing and the authorities were reluctant to provoke a confrontation. In 1795 when agreement was reached regarding the erection of a wall at Bully's Acre, a stone fountain was also provided at this time for the well which was now quite close to the newly constructed South Circular Road.

The pattern was still going strong in 1806 approximately when the young Walter Meyler was brought there by his nursemaid. From his pen we have a splendid account of what a day at this event was like:

> "Once I was allowed to go to a pattern at St John's Well with my nurse and her swain, a soldier on furlough. On our way we passed through the Royal Hospital and strangely did I gaze on the veterans in their singular costumes and cocked hats. The quiet imposing appearance of the place struck me forcibly and then the bustle as we passed from the western gate to John's Well – the booths formed on country carts, covered with blankets and patchwork quilts – turf and bramble fires like gipsey ones, with pots hooked over them; smoking potatoes, cabbages and crubeens, fruit, gingerbread, toys and thimble riggers.
>
> "Then the drinking scenes. Jars of pop and ginger beer, bottles and jars of whiskey. Votaries rushing to the well with tumblers or horn goblets to pay their devotions by mixing the whiskey with its saintly water; then the dancing, reeling, tumbling and reclining from the effects of the well mixture.
>
> "My nurse did not return until her friend promenaded us through "Bully's Acre", pointed out "Brien Ború's grave" and showed, to my terror, the graves desecrated by the "sack-em-ups" and strewn over in several places by shreds of winding sheets".

Here we might mention that Meyler also tells how on a further occasion he was brought to the annual fair in James's Street, an event which likewise originated in Anglo-Norman times.

With the excavation of the railway line in 1846 the source of water for the well was severed, but the spring reappeared directly opposite Bully's Acre on the westside of the South Circular Road, near Saint John's Terrace. Here a new arched surround was provided, but the age-old custom was already in decline, particularly since the permanent closure of Bully's Acre and by the end of the 1880s it had finally come to an end.

The well itself was closed over with a slab. However, a remaining link is the stone surround which by some manner or means was brought to the grounds of the Catholic Church in James's Street, where it can still be seen.

In some parts of Ireland the feast of Saint John is still commemorated by the lighting of bonfires.

Chapter Fourteen

Law, Order and Local Administration

Gallows Hill

The place of public execution at Parkgate Street was not deemed to be a pleasant sight for my lords and ladies towards the end of the seventeenth century as they made their way to the Phoenix Park, then being developed as a recreational area. It was accordingly transferred to the Lower Kilmainham Commons (now the site of the present jail), which had the advantage of being near to the County Jail at Old Kilmainham. The site became known as Gallows Hill, a name which was also used to describe the surrounding area, and for years scores of people were executed here.

There are numerous reports of executions at this venue. One such account tells us that on Saturday 4th November 1768 Denis Toole and his son-in-law Edward Brennan were executed at Gallows Hill for cow stealing pursuant to their sentence.

A more bizarre case is reported for October 1787 in the *Freemans Journal* as follows:

> "WILDE who was hanged yesterday at Kilmainham for stopping and molesting Mr. Gunning with intent to rob him, made at the place of execution ample confession of the many enormities he had committed and declared that if the blunderbuss had gone off he would certainly have shot the person he attacked.
>
> "When cut down a number of fellows laid hold of the body and carried it without a coffin or any other covering along the Circular Road where they several times attempted to restore him to life by rubbing his limbs and trying every other method their sagacity could suggest.
>
> "If the police persist in their exertions, there is not a doubt but the roads leading to this city will soon be cleared of the number of villains who for some time infested them and committed their depradations on the public."

For good measure they added:

> "Early yesterday morning a party of horse set off for Rush and apprehended two notorious robbers whom they safely conducted to town and lodged in Kilmainham Gaol."

Because of the social conditions, the second half of the eighteenth century had seen a tremendous upsurge of crime in Dublin to which the authorities reacted with very stern measures, notably the use of capital punishment and transportation. These penalties were applied not merely for murders but for lesser crimes such as burglary, hold-ups and, as we have seen, cattle rustling.

Bleaching greens were common along river banks such as the Liffey and the Camac. The clothes laid out there were frequently the subject of robberies and one such case is mentioned as having taken place at Blue Bell in 1785.

Our area did not escape the crime wave, but there is on record one incident where the tables were turned on the robber. A well known criminal, Christopher Thompson, robbed a woman with a cocked pistol at the 2nd Lock of the Grand Canal in January 1791. After stealing a guinea from her, he noticed two silver buckles on her shoes which he demanded from her also. She gave him one shoe and, as he examined it, he momentarily put his pistol on the bank of the canal. She quickly grabbed the gun and shot him through the head. For her "determined conduct" she was suitably rewarded.

When work commenced on the building of the new Kilmainham Jail at Gallows Hill in 1787, the place of public execution was changed to a site forming part of the Upper Kilmainham Commons near Rialto Bridge. The first hanging here took place on Saturday 28th April 1787, when four men were executed for robbery and burglary. In the following year, in January 1788, five men and one woman, all part of a gang, were executed for a series of robberies.

The grim work continued at this location until the new jail was opened in 1796, when executions then took place on a balcony over the main door of that building. Then after many more years they were carried out within the jail itself.

The Old Courthouse at Kilmainham

The present courthouse alongside the jail was built in 1820. It replaced a much older courthouse regarding whose location there is very little information, but it is likely to have been on the main street of Kilmainham itself, not far from the old jail. The patriot Anne Devlin in her recollections seems to bear this out when she indicated that the Kilmainham court formed part of the old jail, occupying the ground floor. Whatever about its location, the old courthouse was the scene of many and varied events.

It is also possible that it was the presence of the courthouse which influenced that legal luminary of the time, Sir Simon Bradstreet, to take up residence in 1728 in nearby Riversdale House, later popularly known as Shakespeare House. At the same time another legal gentleman, the judge and future Lord Chancellor of Ireland, John Bowes, was residing at Islandbridge. Both of these men were involved in the local Annesley Case, Bradstreet for the defence and Bowes as one of the trial judges.

Shakespeare House

The very well known public figure Judge John "Bully" Egan, whom we have earlier mentioned, was a Chairman of the County Court at Kilmainham for many years. He was also a member of the Irish Parliament and voted against the Act of Union. His finest hour came in the final debate in the Irish Parliament House on the proposed union between Great Britain and Ireland. Here he delivered a vehement and stirring speech against the Act of Union, finishing with "Ireland, Ireland for ever and damn Kilmainham." Inevitably he was in due course dismissed from his position and he died in Scotland in 1810.

Father Nicholas Sheehy

As a courthouse, this old building witnessed several notable trials which have gone completely from public memory. The most celebrated of these was that of Father Nicholas Sheehy, the Tipperary priest charged in 1766 with complicity in the WHITEBOY agrarian movement in that county. His lawyers rightly maintained that he could not get a fair trial in Tipperary and succeeded in having it transferred to Kilmainham. Following an eleven hour trial in which he was closely cross-examined he was acquitted on all counts by the jury. However, a short time later further trumped up charges were preferred against him and on this occasion he was tried in Clonmel. Found guilty, he was hanged there in 1767.

The County Dublin Grand Jury

Apart from being a courthouse, the building also fulfilled several other functions. At that time the city boundary ended at the top of Mount Brown and County Dublin was administered under the Grand Jury system which was the forerunner of the County Council. The Grand Jury had its headquarters in the courthouse, making Kilmainham the hub of local government administration in County Dublin.

A notable chairman who presided at Grand Jury meetings there was Sir Edward Newenham, an opportunist who changed sides at many times during his varied career. Early on he was Collector of Excises and High Sheriff of County Dublin. He pursued both tax evaders and smugglers with zeal and in the course of doing so made many political enemies. However, he was knighted in 1764 for his services in suppressing riots, thefts and lawlessness in the city. He travelled to Clonmel to be present at Father Sheehy's second trial there and congratulated the prosecution on the result.

For years also he was in the forefront of the campaign to have a new jail built at Kilmainham and it is ironic that when it was built he found himself, because of financial difficulties, committed to the debtors' section of the jail in 1800. He had to remain there, despite a letter to the Lord Lieutenant, until his family endeavoured to raise enough money to clear his debts and secure his release.

The old Courthouse was also the centre where Members of Parliament for County Dublin were elected for the House of Parliament in College Green. The secret ballot was not then in vogue and those entitled to vote, a small proportion of the population, came here and declared publicly the name of the candidate they wished to support. On those occasions, many exciting scenes took place, both inside and outside the building, with the successful candidate usually leading a colourful procession into the city.

A notable by-election here for County Dublin occurred in 1797 when William Brabazon, aged only nineteen, was returned unopposed. The Sheriff very conveniently turned a blind eye to the fact that he was under age. The young man showed his generosity for having been elected by giving an elegant breakfast for all the gentlemen and freeholders who had supported him. Furthermore, he provided £200 for the benefit of debtors held in the Kilmainham Jail and as a result a large number of them were discharged. He was to have a short life however, as at the age of twenty-five he died following wounds received in a duel.

Kilmainham Jails — Old and New

The jail for County Dublin was situated from late in the seventeenth century on a low-lying site bordering the main street of Kilmainham nearly opposite Brookfield Road. There is a fairly early reference to it in a newspaper report of April 1719:

> "On Sunday morning last four popish priests were taken out of the Mass Houses of this city and one of them Conner (registered) was committed to Kilmainham and the rest to Newgate."

In a document of some years earlier still, the following occurs:

> "Order that Hugh Sheridan a Roman Catholic priest in the Gaol of Kilmainham be transported to France within three months from this date.
> E. Budgell, 12 May 1715"

Some of its dungeons were below street level with a grating fronting the side-walk through which the prisoners constantly shouted up at passers-by for food or alms. With the passage of time the buildings were allowed to deteriorate into an intolerable condition and a campaign got under way to have another prison built on another site, but this was put on the long finger for decades. The campaign was encouraged by the well known English prison reformer and Quaker, John Howard, who visited the old jail on several occasions. This great humanitarian was appalled at the conditions there and particularly at the detention of young children alongside hardened criminals. He also noticed the presence of recruiting sergeants outside the jail who endeavoured to enlist released prisoners in the army.

Finally, at the Michelmas Term of 1785, the Kilmainham Grand Jury approved of a plan for a new jail at a different location "as the old jail is situated in a low unhealthy place and unable to contain and keep securely the number of persons committed to it." Notwithstanding this decision, a further eleven years were to elapse before the new jail was built. The Grand Jury had also decided to sell off the old building, but this was not done as we find it pressed into service again in 1803

Kilmainham jail

following the Emmet Rising, when the new jail was already in use for five years. Whether the old jail was totally out of use in the intervening years, we do not know.

In the meantime, shortly after the Grand Jury's decision, a serious breakout occurred at the old jail, reported as follows in *The Hibernian* magazine:

> March 19, 1786
> Fourteen prisoners escaped from the jail at Kilmainham. The felons, including highwaymen and two under sentence of death, had made a hole in the wall near the entrance to the prison underneath a window at which relatives and friends were allowed to talk to them and to pass them food. Two women were observed there the best part of the day sitting at the window but their design was really to cover the work of the prisoners scraping away at the walls.
>
> March 20, 1786
> Through the activity of Mr. McKinley, the Gaoler of Kilmainham, two of the felons were retaken and conducted to their former dwelling.
>
> March 28, 1786
> The two sentinels through whose neglect the felons made their escape from the Gaol of Kilmainham this day received five hundred lashes each in the Barracks.

As neither Islandbridge or Richmond Barracks had yet been built, we do not know where the barracks in question was situated.

The new jail opened its forbidding doors for the first time on the 13th August 1796. It was to enter the annals of Irish revolutionary history and to witness many tragic and heroic deeds until its closure in 1924.

Faulkners Dublin Journal reported:

> "The new County Gaol was completely finished and fit for the reception of prisoners. Those confined in the old were conducted to the new gaol under a strong military guard.
>
> "The first occupancy of this great building, said to be superior to any prison in Europe, was attended by the High Sheriff of the County, the High Sheriffs of the City, several Justices of the Peace and a great number of other gentlemen who afterwards dined by invitation at Harringtons in Grafton Street."

Notwithstanding the new building being described above as a County Gaol, it was in fact built to cater for prisoners from all parts of Ireland, unlike the old premises which served Dublin City and County only.

From the authorities' point of view the completion of the new jail did not come a day too soon as by then they were confronted by the rise of the United Irishmen, many of whose members were the first political prisoners to be held there.

The site at Gallows Hill for the jail was provided by Sir Nicholas Lawless, later Lord Cloncurry, at a yearly rent of £1.

Far Away to Australia

As well as being a prison, the new jail was also used as a holding centre for people from various parts of the country who had been sentenced to transportation to the penal colonies of Australia and elsewhere. These included not only law breakers and political prisoners, but also vagrants who were liable to be indiscriminately taken off the streets.

Starvation and dreadful living conditions for large sections of the population had resulted in increasing crime, and transportation was seen as an additional means of dealing with the problem. Relatively minor transgressions could attract such a penalty. A local example was that of a Ballyfermot man William Keegan who, having sold his cow at Smithfield Market, went on a drinking spree on the way home. He was arrested in a public house near Kilmainham and it was alleged that he had a forged cheque in his possession. He was sentenced to fourteen years transportation, which he appealed to the Lord Lieutenant, but before his letter reached that august person, he was already on the high seas.

All those sentenced to transportation were held at Kilmainham Jail, sometimes for up to two or three years, until such time as ships were available to take them away. One of the saddest sights in those years was the frequent procession of large wagons and other conveyances taking the prisoners, both male and female, under the usual heavy escort on the first leg of their long journey. Yet some of those who survived the rigours of the prison ships and the penal system "down under" were eventually to have a better life than that which they left behind. Many of them, together with those who emigrated voluntarily, helped to form the foundation of the modern Australian nation and to become the bulwark there of the Catholic Church.

Transportation went back to Cromwell's time, but insofar as Kilmainham Jail was involved, it went on from the opening of the jail until as late as 1853.

It brings to mind the words of the well known Irish song "Na Connery's":

"Le linn an aifrinn bímis ag agallamh is ag guí chun Dé
Chun na Connerys a thabhairt abhaile arís
Os na New South Wales"

Chapter Fifteen

1798–1803

MAJOR SIRR

Major Sirr was head of British Intelligence at Dublin Castle during the eventful years of the United Irishmen and the Robert Emmet rebellion. One of his unlikely hobbies was his interest in Irish antiquities, of which he had quite a collection. However, his more immediate task was in the collection of information regarding the leaders and plans of the United Irishmen and towards this end an extensive network of spies and agents were employed. According to Dr Madden, author of *The Lives and Times of the United Irishmen"*, some of these were accommodated in a house nearly in front of Kilmainham Jail, familiarly known to the people as "The Stag House". The word "Stag" was a slang expression at the time for an informer. All trace of this house, which we presume was on Inchicore Road, has vanished.

The following interesting letter from an informer to Major Sirr occurs in the latter's correspondence:

To Major Sirr

Co. Kildare
1.8.1803

Dear Sir,
That the following is authentic information, I beg of you to make no doubt of. There is a man in Kilmainham by the name of Barnwell who keeps a public house nearby opposite the jail and some short time back had regular meetings of United Irishmen at his house from between seven and eight o'clock in the evening until two and three o'clock in the morning. The chairman's name is Peter Brophy; he and his brother, John Brophy, both gardeners, live in the next house to Mr. Dixon, a tanner in Kilmainham. He always takes the chair dressed in a white jacket with green facings and silver epaulettes and a long white wand in his hand.

This Barnwell is a most bigoted Papist.

Yours faithfully,

We do not of course know anything regarding the truth or otherwise of this letter and there is also the possibility that the people mentioned were being "set up" by the writer. However, it does give us an insight into the atmosphere of the period.

James Dixon

The Mr Dixon referred to in the above letter was James Dixon, who had been a member of the famous Catholic Convention held in the Tailor's Hall in Back Lane which sought to redress the grievances of Catholics. He joined the Society of United Irishmen in 1792 and was imprisoned on two occasions. His name appears on a lengthy list of the Dublin members of the society sent to Dublin Castle by another informer. He apparently had a substantial tannery business in Kilmainham and it was at his house there that he provided accommodation for the wives of two of the Belfast leaders when they came to visit their husbands, then imprisoned in Kilmainham Jail.

Another name on this informers list was that of Bartholomew Shannon who likewise was a Kilmainham tanner. This family name is still remembered in Old Kilmainham by Shannon Terrace.

While the 1798 rebellion was planned to commence in Dublin on May 24th of that year, this did not happen but there were several scattered incidents in or near the city. One of these occurred close to the Fox And Geese Inn on the Naas Road, when a party of dragoons intercepted a small number of rebels. In the encounter, several of the latter were killed and two who were captured were brought into Dublin Castle where they were hanged.

The Antrim weaver Jemie Hope, who played such an important role in the 1798/1803 period and who was lucky to survive, made a short stay in Bluebell. He was mainly engaged as an organiser travelling the country and when in Dublin had to keep a low profile, moving frequently from one job to another. Towards the end of this turbulent period he got employment in Bluebell at a bleach yard which was owned by a former member of the United Irishmen. Jemie later told how one day his employer asked him a certain question which aroused his suspicions that the man was now spying for Major Sirr and with the result that he packed up and left Bluebell as quickly as he could.

Another prominent figure associated with this period who had a local connection was Thomas Russell. His father was a soldier and had moved with his family to the Royal Hospital in 1778 when Thomas was eleven years old. As a young man he, like his father, joined the army and saw service in India for three years before returning to Kilmainham. He subsequently became one of the founders of the United Irishmen and was executed in Downpatrick Jail for his part in the Emmet Rising.

Robert Emmet

It was in Nason Browne's tavern in Islandbridge that five of Robert Emmet's followers met for an early morning meal, having first reconnoitered the Artillery Barracks across the road, in the run up to the Rising of 1803. Unfortunately for them their conversation was overheard by the proprietor who lost no time in conveying the information to Dublin Castle. It is believed that this tavern was in more modern times the well known "Gilligans" which closed about thirty years ago.

Following his conviction Robert Emmet was taken from Kilmainham Jail and driven in a coach accompanied by two clergymen to the place of execution at Saint Catherine's Church, Thomas Street. They were escorted by a strong detachment of infantry and cavalry moving at a deliberately slow pace, either for security reasons or in order to overawe the populace. They did not go directly to Thomas Street as one might expect but instead took a circular route which brought them over Islandbridge and along the North Quays.

Robert Emmet's body was laid to rest in Bully's Acre but shortly afterwards was removed to a further burial place, the whereabouts of which still remains one of the great mysteries of Irish history.

Following the abortive revolt the jails, including Kilmainham, were filled to overflowing, so much so that additional "accommodation" had to be provided on ships in Dublin Bay. Apart from Emmet himself, sixteen of his adherents were executed in Dublin City and County and one of these, Felix Rourke from Rathcoole, is buried in Bully's Acre. Another two, Thomas Donnelly and Nicholas Tyrrell, are remembered by a plaque on the side of the West County Hotel, Chapelizod, near where they were executed.

Anne Devlin

In the years before her death in 1851 in Little Elbow Lane in the Coombe, Brother Luke Cullen of the then Carmelite Monastery in Clondalkin recorded the reminiscences of Robert Emmet's faithful servant and confidante, Anne Devlin. These invaluable recollections run to over 200 pages which were painstakingly written in longhand by Brother Cullen. Early on they disclose that when Anne Devlin first came to Dublin she worked for a short time for a lady "in Inchicore not far from the Phoenix Park."

Following the Rising Anne was imprisoned in various jails for a total of four years and despite ill-treatment, threats and bribes, refused to give any information to the authorities. She was being held with her father and young brother (who was allowed to accompany the rest of the family, all of whom had been originally arrested) in the new jail at Kilmainham when it was decided for some reason to transfer her and the young boy to the old jail, which had been put into use again:

> "My round of all the prisons was not yet complete. The low jail of Kilmainham was now for some time lying waste and had gone into a state of

dilapidation but in consequence of the want of room in the other prisons it was fitted up again for the very worst of offenders.

"It was a cold, damp and cheerless evening, not long before Christmas, that we were marched through the mud to this wretched abode. My little brother James who was then nine or ten years old and who was lying very ill in a jail fever, had to rise and accompany me. I went staggering along, my limbs quite stiff and painful, the child shivering and tottering under fever.

"We were going to the abode of fever patients, robbers and wretches that crawled in vice in Dublin. All were now huddled together in this dreary den.

"Even the external view was sickening although the bottom storey was in tolerable repair and here the Chairman of Kilmainham held his court. But in the upper storeys the windows were broken and several of them were entirely out of their frames with nothing left to obstruct the wind and rain but iron bars. The walls were dripping."

She goes on to tell how as they were arriving at the jail a session of the Court was about to be held but when the judge learned that some of the new arrivals had jail fever he immediately adjourned the court and got out as quick as he could.

A short time later the young James died and Anne was transferred back again to the new jail where the only ray of sunshine was the kindness shown to her by Mrs Dunn, the head jailer's wife, when an opportunity presented itself. The Devlin family certainly paid dearly for their involvement in Emmet's Rising.

From a local point of view the recollections have an added value because they are so far the only source of information, however limited, regarding the old court and jail. They give the impression that they both formed part of the one building and that apart from the dungeons there were two or three storeys. One would have thought in view of the reputation of the jail that the court, which was also the venue for elections and meetings of the County Dublin Grand Jury, would have a separate building of its own. Perhaps it had before this particularly disturbed period.

The Stag House Again

Another interesting matter mentioned relates to one of Michael Dwyer's men, a James Cullen, who was very seriously injured while attempting to escape from Dublin Castle. He was brought to the infirmary in Kilmainham Jail but as it was overcrowded he was sent over to the Stag House. Dr Trever, the much hated Governor of Kilmainham Jail, also sent Anne Devlin over ostensibly to help mind the patient but in reality in the hope that some useful conversation might be overheard, James Cullen being another Wicklow person. However the injured man died within a month. Anne also tells us that her mother and two sisters were being detained at the Stag House during this time again because of overcrowding at the jail.

Escape from Kilmainham Jail

One of the very few prisoners to escape from Kilmainham Jail over its long history was an Augustinian from John's Lane. This was Father John Martin, a member of the United Irishmen who was captured in Wicklow in 1798. After three years in Kilmainham he escaped in May 1801 but nothing is known of his subsequent career. *The Dublin Evening Post* had the following notice:

> "Fifty guineas reward for the arrest of John Martin, a priest who broke out of Kilmainham Gaol on 5 May 1801. Description – about fifty years of age, five feet nine inches tall, dark complexion with black hair, a long visage and stoops very much in walking."

Father James Harold P.P. (1744–1831)

Father James Harold, who came from an old Dublin family closely connected with the Dominican Order, was parish priest of Rathcoole in the fateful year of 1798. He had the misfortune to fall foul of the military and his house having been set on fire he was arrested. Indeed it was from the rafters of this house that Felix Rourke, already mentioned, was later hanged.

Father Harold was not charged with any offence but was ordered to be deported to the penal colonies of Australia. He was placed on board the prison ship Minerva and after a voyage of great hardship lasting four and a half months finally arrived in Sydney.

Although not held as a prisoner he was subjected to much harassment by the authorities including his removal to the notorious Norfolk Island, where he was forced to witness the cruel treatment meted out to the prisoners. In 1810 he was granted permission to leave Australia and he sailed for Rio de Janeiro where he spent some time. He later moved to Philadelphia but eventually returned to Ireland in 1810 where he was appointed Parish Priest of Kilcullen.

This much travelled priest who had been so close to many of the events of 1798 died in 1831 aged eighty-seven and was buried in Goldenbridge Cemetery.

The Cloncurrys

Robert Lawless started life selling turf and sticks in the Liberties but went on to become a prosperous woollen merchant. His son Nicholas was born in 1737 and later married Miss Brown, daughter of a wealthy Dublin merchant whose name is remembered by Mount Brown at Old Kilmainham. The Lawless's were a Catholic family but the son, following a dispute with members of his own church while in France, changed over to the Church of England. Back in Ireland he pursued a successful business career and was elected to the Irish Parliament. The government of the day wished to have his support, particularly his financial assistance, and he was elevated to Baron Lord Cloncurry. He took his title from a historic townland in County Kildare.

The new lord had inherited his father's business acumen and was in a position to buy lands in different parts of the country, including the Lyons estate at Newcastle, County Dublin, where he had his mansion. In 1779 he bought the bulk of the lands of Inchicore and Kilmainham, 230 acres in all, and this accounts for his name still appearing on some local leases. At this time also he received the title of "Lord of the Manor of Kilmainham" and here we should explain that the manor was an area rather than a building.

Cloncurry received a major setback in 1798 when his own son, Valentine Brown Lawless, became involved in some way on the fringe of the United Irishmen while in England and he was held on suspicion in London for nearly two years. It has been suggested that the father voted for the Act of Union against his own instincts in order to gain his son's release. Valentine was released, but his father had died in the meantime. In due course however, having in a manner of speaking sown his wild oats, he became acceptable to the establishment and succeeded to his father's title.

As the second Lord Cloncurry he led an active life for many years, both in the commercial world and in managing his estates. He was a director of the Grand Canal Company and, when the new railway was established, he sold a portion of his Inchicore land which was conveniently situated beside the line to the Great Southern & Western Railway for their engineering works and housing estate. A critic said that politically he tended to go a bit of the way with every side, but Daniel O'Connell praised him as a generous landlord. He died in 1853.

Chapter Sixteen

THE NINETEENTH CENTURY

The miserable conditions of the masses were to continue into the nineteenth century, aggravated further by the Act of Union. In addition the population of the country was rising rapidly and would soon reach the 8,000,000 mark. In Dublin the Irish language had by now rapidly declined. However during the first half of the century this district was to witness important developments such as the building of Richmond Barracks and the new Kilmainham Courthouse as well as the opening of Golden Bridge Cemetery and the coming of the railways. Also for some years Golden Bridge had a flourishing spa.

The original courthouse at Old Kilmainham, like the old jail, had fallen into disrepair and was replaced by the present building alongside the new jail in 1820. It was known as The Sessions House and its functions were the same as the previous building, i.e. court proceedings, meetings of the County Dublin Grand Jury and an election centre for parliamentary representatives.

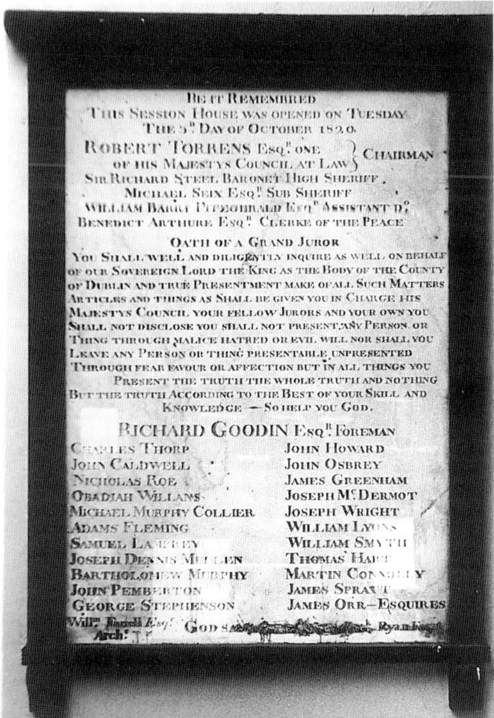

1820 tablet in Kilmainham Courthouse

Immediately to the west of the jail is Richmond View Lodge and a row of cottages once used to accommodate prison warders. They were known as Dunnes Cottages originally, George Dunne being the governor in 1822 and who resided in Richmond View Lodge.

Great excitement occurred in the district when a fire broke out in the west wing of the jail on the afternoon of 3rd December 1817. The fire spread rapidly and had a firm hold as horse drawn fire engines arrived from the city. Troops were summoned immediately and the jail was surrounded to prevent any escape. Lord Dunboyne, with a contingent from the not fully completed Richmond Barracks, escorted prisoners from their cells to the yards and safer parts of the jail, but nevertheless two prisoners lost their lives. The west wing was completely destroyed in the blaze.

Dan Donnelly

The career of Dan Donnelly the Irish prize-fighter coincided with this very gloomy period of Irish history, when Emmet was dead and Daniel O'Connell had not yet appeared on the political scene. It was against such a background that the people looked upon Donnelly as a national hero. This was particularly so following his sensational defeat of George Cooper, the English boxer at the Curragh on 13th December 1815. Incidentally, Cooper travelled out to County Kildare for the contest on a Grand Canal passenger boat. Following his victory Donnelly received a tremendous welcome in the city and the place of his victory at the Curragh has become known as Donnelly's Hollow ever since.

Public houses were anxious to attract boxing celebrities to manage or "front" their business at this period and Dan's services were often called upon. In this context we find that one of his former boxing opponents in England, Jack Carter, took up residence in Dublin in 1819 and "held the licence of the Black Lion at Kilmainham."

When Dan Donnelly died in 1820 there were unprecedented scenes of national mourning, particularly amongst the masses of no property. It was felt that no greater honour could be bestowed upon their hero than that he should be buried in what was believed to be the grave of Brian Ború at Bully's Acre. The *Sporting Magazine* reported that:

> "At least 80,000 men, women and children attended the funeral, the roads and streets leading to the burial ground being covered with a moving mass of rags and wretchedness."

Some days after his burial, Dan's body was removed by the "Sack 'Em Ups", but such was the public outcry that they were sought out and forced to place it back in the grave. An elaborate monument was erected over his grave, but some years later this was vandalised by drunken soldiers. Today his last resting place in Bully's Acre remains unknown and unmarked.

The Enclosure of Kilmainham Commons

By an Act of Parliament of 1821 the Upper Kilmainham Commons, stretching from the top of Brookfield Road to Windsor Motors on the South Circular Road was enclosed – in other words privatised and sold off. The Crown however retained six acres adjoining the city water-course in its possession. One of those who bought up a portion of the Commons was Lord Cloncurry. This Commons had been in existence for six hundred years and had been amongst other things the venue for horse racing and public executions as already related.

Relief Works

The economic slump of 1826 compounded by a typhus fever epidemic had a devastating effect, particularly on the textile manufacturing and weaving colonies in Dublin. The latter were mainly centred in the Liberties, but there were smaller colonies in Bow Bridge, Kilmainham and Islandbridge. The bulk of those who found themselves with no income had to rely on some form of public relief schemes for their existence.

One of these relief schemes involved road works between Bow Bridge and Inchicore Road for which the wages were initially a shilling per day, but this sum was later reduced!

A Rustic Scene

The Reverend Nathaniel Burton, a chaplain at the Royal Hospital, writing in 1843 commented on the rustic and village-like appearance of Old Kilmainham, not yet connected with the city and situated "in the hollow of the Cummogue Vale." He recalled as well, when he first came to Kilmainham about twenty years earlier, seeing the older generation of men wearing their wigs, old fashioned clothes, buckskin breeches and large buckles on their shoes.

The Reverend Burton also referred to the "Boreens of Inchicore and Ballyfermot." Unlike Kilmainham there has never been, as is sometimes asserted, an ancient village of Inchicore. This is borne out further by the historian Dalton, writing a little earlier, who described Inchicore then as "a hamlet scarcely distinguishable by any collection of houses". Nearby however the Golden Bridge area because of its proximity to Richmond Barracks had become a small centre of population. The townland of Inchicore did not become a centre of population until the coming of the railways.

In the meantime however, there had been an increase in the number of stately houses in all the local areas with names such as Rose Dale, Maria Mount, Mons Salutaris, Harcourt Lodge and Susan Vale in addition to the older Golden Bridge House, Inchicore House, Riversdale House, Jamestown House and Stone House. The latter was near what is now the bottom of Landen Road and not too far from the railway line. It was in the Inchicore townland but that location now tends to be referred to as part of Ballyfermot. Otherwise very large fields, usually tree-lined, predominated and there were also quite a few quarries and gravel pits.

Richmond Barracks

Following the recent rebellions and the ever present danger of a French invasion, the British authorities decided to replace the ten temporary barracks in the inner city with two large barracks further out, one at Portobello and the other at Golden Bridge. The building of the latter commenced in 1810 on a twenty-three acre open site between Emmet Road and the Grand Canal and was ready for occupation four years later. Additional blocks on the east and west sides were added in subsequent years. The new barracks was called Richmond Barracks in honour of the Lord Lieutenant, Charles Lennox, Duke of Richmond, who was an advocate of oppressive measures to keep the populace down and who was unsympathetic towards the Catholics. He was also remembered in a street nearby, which was called Lennox Place and is now Thomas Davis Street West. A further thirteen acres of ground on the city side was acquired as a training area and became known as the Barrack Field. It is now the Bulfin Housing Estate. A travellers' guide of 1815 commented:

> "Adjoining to the Great Southern Mail Coach Road an extensive range of Infantry Barracks has been lately erected in an airy secluded situation judiciously selected for the purpose. In a quarry sunk to procure stones for this building a sulphureous calybeate spa has been discovered which will prove an invaluable acquisition to valetudinarians from its contiguity to this populous city."

The barracks had two large parade grounds connected by an archway, over which was a clock tower. The main gate was on Emmet Road, with another gate to the rear on the canal bank. It also had the usual ancillary buildings, military stores, armourer's room, stabling for twenty-five horses, forge, tailor's shop, hospital and a detention centre. A report of 1831 tells us that there were then two regiments in the barracks, consisting of seventy-eight officers, seventy-nine sergeants, twenty-seven drummers, 1,363 privates and a very large number of women and children.

The siting of the barracks at Golden Bridge was the main factor in the development of that area which up to then had been semi-rural.

In the early decades of the century living conditions for the soldiers and their families were very bad, with overcrowding, poor diet and lack of proper sanitation. During an outbreak of cholera in the city in 1847, an edict was issued that "soldiers wives washing linen in the Grand Canal at Richmond or Portobello will be deprived of all indulgences and turned out of barracks".

However from about 1850 onwards, due to a public outcry in England, the lot of soldiers was vastly improved and Richmond shared in this change for the better. It was then that the numbers in rooms were reduced and better married quarters allocated. Also provided was the gymnasium, ball alley, reading and recreation rooms as well as canteens. When the garrison church for Protestant personnel, which also served as a school for soldiers' children, was built is uncertain. The year 1875 has been suggested.

The Fenian Movement in 1867 was attempting with some success to recruit Irishmen in the British Army and in connection with this, one of the leaders, John Devoy, daringly visited Richmond Barracks in a borrowed army uniform. He also laid out detailed plans for the takeover of the barracks, but with the failure of the Fenian Rising these came to naught. Historically, Richmond was not to come into its own until the Rising of 1916.

An interesting resident of Richmond Barracks was "Lennie" Collinge, whose family had quarters there and who was to become an employee of one of Dublin's early cinemas, the "Volta". James Joyce was then the manager of this cinema and "Lennie" became quite an authority on the earlier years of the writer.

Chapter Seventeen

Paper Making at Goldenbridge

One of the most prominent residents of Goldenbridge was Bart Sullivan, who belonged to a well known family of paper makers. His father had been making paper there since 1784 and no doubt had been attracted to this particular location because of the presence of the Camac River and the Grand Canal. As mentioned earlier, a special relationship developed between the new paper mill and the Grand Canal Company.

When the founder died in 1820 his son Bart took over. The latter decided that if he was to compete with imported material, he would have to install more modern machinery. This move made him unpopular with the workers, who refused to handle the new technology. He was forced to bring in Scottish operators who understood the machines and they worked under police protection for three years.

A report of 1833 stated that the Goldenbridge Mills, if in full production, were capable of employing 200 persons and that they were equipped with a steam engine as well as nine rag engines, rags being used as the raw material.

When the Mill commenced in 1784 it was the first major industry to be established in Goldenbridge/Inchicore. At that time paper making was thriving in Dublin, but this was not to last because of the imposition of ever increasing excise duties from 1799 onwards. The mill owners strenuously opposed these duties and the authorities countered with a rigorous system of inspection by excise officers who were known as gaugers. Proprietors had to keep elaborate records of their daily production and every six weeks to make returns verified under oath at the Excise Office. The duty was levied on the weight of the paper, none of which could be moved from the mill without a signed permit or authorised label. Over the years this led to a continual battle of wits between both sides with the mill owners sometimes resorting to false entries and forged labels. Very often parcels of paper without any documentation, "duty free", were smuggled out in carts under loads of hay or straw or vegetables.

Against this background it was not unusual for owners to be heavily fined or imprisoned and Bart Sullivan was no exception. In 1843 he found himself committed for a period to the Debtors' Prison in Marshalsea Lane off Thomas Street at the instance of the Revenue authorities for "smuggling and assaulting gaugers."

Here one of his fellow detainees was our previously mentioned Dublin businessman, Walter Meyler, who once more is able to add to our knowledge. In the

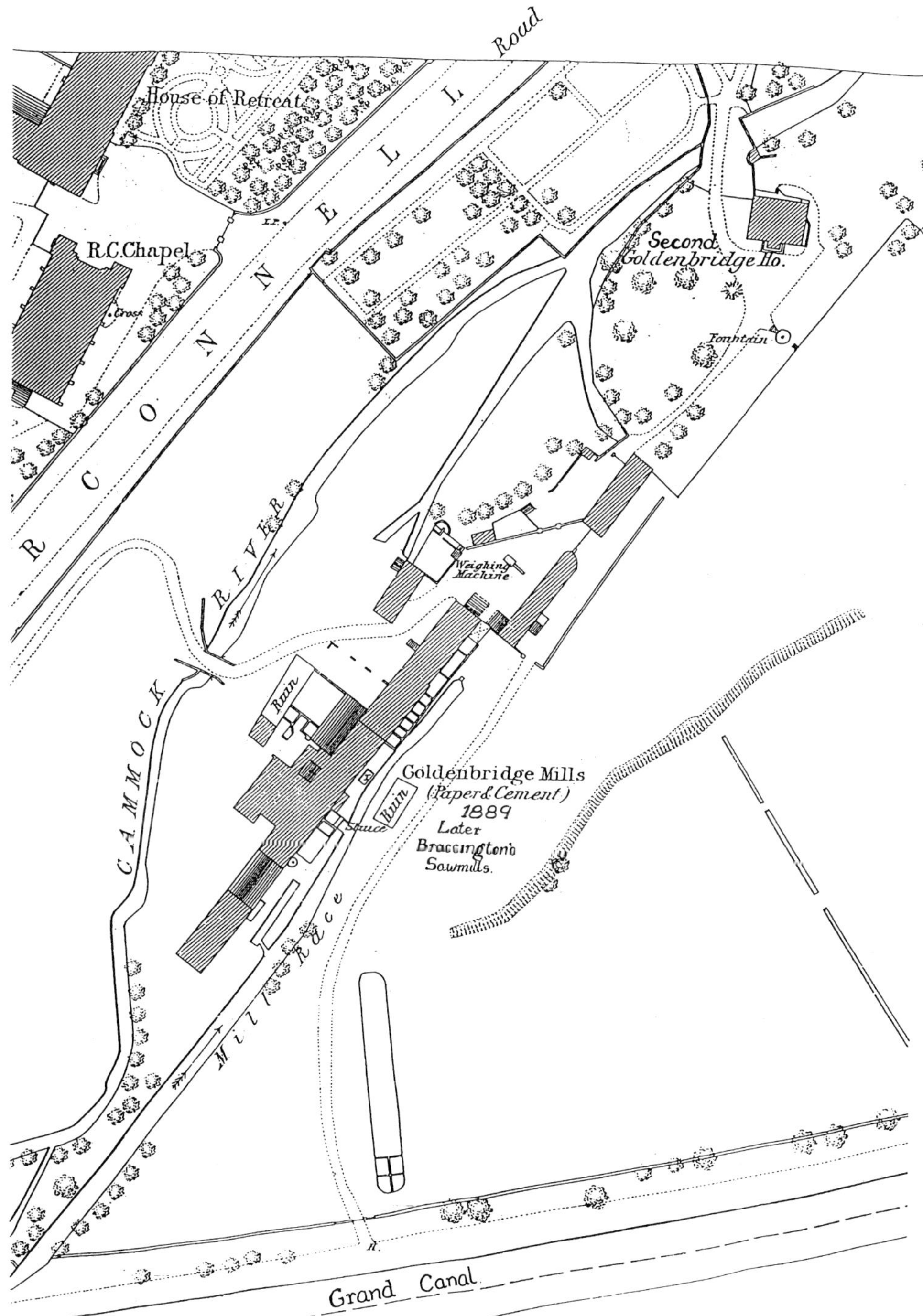
Road
House of Retreat
R.C.Chapel
Cross
R C O N N E L L
Second Goldenbridge Ho.
Fountain
RIVER
Weighing Machine
CAMMOCK
Ruin
Goldenbridge Mills
(Paper & Cement)
1889
Later
Braccington's
Sawmills.
Ruin
Sluice
Mill Race
Grand Canal

Debtors', detainees were not held in close confinement and their families could join them for meals at their own expense. He describes Bart as a sturdy, jolly, good natured fellow and his wife as an amiable and lovely woman. They had a large family of sons and daughters. The former carried on the business while the father was detained and they lived in good style.

However before Meyler was released Sullivan's wife died and, notwithstanding a special plea from the governor, the authorities "refused to allow him to the funeral from her home in Richmond where she died". The area near Goldenbridge was sometimes referred to as Richmond.

The Decline of Paper Making

With the passage of time the Revenue authorities got the upper hand. The mill owners publicly campaigned against the duties for years, but they were not listened to and the industry went into decline. Eventually the duties were abolished in 1860, but the damage had already been done. There were now only twenty-six mills left as against sixty in 1838 and these numbers were to decline further.

The Sullivans continued in business but later the mill passed into several other hands. In 1878 it closed permanently as a paper mill and the well known Brassington family took it over as a saw mill to be known locally as the Bobbin Mills. This family went out of business in 1966 when the large stone building was demolished. The Goldenbridge Industrial Estate now occupies the site.

At one stage there were six paper mills on the Camac River – Sagart, Clondalkin, Killeen, Drimnagh, Goldenbridge and Old Kilmainham, with the first four surviving to modern times.

Chapter Eighteen

Goldenbridge Cemetry

In what was then a quiet backwater between Richmond Barracks and the Grand Canal, Goldenbridge Cemetery was established in 1829. Still somewhat off the beaten track it is relatively unknown to most Dubliners and although not an ancient cemetery it has its own historic significance, being the first Catholic burial place in Dublin since the Reformation.

Prior to its opening the Catholic clergy had to apply for and obtain written permission before they were allowed to say the prayers for the dead in the existing cemeteries. Sometimes they were even prevented from saying these prayers – something which caused deep distress to mourners. For many decades all of this was the subject of much anger and dissatisfaction amongst the Catholic population. As a result, the Catholic Association under its chairman, Daniel O'Connell, who was already championing the cause of Catholic Emancipation, commenced an energetic campaign to acquire a burial ground of their own. This task took a long time to achieve as there was a reluctance to sell land to Catholics and many obstacles were put in the way. In the end, through the efforts of Mathias O'Kelly, a leading member of the Catholic Association and a tireless worker in the cause of Catholic civil rights, a three acre site at Goldenbridge was acquired in 1828 from a "friendly Protestant" whose name we do not know. For the purpose of administering the new venture the Dublin Catholic Cemeteries Committee was formed and Daniel O'Connell was one of the first trustees.

A long held ambition of having a burial ground where Catholics might have the funeral rites of their Church solemnised without fear of disturbance had at last been achieved. Nevertheless those first trustees struck an ecumenical note when they declared that all religious denominations were free to use the ground and to perform whatever religious ceremonies they wished.

Consecration Ceremonies

The work of laying out the ground proceeded rapidly and the official consecration took place on Thursday 15th October 1829 within six months of the passing of the Act of Catholic Emancipation. The *Freemans Journal* reported as follows:

> "Yesterday this really Catholic cemetery was consecrated. The field which contains two Irish acres is situated between Richmond Barracks and the

Grand Canal and is well enclosed by a stone wall about nine feet high. A house is provided for the sexton.

"The ground is nearly square and is intersected with neat gravel walks and a number of young trees comprising willows, weeping ash, larch and sycamore are planted at distances of eight feet in straight lines. In the centre is a small eclipse within which there is to be erected a chapel, the foundation of which is already laid.

"The Catholic Archbishop having been unable to attend, the ceremony of consecration was performed by the Rev. Father Canavan, curate of St James's, who also officiated at the solemn Mass which was celebrated in a temporary chapel erected for the occasion. The clergy present attended in soutanes, surplices and stoles. The parochial choir which is an excellent one was also in attendance. The price of admission was 2/6d and the proceeds are to go to the Parochial Free School Fund.

"There were about two hundred persons present besides a few officers and a good many soldiers from whom no money would be received. The ceremony was over about three o'clock when the assemblage separated in the most perfect order.

"Too much praise cannot be given to Mr. J. Browne and Mr. O'Kelly of James's St. for the unceasing pains they took with this splendid undertaking from the moment the foundation stone was laid until the work was completed."

Amongst the clergy present that day were those two remarkable priests, Father Henry Young and Father John Spratt, both notable champions of the poor.

The presence of the soldiers is surprising in view of the subsequent animosity which developed between Richmond Barracks and the trustees of the cemetery. We can only assume that they were present in their individual capacities as Catholics.

Immediately after the consecration ceremony, four burials took place in the outer sections of the cemetery.

CATHOLIC BURIAL GROUND,
GOLDEN BRIDGE.

THE Consecration of the above will take place on THURSDAY, the 15th inst., at Twelve o'Clock.— The Public are invited to be present at this solemn Ceremony, for which Tickets at 2s. 6d. each can be had at the Chapel House, James's-street; Mr. Coyne's, Capel-street; and on the ground

The Freeman's Journal, 12 October 1829

Further Occasion

What appears to have been a more public occasion took place a few days later on Sunday 18th October 1829. This was the re-burial of Father Lawrence Sylvester Whelan, who had in earlier decades ministered at the old chapel at Dolphin's Barn and had originally been buried under the earthen floor of that building. The newspaper report tells us his remains were removed from Dolphin's Barn Chapel to Goldenbridge Cemetery "attended by many thousands of people".

Unfortunately we do not have any further details of this occasion, but it does indicate that Father Whelan was not the first person to be buried in Goldenbridge, as has so often been stated before.

Shortly afterwards an open plan mortuary chapel, approached by two granite steps and supported by pillars, resembling a classic temple, was built. Under this a cellar was provided to accommodate gravewatchers who were on duty at night to prevent bodysnatching and who were provided with firearms and Cuban bloodhounds to assist them in their task. As a result of these stringent precautions no attempts to interfere with the graves have been recorded. A contributory factor also was the coming in to force of the Anatomy Act of 1832, which outlawed the practice and gradually brought it to an end.

Opposition from the Military

There was a tremendous demand for burials at the new cemetery and within the first two years alone 12,000 people were interred there. These included many of the Catholic middle classes from all parts of the city as well as some members of the religious orders such as the Augustinians and Dominicans. When it was realised that Goldenbridge would not be large enough to meet the demand, particularly with the closure of Bully's Acre, it was decided to establish a second cemetery at Glasnevin which opened in 1832.

From the outset the military at Richmond Barracks were very much opposed to the siting of Goldenbridge so near their own premises. They claimed that the constant funeral processions along Emmet Road and Vincent Street, particularly in the earlier years, interfered with their exercises and marches. They also maintained that there were problems of hygiene, something which was strongly denied by the trustees. With the opening of Glasnevin, the number of funerals decreased to about 300 a year, but the army kept up the pressure over the years. Finally, at the behest of the War Office in London, and much to the annoyance of the local community, the cemetery was closed in 1869, except for those who had rights there.

THE TEMPLE, GOLDEN BRIDGE CEMETERY.

The Many Headstones

The graves surrounding the mortuary chapel and which tended to have larger tombstones were known as the "chapel circle." The inscriptions on 1,100 headstones in the cemetery have in recent years been recorded through the magnificent work of the members of the Irish Genealogical Society, but there are still further stones which are embedded below ground level. In the north-eastern corner are the mass graves of cholera and other such victims.

As mentioned earlier Father James Harold of the 1798 period is buried in this cemetery. The now illegible inscription on his tombstone and which gives no clue to his adventurous life once read as follows:

> "Beneath this stone lie entombed the mortal remains of the Revd. James Harold and the Revd. William D. Harold. The former was during many years Parish Priest in this Archdiocese. He died on the 15th of August, 1830, in the 85th year of his age, a faithful Christian and a firm friend. The latter was of the Order of Preachers, and a member of their house in Denmark-street. The few years of his public ministry were spent in the zealous discharge of all his sacred duties. Pious, upright, and benevolent, he expired on the 15th

December, 1830, in his 29th year, leaving many who revere his memory and deplore his death.

"Here also lie interred the mortal remains of the Revd. John Raymond Tommins, O.P., whose career as a truly virtuous and exemplary priest was brought to a close in the Convent of St. Saviour, on the 14th May, 1842, in his 40th year.

"The Revd. William V. Harold, D.D., of the same order, who, both in Ireland and in foreign lands, did good service to religion, being held in high repute for his accomplishments as a scholar, his eloquence as a preacher, and the purity of his life. He died at the age of 80, on the 29th of January, 1856.

"The Revd. Laurence Cremmin, whose name as a Dominican Friar was held in loving veneration by the many he had guided in the ways of repentance and salvation to the very day before his death. He finished his course on the 10th June, 1866, in his 72nd year.

"Blessed are the dead who die in the Lord."

The unmarked grave of a United Irishman, Thomas O'Flanagan, provides another link with that period. He was a printer of revolutionary journals for several generations from Lord Edward to the Young Irelanders. He died at the age of ninety.

Mr William T. Cosgrave, a participant in the 1916 Rising and first President of the Irish Free State from 1922 to 1932, was buried in Goldenbridge in November 1965. His wife, the former Louisa Flanagan, also buried here, was the daughter of Alderman Flanagan of Portmahon House, Rialto who engaged extensively in market gardening on the lands of Drimnagh and Walkinstown.

Other family members buried here are Philip Cosgrave, also a veteran of the Easter Rising, and Patrick J. Cosgrave. The latter was shot dead during the Civil War in the family's licensed premises directly opposite Saint James's Hospital.

The Dublin Cemeteries Committee

This unique voluntary association has continued its unbroken work from 1829 down to the present time. It is self-financing and independent of state funding. Right from the start it was its policy, as recommended by the "Liberator" himself, to use any surplus income from burial fees for the benefit of Catholic schools and orphanages then struggling to get on their feet. As we have seen from the newspaper report of the official opening an admission charge of 2/6 was made for the benefit of the Parochial Free School Fund, the cost of acquiring the ground having already been borne by O'Connell's Catholic Association. This policy was carried out for very many years and old records show that £10 was awarded to Goldenbridge Reformatory in 1865 and £25 in the same year to the Oblate Fathers.

Goldenbridge cemetery has suffered from vandalism in recent years but plans are now afoot for a major upgrading of this historic burial place.

Post-Famine Kilmainham Jail

Dublin was not directly affected by the Great Famine but many people from the countryside made their way into the city. For the five years after this event the number of admissions to Kilmainham Jail increased dramatically. This was often brought about by hungry people who deliberately committed some offence in order to be sure of getting a meal, however meagre, within the jail. A contributing factor also was the passing of the Vagrancy Act of 1847. It is hard to believe that an act such as this which made it an offence to beg on the street was passed when the famine was at its worst.

SOME RESIDENTS OF OLD KILMAINHAM 1850

John Moran, Car Owner
Michael Minch, Draymaker
Francis Tuite, Miller
John Leonard, Cattle Dealer
Peter Lacy, Workman
Michael Short, Dairy
Patrick Monaghan, Tanner
James Smyth, Master Tanner
Thomas Kenny, Corn Chandler
Stephen Barnwell, Vintner
Joseph Kelly, Caretaker
Patrick Littleton, Provision Dealer
Thomas Sheridan, Dairyman
Jas Radcliffe, Tanner and Currier
Alex Corcoran, Smith
Mrs. Andrews & Son, Tanners
E. Butler, Bonnet Maker
Peter Dunn, Tanner
Catherine Dunn, Washerwoman
William Nicholl, Builder

Also listed are twenty-six tenements, several cabins, six cottages built within the foundation of the old gaol and a building that is described as "Officers' Lodgings".

Chapter Nineteen

The Great Southern and Western Railway Company

The greatest local development of the nineteenth century was undoubtedly the establishment of the Great Southern and Western Railway Company. It not only brought the new railway line through the area, but also established its engineering works there as well as a housing estate for its employees. It was in fact one of the biggest industrial enterprises in Ireland at that time.

The company was formed by a group of Dublin businessmen headed by Peter Purcell, a wealthy landowner and operator of mail coaches. He became the first chairman of the company but did not live to see the line opened. An Act for the making and maintenance of a railway, which was to commence "in a field at or near the King's Bridge" and to run to the town of Cashel with a branch to the town of Carlow, was passed in 1844.

Work proceeded rapidly in spite of opposition by the Royal Hospital and the military at Islandbridge Barracks, neither of whom wished to cede a portion of their land for the new project. The first passenger service commenced on the 4th of August 1846 with a journey to Carlow and the newspapers tell us that the carriages were densely crowded. Shortly afterwards the main line proper to Cashel was opened and the terminus at King's Bridge became known as the Cashel Station. Because of this terminus the old right of way from Islandbridge to Steevens' Lane which had caused such conflict in the previous century had to be closed off in the decades which followed. Another development was the construction of a new road parallel to the railway line which we now know as Saint John's Road.

The continuation of the line to Cork was not completed until October 1849 because of many difficulties encountered, not least being the effects of the Great Famine.

The Inchicore Railway Works

Inchicore at that time was a totally undeveloped area of fields and pastures about three and a half miles from the centre of the city, but all that was to change. Simultaneously with the laying of the railway line, the company had acquired a

40

GREAT SOUTHERN AND WESTERN RAILWAY,

LOCOMOTIVE ENGINEER'S OFFICE,

INCHICORE,

DUBLIN, July 21st 1886

I HEREBY acknowledge to have received from Wm Woolfull — the sum of Five Pounds (£5) being the Indenture Fee of his Son William Woolfull whom I have consented to take into these works as an Apprentice for the term of Five years, commencing 21st July 1886

Indentures will be given by me if desired at the termination of the Apprenticeship, at the expense of the said Apprentice, but it must be distinctly understood that I reserve to myself the right of dismissing the said Apprentice at any time, if, from misconduct or any other cause, I should think fit to do so, but the fee in no case will be returned.

I also reserve to myself the right of arranging the wages of the said Apprentice during the term of his Apprenticeship, and if he is attentive, and conducts himself to my satisfaction, the rate of his wages will be—

First year	... ...	5/- per week.
Second "	... ...	7/- "
Third "	... ...	9/- "
Fourth "	... ...	11/- "
Fifth "	... ...	13/- "

John A. F. Aspinall

Railway indentures 1886

seventy-three acre site alongside the tracks, some of it from Lord Cloncurry. On a portion of this ground they built the engineering workshops to the design of the architect Sancton Wood and commenced operations with thirty-nine employees in

April 1846, four months before the rail service started. Over the years these workshops were greatly expanded and employment was to reach a peak of nearly 2,000.

All the original engine drivers and much of the mechanical staff had to be recruited in England where advertisements had been placed in the newspapers. Many of the Irish workers had at that stage never even seen a railway engine, but as Father Cooke O.M.I. later showed, quite a number of Irishmen who had been employed in English engineering plants also came over to work in the new project. The newcomers settled down in what must have been a very strange environment, particularly for the English workers, and got the services going both on the lines and in the workshops, pending the training of local labour. An engine driver was deemed to be very well paid at £2 per week, in contrast to 60 pence for a plate-layer.

Progress at the works was such that by 1852 they were able to turn out their first locomotive, the "No. 57." Playing a very significant role in these formative years was the engineer, John Wakefield.

He was succeeded by another notable of the age of steam locomotion, the Dublin born Alexander McDonnell, of whom it was said that he made the name of Inchicore great. During his term of office from 1864 to 1882, skill in design and construction continued to develop. He left a marked influence on the works and some of the locos he inspired were to last down to the diesel era. As well as his engineering abilities he

Inchicore railway works 1906

was also an able administrator and all of this is reflected in the address which was presented to him on leaving the company in October 1882.

> "We the employees of the Great Southern and Western Railway Company in the departments under your charge beg to tender to you our congratulations on your receiving the new and more important appointment of Locomotive Carriage and Wagon Superintendent of the North-Eastern Railway of England.
>
> "You have succeeded in extending and converting our once infant works into a model manufactory where we now see accomplished your expressed desire of building all your own rolling stock, giving thus to our country an example of the possibility of Irish manufacture and leaving us a factory of which we all feel proud."

Other talented men were to follow who continued the standards laid down in the early years. A wide range of skills were developed involving boiler makers, fitters, brass finishers, blacksmiths, coppersmiths, tinsmiths, moulders, carpenters, carriage and wagon builders, painters and upholsterers. The nerve centre of the works was the "Drawing Office" where loco and other draughtsmen produced and developed the necessary mechanical drawings. Also spread throughout the complex were other depots such as the Running Shed, the Coal Bank, the Foundry, the Sawmill, the Smithies, Stores Department and the Gasworks, which made gas to light the carriages, the housing estate and the Kingsbridge Terminus.

The Housing Estate

As there was no housing available in the district for the influx of workers it was necessary for the company to build its own houses. They commenced with Inchicore Terrace North and South, as well as Inchicore Square. The other terraces i.e. Abercorn, Granite, West, Saint Patrick's and Saint George's Villas were added later. Although they were sizeable two storey dwellings, they were officially known as the "Company's Cottages," perhaps because of the cottage style doorways on many of them. Rents were deducted from employees' wages and it was a condition that they were not to keep goats or pigs!

A Dining Hall, Library and Recreation Centre collectively known as the Institute was built on one side of Inchicore Square. Other later features were a doctor's surgery, as well as that very old Inchicore institution known as "The Sewing Class". Here women and girls were employed to make railway uniforms as well as suits and clothes for employees, with payment for these being deducted from the weekly wages over a number of months. Nearby, a fine building known as "The Dormitory" up to recently provided overnight accommodation for provincial train crews. In this area also was the ball alley where many great exponents of the game once performed but which remained silent and deserted for decades until its recent demolition.

A cricket and athletic ground was laid out in the "top fields" which were situated above the works on the Ballyfermot side.

In different locations outside the estate, but close to the railway line, the company built several very large houses for some of their officials and were named as "Floraville", "Mount Vernon", "St. John's Gardens" and "Sevenoaks". Only the latter now survives and it had up to very recently been occupied by the Little Sisters of the Assumption who for over forty years provided there a very valuable service for the elderly and under-priveleged of the area.

Horse Buses and Trams

The "Inchicore Enterprise Omnibus Company" which was the first regular public transport service in the area came into existence in 1848. The bus in question was an enclosed vehicle with small windows and an open-air upper deck, drawn by two horses. It promised a service every half hour between the city and Inchicore and the fare was two pence. Already on the road at that time were licensed cabs, carriages and side cars also known as jaunting cars. The commencement of this horse drawn bus service was ironically influenced by the building of the Railway Works and housing estate and the consequent need for a transport service to and from the city.

In 1878 the horse buses were replaced by horse trams for which tram rails were laid on the roadway and the terminus was at the Black Lion. The proprietors were the Central Tram Company later known as the Dublin United Tram Company. Two horses were used to draw the trams, but at steep gradients such as Mount Brown an extra "tip" horse had to be employed.

Some time later the D.U.T.C. built their tram sheds and assembly works at Emmet Road/Spa Road which was another major step in the development of the area. The electric tram took over in 1899 and continued on the Inchicore line until 1940.

The side-cars continued to ply from a "hazard" on Emmet Road outside the barracks until the early years of the present century and some of the families associated with these cars such as the McGraths, Coombes and Neills are still remembered by very old residents.

The Rail Services

The G.S. & W.R. services, both passenger and goods, expanded steadily throughout the nineteenth century on routes to the south and south west. They failed, however, to obtain the franchise for the west of Ireland as originally intended and as indicated in their title. This was a disappointment to the directors and led to much feuding with their principal rivals, the Midland Great Western. Nevertheless the G.S. & W.R.

"Macha" at the Inchicore loco shed

became the major railway company in Ireland and by 1900 was carrying 4,000,000 passengers per year.

The outbreak of war in 1914 was to see a downturn in their fortunes, but we shall come back to their story when dealing with the twentieth century.

Joseph O'Callaghan, Tyrconnell Road. Résumé of interview with the late John Holden of C.I.E. (Link magazine 1953)

> "In 1889 a young monitor attached to Inchicore schools was dissatisfied with his pay – five shillings weekly, paid quarterly – and he sought another post, soon finding himself on the clerical staff of the Great Southern and Western Railway at Inchicore Works. His name was Joseph O'Callaghan.
>
> "At that time Inchicore was a long way from the city, so to speak. Horse-drawn trams gave a passenger service from Inchicore citywards, the through fare being four pence. So also was a glass of whiskey. Bicycles of a sort were replacing the penny farthing model. But these contraptions were not in favour. Further, pot-holed roads and solid tyres provided a strong argument against them.

"During a fireside chat, I found that Mr. O'Callaghan had served for 50 years on the clerical staff, remaining all the time in the locomotive office. His father had been employed by the G.S.W.R. for the remarkably long period of 66 years in the Permanent Way Department.

"Mrs. O'Callaghan's grandfather, Joseph Kelly, was in charge of the G.S.W.R. Coal Bank at Inchicore and lived to 104 years of age. In 1840 the same Joe Kelly, then pushing on to his forties, marched at the head of 150 G.S.W.R. employees from Inchicore to St Catherine's Church, outside of which they knelt in batches and took the total abstinence pledge from Father Matthew himself.

"The records I examined showed that people of all classes and creeds combined in their activities for the betterment of Inchicore and I venture to say that it was this splendid spirit that gave Inchicore one of the finest heavy industries in the country and one that provided skilled executives to transport the world over.

"From documents sorted out by Mr. O'Callaghan I gathered that in the early days of the Works, one of the first – if not the first – superintendent's name was Mr. Wakefield. He resided in "Silverdale" (facing St Jude's Church) and arrived each morning at the works on horseback.

"Engineers to follow him were Mr. A McDonnell – about the year 1864. After him came J.A.F. Aspinall in 1882, followed by H.A. Ivatt, R. Coey, R.E.L. Maunsell, E.A. Watson. Mr. Aspinall arranged that on all holidays of obligation a Mass was celebrated at 5.00 am by the Oblate Fathers, which the works staff attended.

"The working hours then were 54 weekly, from 6.00 am to 5.15 p.m. and on Saturdays (pay-day) 12 noon.

"Every Saturday when leaving for home, to any man who required them, the Stores Department sold penny bundles of firewood, made up during the week from all waste timber in the Saw Mill and other shops."

Chapter Twenty

The Coming of The Oblate Fathers

The Wooden Church

The arrival of the Oblate Fathers in Inchicore in 1856 was to have an enormous influence on the spiritual life of the area, right down to the present day.

The founder, Bishop – and recently Saint – Eugene de Mazenod, was anxious to extend the order to Ireland and, following a retreat in John's Lane Church, Father Robert Francis Cooke OMI, a Waterford man, succeeded in bringing this about in June 1856. This priest, by means of a loan provided by a well wisher, secured a property on Tyrconnell Road directly opposite Bart Sullivan's papermills, which consisted of a residence and an adjoining thirty-one acre farm-holding. The opening of the Railway Works ten years previously brought a large number of workers and their families to Inchicore, but there was no Catholic church between James's Street and Clondalkin. Father Cooke has written of those early times and the following are some extracts:

> "A thousand men were employed in these works who resided in great numbers in Inchicore in cottages built by the company. The railway company selected these men in large measure from the foundries and railway works of England. They were Irishmen for the most part and all clever and highly intelligent men, but many of them had been living for years in the neglect of their religious duties. There were some apostles of infidelity among the body of workingmen at Inchicore who sought by public lectures and private propaganda to spread their wicked teachings. Inchicore lay at the extremity of St James's Parish, a mile and a half from the parish church and many of the men never went to Mass. Such was the population in the midst of which the hand of God placed the first Oblates of Mary Immaculate in Ireland".

Within a week of its purchase, Sunday Mass was said in the parlour of the private residence. Father Cooke goes on:

> "Judging that increased accommodation would be necessary for the larger congregation which would be sure to assemble on the following Sunday, I took the opinion of some practical workingmen as to the best means of providing it. A young carpenter who was present undertook to have a large wooden

Saint Eugene de Mazenod

chapel erected by them, provided that the men of the railway works lent their aid in constructing it. A cheerful response came from the railway men. Materials for the temporary building were on the ground on Tuesday the 24th June. That evening at six o'clock after their day's work, seven hundred men from both the railway works and the neighbourhood of Inchicore offered their services for the project. They were all skilled workmen and worked from six to nine every evening at the new building. They completed their labour of love by ten o'clock on Saturday evening and a building capable of accommodating seven or eight hundred people was raised by these devoted men in sixteen hours.

"The following morning, Sunday the 29th June, High Mass was sung in the new temporary Church of Mary Immaculate in the presence of an overflowing congregation. But the most gratifying feature of the whole proceedings was the wonderful reawakening of dormant faith and practical religion.

"Shortly afterwards a mission was held in this building and was attended by the men of the railway works in crowds. There was a large attendance also of railway guards, engine drivers and stokers. The Fathers at Inchicore have always taken a special interest in these excellent men upon whose steady conduct and conscientious discharge of duties the very lives of many depend".

Father Cooke, as well as being a renowned preacher, was also a man of great sanctity and self-denial, to whom many favours were attributed.

Brother William Costigan, O.M.I. (1828–1902)

There are still surviving links in the area with that first little church. Brother William Costigan, a skilled carpenter who was probably born near Bow Bridge, was one of the first adherents to the new Oblate community at Inchicore. There is a strong family tradition that he was involved in the building of the wooden church and his great-grand nephew, Ray McGovern of Jamestown Road, told me that his name was always held in esteem down the years by his relatives. A younger brother, Patrick, born in 1834, worked all his life as a fitter in the railway works. It was Brother Costigan who made the original furniture for the House of Retreat and for very many years taught carpentry. He is buried in the community cemetery in Inchicore.

There is another association through local man Dermot Larkin who was a third generation railway employee until his retirement some years ago. His grandfather Nicholas Larkin, who hailed from Balbriggan, was one of the many who secured employment in the early years of the Works. Nicholas was a carpenter also and his plane and saw, which again according to strong family tradition were used by him in the building of the church, are still in Dermot's proud possession.

Further Developments

Six months later, in January 1857, the new community were able to open a school in a spacious and well preserved coach house which they had reconditioned. Night classes were also held for adults, among whom there was a high rate of illiteracy.

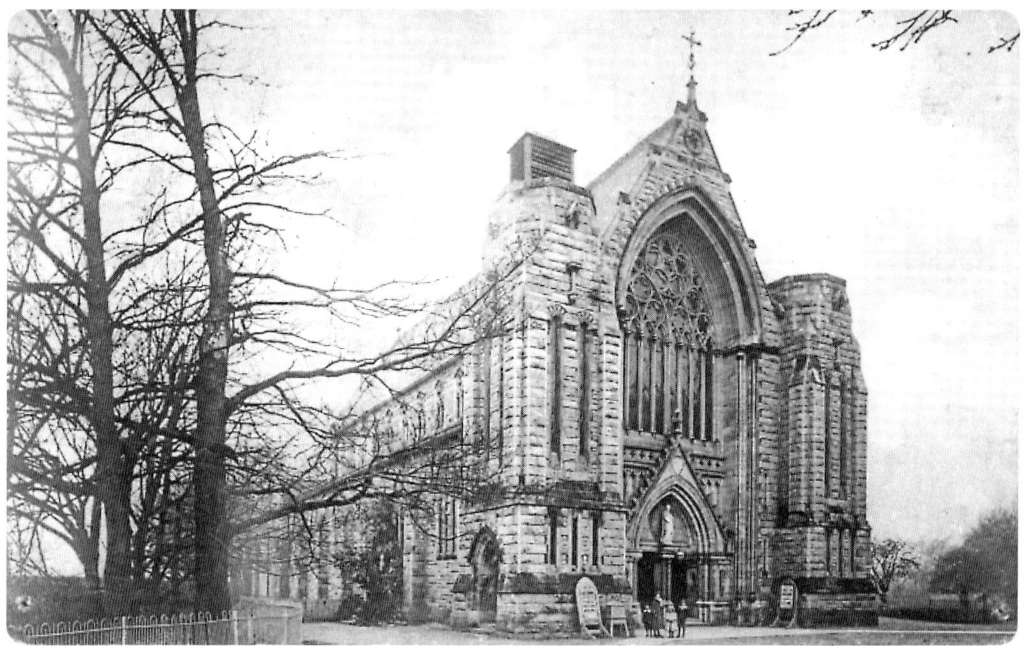

An early view of the Church of Mary Immaculate

The large House of Retreat intended for enclosed retreats for the laity, was commenced in 1858 and completed in 1861. Saint Eugene de Mazenod paid a short visit to Inchicore in 1858, when he said Mass in the temporary church and also made a tour of the railway works.

A new school was built in 1864 and until its eventual replacement seventy years later it was known as the "Chapel School". The Commissioners of Education stipulated that religious objects such as statues and crucifixes should be kept in presses and only displayed at the times of prayer and religious instruction.

The wooden chapel, which incidentally was on the site of the present Áras Mhuire, was eventually rebuilt in stone and enlarged somewhat. However it was still not big enough and the large Church of Mary Immaculate as we know it today was planned. Work commenced in 1876, but could not be completed for various reasons. It was decided to use the church in its uncompleted state and the first Mass was celebrated there on 8th December 1878. It was almost another fifteen years before the work could be nearly completed in 1892, and even then the spires had not been built. The High Altar, one of the finest of its kind, is the work of Padraig Pearse's father.

A great friend and advisor to the first Oblate community in Inchicore was the Irish speaking Augustinian Bishop, Dr Donal O'Connor, who had previously been the representative of the Holy See in Madras, India. Eugene de Mazenod acknowledged this in a letter of 1861: "I am most anxious to thank in person the Augustinian Fathers, and especially the worthy bishop of the Order, Dr. O'Connor,

The "Chapel School", Tyrconnell Road 1937. Also note the little milestone.

for their many kindnesses towards our fathers and having been of such great help in getting us established in Dublin".

French Refugees

In 1880, during an anti-clerical period in France, many religious orders were expelled. Amongst these were an Oblate community in Burgundy, who were offered hospitality by their brethren at Inchicore. The party, consisting of about forty priests, brothers and scholastics, arrived at the North Wall in November 1880 and moved to Inchicore with all their gear in a procession of twenty carts and carriages. On the last part of the journey they were escorted by a huge crowd of people who gathered outside the House of Retreat, where a band was playing and speeches of welcome were made.

The visitors were housed on the top floor of the House of Retreat, where the students continued their courses for the next four years. More suitable accommodation was then secured for them at Belcamp, Raheny, but it was to be a further four years before they were able to return to the continent.

The previous old church and first crib

The Inchicore Crib

The original Inchicore crib was the most acclaimed crib in Ireland, and down the years was visited annually at Christmas time by thousands of people from far and near. It had been at first intended for the Basilica of the Sacred Heart at Montmartre in Paris, with which the Oblates were associated, but it did not fit in with the architect's plans for that building. The wax figures were the work of a French artist who had gone to the Holy Land to model them on local people. The crib was brought to Inchicore in 1885 and laid out in the old church which was now disused. It consisted of twenty-seven lifelike figures which were presented in a series of nativity scenes. "With its feeling of reality and the delicacy and authenticity of expression with which the artist had enlivened the figures, the crib grew more and more into the hearts of succeeding generations of Dubliners."

In 1937 because of new developments the crib had to be moved to another nearby building known as the Leo Hall where, tragically, due to an accidental fire it was totally destroyed on Christmas Day 1948.

Father W. Ring (1834–1919)

Father William Ring was one of the foremost among many remarkable Oblate Superiors. A County Derry man, he was a born leader and organiser with a tremendous capacity for work. Socially concerned, he did prodigious work on behalf of the underprivileged in the slums of London. He preached missions, not only in Ireland and England, but also throughout the USA and Canada, at a time when travel was infinitely more laborious than it is today. Father Ring initiated the Inchicore pilgrimages to Lourdes and such was his reputation that he was invited by Cardinal Logue to organise a national pilgrimage to Rome in 1892, something which he did with great success.

Ring Street and Ring Terrace, in the shadow of the Church of Mary Immaculate, honour his name.

Chapter Twenty-One

The Township Commissioners

As Dublin City continued to expand in the second half of the nineteenth century, district councils with strictly limited powers and known as Townships were established in some of the suburbs, such as Rathmines, Pembroke and Drumcondra. The initiative for one of these councils for our area came mainly from local industrialists, mill owners and business people, all of whom were concerned at the lack of proper water and other services. A meeting towards this end was held somewhere in the district in May 1868. The Chairman of the meeting, Dr E. Kennedy, J.P., while praising the good points of the locality, also painted a rather stark picture of some of its shortcomings.

First of all he said there was a need for more villa residences for the trading population, but their second grievance was of a more serious nature. They had, he said, a horrible nuisance that existed beside them. It was a nuisance that was destructive to health and even to human life. He alluded to the open sewer into which was discharged the sewage of Richmond Barracks. Within the last few years they had three epidemics traceable to that nuisance, cholera, fever and even lately some cases of black death. When that nuisance was removed, he did not hesitate to say that the district would be the most salubrious and healthy part of Dublin.

Further objectives would be a proper water supply and a decent approach to the City. He would expect financial assistance from the Government, particularly in view of the presence of a garrison.

A debate followed regarding the title of the proposed township and the names mentioned were New Kilmainham, Inchicore and Richmond, the latter no doubt being suggested by pro-British elements. Dr Kennedy favoured Inchicore because he contended that that area would contribute the greater portion of the rates. Also, he went on, "Inchicore is a good Irish name and we should be proud of it. With regard to Richmond, there is no necessity to go outside of Ireland for a name". We do not know which name was favoured by the meeting. However when as a result of these local efforts township status was granted, it was referred to as New Kilmainham.

The New Kilmainham Township Act (1868)

The Act giving effect to the new township was passed by the British Parliament in 1868 and elections for same followed later in that year. The area covered was New

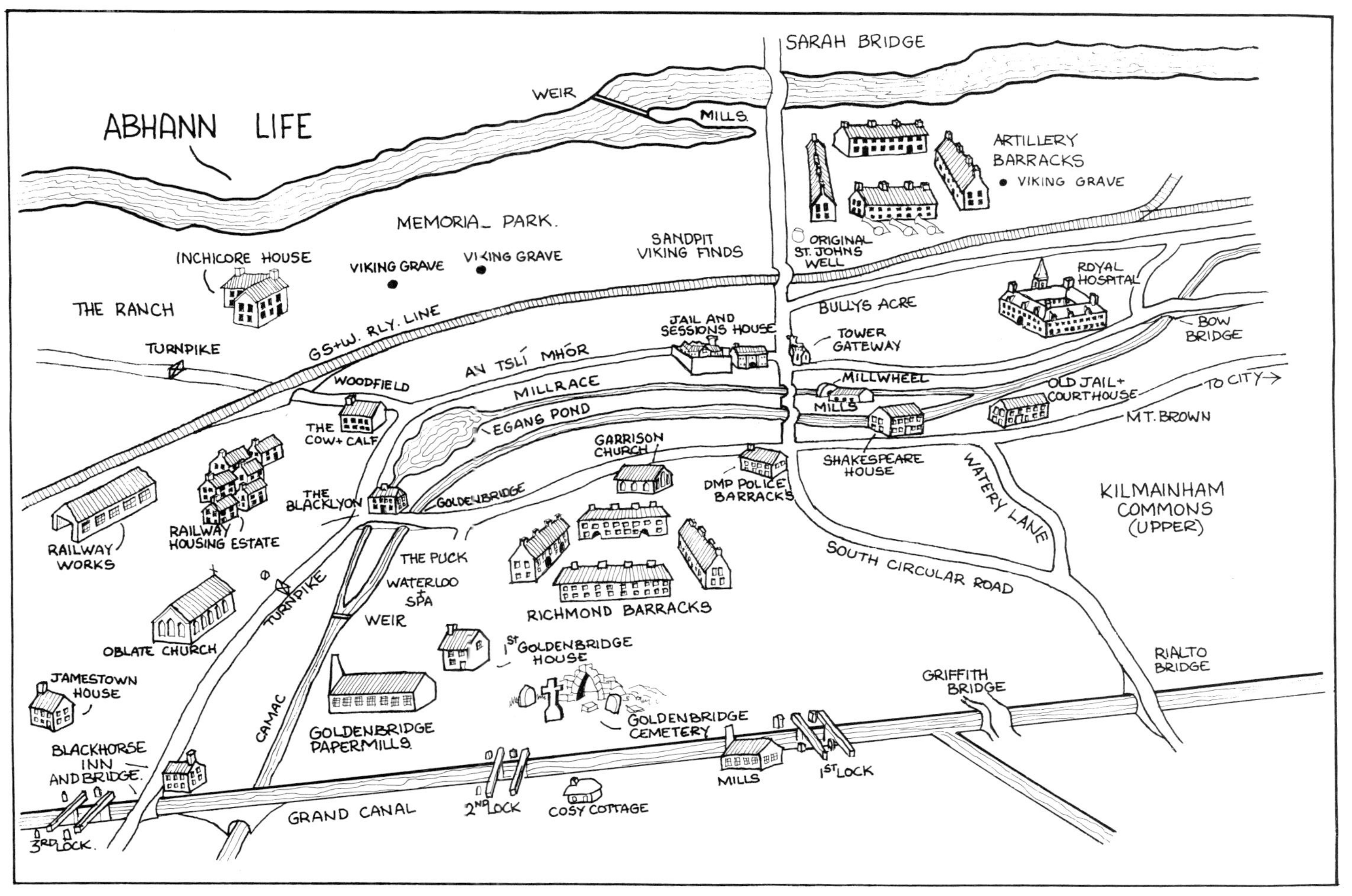
ABHANN LIFE
WEIR
MILLS
SARAH BRIDGE
ARTILLERY BARRACKS
VIKING GRAVE
MEMORIA_ PARK.
INCHICORE HOUSE
VIKING GRAVE
VIKING GRAVE
SANDPIT VIKING FINDS
ORIGINAL ST. JOHNS WELL
ROYAL HOSPITAL
THE RANCH
BULLYS ACRE
GS+W. RLY. LINE
JAIL AND SESSIONS HOUSE
BOW BRIDGE
TURNPIKE
TOWER GATEWAY
AN TSLI MHÓR
WOODFIELD
MILLRACE
MILLWHEEL
MILLS
OLD JAIL + COURTHOUSE
TO CITY→
EGANS POND
MT. BROWN
THE COW + CALF
GARRISON CHURCH
SHAKESPEARE HOUSE
WATERY LANE
THE BLACKLYON
GOLDENBRIDGE
DMP POLICE BARRACKS
KILMAINHAM COMMONS (UPPER)
RAILWAY HOUSING ESTATE
RAILWAY WORKS
THE PUCK
SOUTH CIRCULAR ROAD
WATERLOO SPA
TURNPIKE
RICHMOND BARRACKS
WEIR
OBLATE CHURCH
1ST GOLDENBRIDGE HOUSE
RIALTO BRIDGE
JAMESTOWN HOUSE
GRIFFITH BRIDGE
CAMAC
GOLDENBRIDGE CEMETERY
GOLDENBRIDGE PAPERMILLS
BLACKHORSE INN AND BRIDGE
MILLS
1ST LOCK
GRAND CANAL
2ND LOCK
COSY COTTAGE
3RD LOCK.

Kilmainham, i.e. the district near the jail, Inchicore, Goldenbridge and Islandbridge, all of which had previously been under the jurisdiction of the Grand Jury of County Dublin. Old Kilmainham was to continue under Dublin Corporation as heretofore, the City boundary ending at Kilmainham crossroads – now Kilmainham traffic lights.

The township was a homogeneous area with many distinctive features such as Richmond Barracks, Kilmainham Jail and Courthouse, Inchicore Railway Works and housing estate, the tram works, several mills, the Oblate Church and House of Retreat, several other churches and schools and an orphanage, Goldenbridge "Village", the Grand Canal and the Camac river. New houses had begun to emerge by degrees on Emmet Road, Tyrconnell Road, Woodfield and The Ranch, while ascendancy and military types came to live in very large houses on Inchicore Road. Many "yards" of small cottages sprang up off several of the main roads, although some of these, mainly in Goldenbridge, had been there since the early days of Richmond Barracks.

While it was predominantly working class, it differed from the city insofar as many of the employees were in relatively secure employment. Another aspect was that Protestants formed a strong minority of the population due to the number of English workers originally required to establish the railways and also due to the military presence.

The franchise for the election of nine Township Commissioners was limited to male adults, who owned property in the area with a poor law valuation of at least £4. Amongst those first commissioners were well-known businessmen David McBirney (Chairman), Francis Moore Scott and William Ryan, who had recently taken over the Goldenbridge Paper Mills from the Sullivan family, and two officials of the Great Southern and Western Railway Company. Strangely, for some unknown reason, the railway company had originally opposed the setting up of the township.

The Commissioners had quite limited powers. They were responsible for roads, bridges and footpaths, with the administration of the township being financed by rates. Also they were supplied with water by Dublin Corporation and a special water rate was levied by the Commissioners on property owners in the area, which was used to reimburse the Corporation. We can only presume that they also succeeded in dealing with the sanitation problems. Unfortunately, the New Kilmainham minute books, unlike those of the other townships, have not been found to date. If they ever surface, they will provide much valuable information on the administration of the area during the latter years of the last century.

The Commissioners were given authority to build a Town Hall, but this never came to pass, their meetings being held in Kilmainham Courthouse. Here also they had office accommodation for a town clerk, surveyor, sanitary officers and medical officer.

The Commissioners did not have any political function, but it is interesting to note that when Parnell visited Inchicore in 1891, the current Township Commissioners presented him with an address of welcome. Only one of them whose name we do not know refused to sign the address. It is also interesting that a local supporter of Parnell, Mr Edward Holohan of Inchicore House, had been elected as Chairman of the Township Commissioners at that time. This support for the Home Rule Leader in an area so dominated by British officialdom and power comes as a surprise, but it probably reflects the growing influence of Catholics/Nationalists in the administrative life of Dublin generally as the century came to an end.

In 1889, the Township was upgraded to an Urban District Council and with a more liberal election franchise, but unfortunately this new-found status only lasted for two years. In 1900, the New Kilmainham U.D.C., in common with a number of other similar bodies on the fringes of the city, was abolished and placed under Dublin Corporation. The new city boundary was accordingly extended out as far as the Third Lock (Black Horse) Bridge.

It is regrettable that this exercise, however limited, in devolved local administration, was not allowed to grow and flourish over the past ninety-nine years.

Chapter Twenty-Two

The Invincibles

It was on Saturday evening 6th May 1882 that members of the secret society known as the Irish National Invincibles assassinated Lord Frederick Cavendish, the newly appointed Chief Secretary for Ireland, and Thomas Burke, the Under-Secretary, on the main road of the Phoenix Park as the two of them strolled without an escort towards the Vice-Regal Lodge, now Áras An Uachtaráin. The killings, which became known as the Park Murders, caused consternation in Ireland and England and brought widespread repercussions in their wake.

The affair was seen by quite a number of people who were about but not all of them fully realised what was afoot. Amongst those who were passing at the time were two men, a brass finisher and a boiler maker from the Inchicore Railway Works who lived in the company's cottages. They were getting in some cycling practice in the Park and by mere chance rode into the middle of the affray. They managed to keep going however and continued down the main road. Soon they saw a cab ahead of them into which four men had entered. They, as it turned out, were part of the Invincible group, the cabbie being "Skin the Goat" Fitzharris who stood up to whip on the horse. The cyclists were very agitated but decided to say nothing at this stage, preferring to think that they had just seen a rough and tumble tussle.

In the meantime a second group of four Invincibles, which included Joe Brady and Tim Kelly who had actually committed the fatal stabbing, left the Park by the Chapelizod Gate at a fast pace on Myles Kavanagh's outside-car. They crossed over Chapelizod Bridge and, proceeding up Sarsfield Road, turned at the Model School corner into Grattan Crescent before travelling out the Naas Road. Somewhere near Fox and Geese they turned off again and entered the city via Terenure.

The Inchicore Witnesses

The two railway men spent a very uneasy weekend, but when they saw the story in the newspaper they decided to consult their superior, Mr Aspinal. He advised them to contact the police, which they did. All of this was to become the subject of much speculation and rumour in Inchicore, particularly in the Works.

Widespread investigations and searches went on for months in city and county, but while they had their suspicions the authorities were not yet able to secure incriminating evidence. They then enlisted the services of a special magistrate, Mr John Adye Curran. He had all the people who were in the Park brought to Dublin Castle, where he examined each one of them closely and obtained sworn statements from them on the 19th of December. The following are some points from the statements of the Inchicore men, both of whom initially saw a side-car with its driver parked near the Phoenix monument, but took no heed of it.

The first cyclist, who was several yards ahead of his companion, saw four men scuffling on the footpath and two of them staggered down the slope and fell on to the road within two yards of his machine. He had to pull over to the other side of the road to get out of their way.

The second cyclist told how he saw four men in a group and a man lying on the ground. Then about four or five yards from the monument "I saw two men standing and one had a knife in his hand. There were people all along looking about.

> "As I went on I saw by the side of my eye one of these men raise his hand several times and I saw a form fall. I could not give the least description of the appearance of any of the men."

Finally after further painstaking police work and with the benefit of information supplied by informers, a large number of suspects were arrested in mid-January. Eight of these were charged and brought to Kilmainham Courthouse for identification purposes on the 15th of February 1883. In a deposition taken in the presence of the prisoners the first cyclist stated that he recognised Joe Brady as one of the men he had seen on the footpath in the Phoenix Park. His colleague was not called, probably because of his previous definite statement that he could not recognise any of the men. We do know that this man was very frightened and there was a story in the Works as we shall see later that he fled to America.

Lengthy and sensational trials were to follow which went on for months at Green Street Courthouse. The second of the trials had taken place in Kilmainham Courthouse amidst extraordinary security, but it was too small in view of the number of the accused. In the end five of the Invincibles were hanged at Kilmainham Jail in May/June 1883. Others received lengthy prison sentences, one of these being a shoemaker from Old Kilmainham.

Contemporary artists impression of the Park Murders

My next door neighbour, Anthony Byrne, told me that his father remembered going with other young boys down to the bottom of Emmet Road to see a black flag being flown on the top of the jail wall following the executions.

Catherine Tynan

The poet and novelist Catherine Tynan makes a number of local references to the Invincible period in her memoirs. She was living then at Belgard in the family home, "White Hall", which together with its adjoining farm was occupied up to a few years ago. It was at this residence in later times that she hosted frequent literary gatherings attended by such notables as William Butler Yeats and Dr Douglas Hyde. Regrettably this historic house has been vandalised in recent times but the Catherine Tynan Society are campaigning to have it restored.

She tells us that on that fateful evening of the 6th of May 1882 her younger brother and sister were walking home from Dublin and had reached the quiet winding lanes of Ballymount. Suddenly they were pushed back against a wall by a carload of men which was being driven furiously. After they recovered they proceeded on their way until they came to the Coolfan stream between the Red Cow and Ballymount. Here the car had stopped and a number of the men were washing something in the water. Catherine expresses the view that they were washing the knives used in the Phoenix Park murders only a few hours previously.

She recalls another incident some short time after the trial of the Invincibles at which James Carey had given evidence against his former colleagues. She was travelling from the city on the Inchicore horse tram which stopped in Thomas Street to take on a woman with a small child. A hubbub broke out on the tram and there were demands that the woman should be put off. The agitated conductor pleaded that he could not do so as she had paid her fare at which some of the passengers got off. The tram proceeded then and the woman sat in a corner by herself. "She alighted at one of a little red-brick row of houses in the shadow of Kilmainham Jail. It was a dreadful little house with a dirty curtain pulled across. Some women cursed as she went out and one or two spat after her. It was James Carey's wretched wife, poor creature."

It has to be said that Carey was to some extent tricked by the police into testifying against his accomplices but this would not have been known to the public at large.

The Careys did not live at Kilmainham and we must assume that his wife and family moved there when he was arrested. Very soon however after the completion of the trials the British government as previously promised quietly arranged for the passage of James Carey, his wife and six children to South Africa. As they neared their destination Carey was shot dead on board ship by a Donegal Fenian, Pat O'Donnell, who accidentally discovered his identity.

Catherine Tynan also tells us in her memoirs that her father was President of the Inchicore United Workingmen's Club on Emmet Road about 1890.

> "We were always going to meetings of one kind or another. My father had accepted the Presidency of the Working Men's Club at Inchicore, the members of which were mainly the skilled artisans employed in the great railway works. He was very much beloved by these men and he never missed a meeting. The meetings took place in the evenings and were often prolonged to a late hour. I used to sit more or less patiently waiting for him in the little pony-trap outside.
>
> "I remember a night of full moon, one side of the street bright as day, the other in velvety black shadow. Suddenly from the blackness there was projected upon the bright space a number of queer shadows coming in a procession. I watched with half-alarmed curiosity. Presently the shadows resolved themselves into a man carrying a table on his head, a woman carrying a shapeless bundle and three children carrying respectively a chair, a sweeping brush and a teapot. I remembered then that it was the eve of a Quarter-day (when rents would be due) and this was a flitting."

She does not offer any explanation as to how her father, who was a farmer and landowner, became involved with the club.

Chapter Twenty-Three

From Tyrconnell Park to Croke Park

Spendloves Field

The ground where Tyrconnell Park now stands is described in old deeds as being part of the lands of Inchicore in the possession of one Joseph Moore Labarte. It was only when the houses were built there in 1934 that it was given the name of Tyrconnell Park. However it had previously been known to old timers in the district as Spendloves Field (not to be confused with Spendloves Bank which was a location within the railway works). One of these, the late Charlie Dowdall, well known League of Ireland and James's Gate player, told me that it was in Spendloves Field that he first kicked a ball when playing for a juvenile soccer team. He also remembered it being used for hockey matches in the early 1900s and the small stream which crossed through it up towards the "Bungalow" end. Later it was used for plots and allotments, particularly during World War I, and for years afterwards, by which time it was owned by Alderman James Flanagan of Portmahon House, Rialto. The field, as sometimes thought, did not form part of the railway estate from which it is divided by a high wall.

However, back in the previous century, it was the playing pitch of the Saint Patrick's Hurling and Football Club. This was the most notable G.A.A. team in the district and was founded in 1886. They had previous grounds at Goldenbridge and the 2nd Lock, but in 1888 moved to the Tyrconnell Road field, which became known as the Saint Patrick's Ground. They only remained here for two years, but during this short time, they packed in an amazing series of hurling, football and athletic events, as well as two early "All Irelands". It was always believed that the latter were played at this location, but up to now there was no documentary proof. However, the following news item of March 1889 provides the necessary confirmation:

> "The Dublin County Board earnestly urges players and spectators attending the Inchicore matches to preserve orderly demeanour and refrain altogether from shouting or cheering during religious services in the neighbouring Catholic and Methodist Churches."

As we know, Tyrconnell Park was situated between the two churches indicated in this report, but the Methodist one has very recently been demolished. It should be mentioned here also that many of the games commenced at 11.00 a.m. on Sunday mornings.

Teams in those days consisted of twenty-one players, while points were scored through side posts. "Over the Bar" had not yet arrived and it took five points to equal a goal.

Whitsuntide, 9th and 10th June 1889

What was described as a Whitsuntide Carnival of hurling, football and athletics was held at the ground on Sunday and Monday the 9th and 10th June 1889. This was a most ambitious tournament involving eight teams from Leinster and County Tipperary, as well as well known athletes.

At that time, County Tipperary was noted not only for its hurling ability, but also for its famous Bohercrowe football team, which was one of the attractions of the weekend. This team arrived by train at Kingsbridge on the Saturday night and was greeted at the station by the playing of the Inchicore Brass Band as well as by a large crowd of city based followers, who gave them a hearty welcome.

It has to be said that the result of the match between the Tipperary footballers and Erin's Isle on the next day was not altogether satisfactory because of a disputed goal by the latter in the last three minutes of the game. The committee asked both teams to replay the match, but as Erin's Isle were not agreeable, it was awarded to Bohercrowe.

Otherwise, it was a very enjoyable week-end. The sporting correspondent of the *Freeman's Journal* commented that with the beautiful day, the brilliant play and the big gathering of spectators of both sexes, some four thousand souls, those who visited Inchicore on that Sunday were well rewarded for their trouble. He also went on to compliment the Inchicore Band for attending and rendering such an admirable selection of music.

In the other games, greatest interest centred on the Thurles Hurling Club, who had won the 1887 All-Ireland. In playing against the host team, Saint Patrick's, whom they defeated, they gave a tremendous exhibition and the correspondent wrote that it was no exaggeration to say that such brilliant hurling had not been seen in Dublin before.

> "It was delightful to see the certain easy graceful manner in which they used their hurleys, while their air pucking, neatness in striking and agility evoked rounds of applause from the large gathering of people who throughout were kept spellbound by the fleet-footed Tipperary men".

In a competition of the long puck, Pat Browne of Saint Patrick's achieved a splendid distance of 198′ 6″. "All his three pucks were of similar length and were straight as an arrow and mainly against the wind".

A tough tussle took place in the tug-of-war competition between the Wolfe Tones from Blue Bell and Young Irelands. The Blue Bell men, who already had ten medals to their credit, won after a splendid contest.

This completed the programme for the Sunday. Time did not permit the completion of the Hurling and Football tournament and it was postponed for some weeks. The athletics were held as arranged on the next day, Whit Monday.

Completion of Tournament – 21st July 1889

The finals of the Whit Tournament were held on Sunday 21st July 1889 between Bohercrowe and Drogheda Gaels in football and between Thurles and Rathdowney in hurling. In addition, two other matches were played as well, giving patrons wonderful value for their money. There was a large attendance of approximately 3,000 people, nearly half of whom were country folk and this number would have been greater still were it not for a wet and windy morning. A special excursion train brought the Tipperary and Laois supporters to Kingsbridge station that morning.

One of the games played as a curtain raiser was the semi-final of the County Tipperary hurling championship between Toomevara and Holycross, because a neutral venue could not be agreed upon within that county. "Toomevara, tall strapping fellows, showed the way on to the ground and the moment they appeared, they took the fancy of the crowd". In a closely fought match, they defeated Holycross by one goal to one point.

The correspondent could not contain his admiration for the victors. "They are wonderfully sure, hit terribly hard and can take lightning balls either in the air or on the ground."

In a further game, two County Louth football teams played in a challenge.

The sporting correspondent reported as follows regarding the tournament finals themselves:

> "It was only when the two finalists, Bohercrowe and Drogheda Gaels, took the field that the real enthusiasm of the spectators manifested itself and the excitement from the moment the ball was thrown in until the final whistle could not reach a higher pitch. This was not to be wondered at, as the teams playing with great brilliance and earnestness caused the game to be of the most wildly exciting description.
>
> "Bohercrowe won with a score of 1 goal and 1 point against their opponents' 1 point. It was their fierce charging and fast play that won the game for them. However, Drogheda need not hang their heads in shame, they can be proud of their brilliant and skillful play. It is questionable after this contest if the Tipps. have any superiors as footballers in Ireland.
>
> "In the Hurling Final, Thurles hurled a magnificent game to beat Rathdowney 1 goal and 9 points to 1 point.

"After the games, Miss Ryan, one of Tipperary's fairest daughters, very kindly and gracefully distributed the medals to the winning teams".
It was certainly Tipp. all the way.

The Oblate Connection

The Oblate Fathers' Church of Mary Immaculate was first put into use in 1878, although not fully completed. Because of lack of funds, it was to be many years before the work could be brought to fruition. The two tournaments mentioned were in fact part of the fund-raising campaign and were very successful towards this end. This information has come to hand in Canon Fogarty's book, *Tipperary's G.A.A. Story*, published in 1960, in which he tells us:

> "The Bohercrowe Club was founded in 1887 and up to the All Ireland Final of 1889 had played in thirty six matches of every description. Some of these were in a big tournament in Inchicore in which they won a set of gold crosses from the crack teams of Leinster. The tournament was run to raise funds for the building of the new Oblate Church, which was sometimes referred to as the Bohercrowe Church".

The newspaper reports did not give this information, but their reference to the teams being in the final rounds "for the crosses" is significant in the light of Canon Fogarty's statement.

Mr Tom O'Donoghue of Tipperary has told me that there is a tradition in that town that a plaque was erected in the Oblate Church following the tournament acknowledging the help of Bohercrowe, but no record of this now exists.

"All Ireland" Background

The G.A.A. was founded in 1884. The first "All" Irelands were held in 1887, but none took place in 1888. The Central Council continued with their efforts and selected Saint Patrick's Ground in Inchicore for the football and hurling finals of 1889, as well as the preceding semi-finals. Clubs were flourishing by this time all over the country, but because of disagreements and other reasons only a handful of counties, represented by their club champions, took part in the championship series. Notwithstanding this, the Inchicore finals of 1889 were an important link in the evolution of the G.A.A. and it was a tribute to the local Saint Patrick's Club that their ground was chosen for these games.

Only three football teams were in contention for the Leinster Final. The matches were played at Saint Patrick's Ground on the 13th October 1889, which was a beautiful autumn Sunday.

In the first game, Maryboro' defeated Bray by nine points to four and after an hour's rest these mighty men lined up again to meet the Drogheda Blues, whom they defeated by three points to two. The reporter commented on the winners:

> "In point of physique, it would be hard to beat them, all splendid specimens of bone and muscle looking extremely well in their green jerseys and stockings and white buckskin breeches".

He went on to say that it was a highly exciting encounter, but one of the roughest matches yet played at Inchicore, with too much tripping and general fouling.

The Leinster Hurling Final should also have been played on the same day but as Rathdowney did not turn up the Dublin side, Kickhams were given a walkover.

The All Ireland Football Finals

The next week-end, Saturday and Sunday the 19th and 20th October 1889, were to have been big days at Inchicore, but things did not work out as planned. It was originally announced that the All-Ireland semi-finals in both hurling and football would take place at Saint Patrick's Ground on the Saturday, to be followed by the finals on the Sunday. However, neither the hurling or football champions of Connaught or Ulster put in an appearance and neither had the Munster hurling championship been completed in time. The organisers had no alternative but to postpone the hurling final and only play the football final on the Sunday between the two teams that turned up, i.e. Bohercrowe, representing Tipperary, and Maryboro', representing Laois. One way or the other, it would not have been possible to play any games on the Saturday, as the rain fell in torrents from early morning until nightfall.

On Sunday morning it was still raining heavily but cleared up by mid-day. Shortly after this the game got under way before an attendance of about 2,000 people. The ground was in dreadful condition and so slippy that the players had great difficulty in keeping on their feet.

The Maryboro' men had the advantage in physique, but in comparison to their opponents they showed a great lack of skill. According to the newspaper account the punting, passing and all round kicking of the Bohercrowe's was astonishing considering the state of the ground. While Maryboro' played a dashing and determined game, Bohercrowe had the upper hand in both halves of the game. The report went on to say that the game was characterised by too much roughness and viciousness and that one or two scenes occurred which they did not care to dwell upon! Furthermore the lack of proper stewarding left the referee with a most difficult task. As soon as the smallest dispute arose between the players, the crowd flocked on to the field, causing the game to be suspended for several minutes.

The final score was Bohercrowe three goals six points, Maryboro' nil, with Tipperary being declared the All-Ireland football champions of 1889.

The All Ireland Hurling Final

The postponed All Ireland hurling final was played on Sunday the 3rd November 1889, between Tulla, representing Clare, and Kickham's, representing Dublin, before a crowd of 1,500 people. Like the football final, recent heavy rain had again left the pitch in a wretched condition, so much so that Tulla elected to play in their stocking feet. Unlike the football, however, this game was conducted in a very sporting manner and free of incidents.

Notwithstanding the adverse conditions underfoot, a tremendous game was provided by both teams. It was described as the finest display of hurling witnessed, not only in Dublin, but probably throughout the length and breadth of Ireland, since the G.A.A. was founded. Tulla were the favourites and had the upper hand in the first half. After the interval Kickhams "hurled in the most brilliant fashion imaginable" and became the 1889 champions, with a score of five goals and one point against Tulla's one goal and six points. Clare would have to wait until 1914 to achieve their first All-Ireland hurling title.

In the concluding report of the game, the Dublin County Board were praised for the manner in which the arrangements were carried out and which reflected great credit on all concerned.

Secret Service

All national organisations including the G.A.A. were under surveillance by the members of the D.M.P. and the R.I.C., who were the eyes and ears of the British authorities. As a matter of routine, plain clothes men were in attendance at all the matches and sent in reports to police headquarters of which the following extract is a typical example:

CRIME SPECIAL - COUNTY OF DUBLIN

4 April 1889

"I beg to report that I have during the past month attended at the football championships at Inchicore and Tallaght on Sundays. I entered into conversation with those present and the only person whom I have seen attending these matches is William Fields of Blackrock on the 3rd ult. at Inchicore.

"As far as I can yet ascertain, there is no secret illegal organisation in Co. Dublin. However, I am informed that within the last three weeks, there has been an effort made etc., etc."

Yours etc,

______ Sgt

William Fields was suspected of being a member of the Fenians.

Blue Bell Tournament

Only a few weeks after the All-Ireland Hurling Final, the Blue Bell Club, the "Wolfe Tones", held a very successful one-day fund-raising football and hurling tournament on Sunday 17th November at Saint Patrick's Ground. Much of the credit was given to the club's able Chairman and veteran Gael, Matt Murphy, as well as the Secretary, M. T. Kelly of Jamestown Cottage. They were blessed with fine weather and on this occasion, the ground was in splendid condition, with an attendance of about two thousand people. Commencing in the morning, four games in all were played.

Athletics

Sports and athletic meetings were a very popular pastime throughout Ireland and Inchicore was no exception. Here patrons were well catered for by frequent events at local venues including Saint Patrick's Ground. Nearly all these meetings had a very comprehensive programme which took in a wide range of running competitions as well as weight throwing, hammer throwing and putting the shot, hop, step and

The Ivy Cycling club outside the Dining Hall 1881
Amongst this group are John Owens, Tom Bryan, Tom Owens, Tim Coughlan, James Griffiths, Joe Byrne, Harry Garnett, Fred Caswell, John Dillon, Robert Prendergast, James Clarke, Jack Davis and Railway Engineer, Harold Ivatt

jump, hurdle race, high jump, walking race, place kicking, long puck, tug of war and cycle races.

However, at the Saint Patrick's Sports in their grounds at Tyrconnell Road in early October 1889, the order was stated to be very bad and because of spectators crowding in, it was difficult to carry out the events. The most exciting event of the day was declared to be a three-mile cycle race in which the winner had less than two yards to spare from his nearest rival.

Another very active club in the district, although not as spectacular as Saint Patrick's, was the Henry Grattans. They also appear to have had a ground of their own which possibly was at Jamestown. It was certainly at that venue that they too organised a large-scale sports. The programme included a pony race and much excitement was caused when several of the ponies bolted.

In those early pioneering days of cycling, Inchicore had their own Iveagh Cycling Club which was notable for the fact that their members were drawn from both the Catholic and Protestant communities. They had committee rooms at "Independence Cottage" on Emmet Road where Centra Food Market now stands.

Change of Venue

Saint Patrick's continued their games at the Tyrconnell Road pitch up to about May or June 1890. Perhaps the lease had expired, but for whatever reason, they moved then to a somewhat smaller ground at Emmet Road, which is now Richmond Park, the home of Saint Patrick's Athletic. Is it a coincidence that although a different code, the present club bears the same name?

It was reported in the *Freeman's Journal* towards the end of April 1890 that the Dublin County Board were in negotiation with the Inchicore Race Committee for the use of their racecourse. It is likely that as the ground at Tyrconnell Road would no longer be available, the County Board were seeking an alternative venue for the All Ireland Finals of that year. This report is in line with the story that the late Simon Quigley told me that originally the G.A.A. intended to have their major venue at a site not far from the Naas Road. However, the negotiations fell through, as the race committee for some strange reason stipulated that the name of their ground, which was situated at Jamestown, would not be used publicly. The G.A.A. then secured Clonturk Park in Drumcondra, where All-Ireland Finals were played until the eventual move to Croke Park.

Saint Patrick's made quite a lot of use of their new ground at Emmet Road, where they remained for three years. However, in 1893 they suddenly went out of existence at a time when a general decline in Dublin G.A.A. clubs set in. Two of their most energetic officials over the years had been Mr Peter Ryan of Emmet House and Mr J. Drea. The other local team, the Henry Grattans, kept going until 1912.

Today "Liffey Gaels" continue these early traditions of Gaelic games in the district at their own playing fields and club-hall at Sarsfield Road.

Chapter Twenty-Four

JAMESTOWN RACES

Pony racing took place at Jamestown for several years, commencing in October 1889 between the dates of the two All-Ireland Finals at Tyrconnell Park. What with hurling, football, athletics, cycling and now racing, sportsmen were being very well looked after during this era in Inchicore. The only person I heard very many years ago mentioning these races was old Paddy Cardiff from East Square, who told how he backed a horse there called "Scene Shifter". Otherwise all local knowledge of this race course has died out. It was situated at the top of Jamestown Road on the lands of Jamestown House, some of which were known as Kane's Fields in the not too distant past.

It was the pony race at the Henry Grattan Sports in 1888, already mentioned, which gave some local gentlemen the idea of having full-scale races the following year. A race committee was formed to make the necessary arrangements and one of the principals here was the Parnellite, Michael Flood, of Stone House. They went to a lot of trouble to provide good amenities such as a substantial stand which, along with an enclosure, could accommodate up to 200 people. They also provided comfortable dressing rooms and a weigh room for the participants. The course itself was three quarters of a mile in circumference, It was stated to be perfectly flat, affording excellent going except in the gaps of the boundary hedges, where the gates had been removed.

INCHICORE

(Co Dublin)

PONY RACES

(under Turf Club rules of racing)

will be held on the

JAMESTOWN COURSE

MONDAY 21st OCTOBER

The Course is situated within three minutes walk of the Inchicore Tram

Programme to be had at "Sport" Office

P.B. Kirwan, Manager 12th Oct. 1889

The first meeting was advertised for Monday 21st October 1889, which was the day after the All-Ireland football final, but due to circumstances outside their control, the committee were forced to postpone it to Thursday 24th October. The Thursday was not regarded as being as good a day as Monday and furthermore it clashed with the Cambridgeshire in England, but the attendance was reported as being fairly good. The committee showed much initiative in having a telegraph board installed at the course on which the results from the Cambridgeshire were received for the benefits of the patrons.

At this first meeting which commenced at 1.00 p.m., the races were on the flat, but in subsequent years, when the date was changed to the 29th June, they were all hurdle races. The principal race, "The Inchicore Plate", over two miles had to be run twice because of some objection but the final result was exactly the same as the first!

The winner was "Hard Cash" at two to one.

Chapter Twenty-Five

Parnell at Inchicore

Sunday June 7th, 1891, was a beautiful summer's day when the Irish leader, Charles Stewart Parnell, addressed a very large election meeting on the lawn of Inchicore House. In fact it was the largest political gathering ever held in Inchicore, before or since. Perhaps the fine weather played some part in that as well.

The house in question – a tall, old-world building which survived up to about twenty-five years ago – was situated in picturesque surroundings overlooking the river Liffey and had a commanding view across to the Phoenix Park. Older readers will recall the Gate Lodge on Sarsfield Road, the winding avenue up to the house, and the large field adjoining The Ranch. The gate piers were surmounted by two large stone eagles which caused the house itself to be sometimes mistakenly called Eagle House. The latter however was another old house situated in Goldenbridge beside that other well-known landmark, Cambridge House. Today Liffey Gaels' Clubhouse and playing fields occupy some of the lands of Inchicore House while the new dual carriageway traverses the site of the house. A short distance away, on the other side of the road, then as now, was the narrow "Khyber Pass" pedestrian entrance to the extensive railway works.

One hundred and eight years ago Ireland was going through the turmoil of the bitter dissension within the Irish Parliamentary Party, with the country divided for and against Parnell. The Irish leader's political fortunes were on the wane, but Dublin remained loyal to him. It was against this background that Mr Edward Holohan of Inchicore House, who was also chairman of the then Local Authority, Kilmainham Township Commissioners, invited Parnell to hold a public meeting in his grounds.

Down at the Fountain

The proceedings on that historic day commenced down in James's Street where Mr Parnell and his colleagues arrived in a wagonette drawn by two horses, not far from the Fountain at 2.00 p.m. A large crowd was waiting here to greet him with many standing on the steps of the Catholic Church to get a better view, and soon the horse tram and other traffic were unable to pass to and from Inchicore.

Addresses of welcome and expressions of confidence in the leadership of Parnell were presented by various organisations, with a young American girl, a Miss Trainor, offering a bouquet of flowers. Parnell responded with a short speech, his wagonette being used as an impromptu platform. In the course of this he said that it was useless to struggle for "Ireland a Nation" if Ireland's people are to disappear from the face of their own country. "Also every effort must be made to keep our people at home to afford them a career in Ireland so that we may be able to say that we still have a nation for which to fight".

The procession was then marshalled and with twelve bands in attendance set out for Inchicore. What a stirring sight this procession must have been as it made its way down Mount Brown and along Old Kilmainham with the bands playing patriotic airs all along the route.

At that time nearly every district had its own band which very often was the heart and soul of the community. It is interesting to note those that took part on that occasion:

Bluebell Fife and Drum; Green Flag, Chapelizod; Saint Brigid's, Blanchardstown; Inchicore Brass Band; Clondalkin Pipers; Saint Catherine's, Thomas Street; Amalgamated Carpenters; Saint Kevin's, Bray; Lord Edward, Harold's Cross; Workman's Club, York Street; Dublin United Labourers, Francis Street; Saint Patrick's, Rathmines.

Haunting Memories

Mr Parnell was cheered at various points and from the windows of some of the houses the occupants waved white handkerchiefs or green banners. At the township boundary at Kilmainham Cross, evergreens and streamers with slogans were stretched across the road. Then as the grim walls of Kilmainham Jail came into view, memories no doubt were flooding back to Parnell of his short sojourn in that establishment ten years earlier during the height of the Land War and of the ensuing Kilmainham Treaty.

Shortly afterwards the procession passed Inchicore's oldest school – the Model – before going under the railway bridge and then turning into Inchicore House. Several thousand people had already gathered around the platform on the lawn of the house together with a deep fringe of horse cars, and greeted the Chief's arrival with enthusiastic cheering. Amongst those on the platform was Councillor Michael Flood of Stone House just across the fields.

At a brief reception in the house Mr Parnell said that "it was a privilege to find themselves in that beautiful country where some of the most beautiful scenery in Ireland was at the door of their host, Mr Holohan". Even allowing for the euphoria of election time this gives some idea of the unspoiled nature of the district then.

Before the meeting proper got under way, a large effigy of Mr Parnell's arch political enemy, Tim Healy, was carried round the field, beaten with sticks, and finally torn to shreds. Such were the political passions of the time.

An address from the Kilmainham Commissioners was read and this had been signed by all the commissioners except one. Mr Parnell then came forward and was again greeted with enthusiastic cheering. A contemporary report claimed that "he appeared invigorated by the splendid array of men around him and delivered his speech with a fire which shows that his health is not impaired by his campaign". His speech is too long to repeat here but the following are some noteworthy extracts:

In Praise of Railway Workers

"There is another reason why I am pleased to address this meeting and it is because it is largely composed of the men of Inchicore, comprising amongst them the best mechanical and engineering talents in Ireland.

"I know that the men of Inchicore can turn out work in the engineering workshops of Inchicore unequalled by the work of artisans anywhere in the world. The locomotives and railway carriages and wagons they produce are excelled by no others and are an example of what Irishmen can do in these great industrial pursuits if they were only given the opportunity.

"How we are taunted with a decrease in the population of our own country. It has decreased because the manufacturing resources of Ireland, crippled in the last century by penal legislation, lost the start in the great race which is producing the industrial prosperity of other nations. Inchicore has had its chance. In the 10-year period which has seen Ireland's population reduced by half a million, the population of Inchicore has increased from 7,000 to 11,000.

"Give me a hundred Inchicores throughout Ireland, one hundred places where the integrity, the talent and the industry of our people can have fair play and I predict that within the next 10-year period we shall make up for the losses of the last 10 years."

How accurate the population figures for Inchicore are we do not know and might require further study.

The National Question

"I cannot say that liberty will come undoubtedly. It will not come tomorrow, it will not come next year. It will be a work of time, it will come by degrees. It will come by struggle, by effort and by exertion on the part of the people of Ireland. But it will never come if you allow the strong weapon of constitutional force which you hold in your hands to be perverted from the interests of Ireland to the interests of any English political party.

"Believe me my fellow countrymen – our cause is not a despairing one. It is not dead, but very much alive."

Towards the end of the meeting, Dr Kenny MP, one of the six MPs present, congratulated all present "on having assembled in thousands to accord that splendid reception to Mr Parnell and to welcome the man who had led them out of bondage and who would lead them to the Promised Land, to liberty."

However, within four months the Chief was dead. He died on October 4th, 1891 and many of those who had assembled at Inchicore now followed him on his last journey to Glasnevin Cemetery.

One hundred and eight years on, the memory of Parnell's visit to Inchicore has almost faded – except perhaps in the Ranch – where it still flickers, however faintly.

Chapter Twenty-Six

INCHICORE HOUSE

Inchicore House, with its associations with the Annesley Case and the Parnell Meeting, was visited by the Dublin historian W. A. Henderson in 1919 some time after Mr Cant and his family had taken up residence there and he recorded the following valuable account of his visit:

> "The house stood between the Liffey and the turnpike road which ran from Kilmainham and which was re-named Sarsfield Rd about twenty years ago. Starting from the towered gateway of the Old Man's House, as the Royal Hospital is locally called, the road runs straight for about a mile to the Railway Bridge. Beyond it on the right hand side stand two square perpendicular piers set wide apart which unmistakeably indicates the entrance to a seat of high nobility. The inner gates with spread eagles on pedestals bear marks of the erosion of age and weather. An extensive green lawn and a group of silver beeches can be seen from the entrance.
>
> "This was undoubtedly the residence of Arthur Annesley, 4th Lord Altham. He probably built the house and lived in it until his death in 1729.
>
> "The front of the modern house with large windows stands on the verge of the Liffey ridge and commands an exquisite view of the Phoenix Park. Attached to it on the east end stands a three storied house considerably older, roughly build of brick and mortar, which has many apartments and a large flagged kitchen with a great fireplace now fitted with a modern range. The stables are extensive and the loft is reached by a heavy flagged staircase with thick iron ballustrades.
>
> "Mr. Cant pointed out a pathway near the house which was known as the Friar's Walk. Earlier residents verified this and the popular tradition is that a monastery stood on the grounds."

He then goes on to relate details of the Annesley case but does not mention the Parnell Meeting.

Inchicore House was in fact two houses in one and this is shown clearly in the aerial photograph. The older building is almost certain to have been the brick house at "Inchycore" mentioned in the Civil Survey of 1654 and at the time of its demolition in 1960 was by far the oldest dwelling in the whole area. Also the Down Survey Map of 1659 clearly indicates a building or monument on this site.

Inchicore House, Sarsfield Road, overlooking the Liffey 1951

Whether there is any substance in the reference to a monastery we do not know, but it seems unlikely. The surrounding lands formed part of the estates of Kilmainham Priory and perhaps the Knights Hospitallers had an involvement of some kind there, but if so, it is not mentioned in the *Extent of Kilmainham*. Another possibility, given its commanding location, is that the old building was a fortified mansion in Anglo-Norman times and, as mentioned in the opening chapter, that there may originally have been a pre-historic presence at this location.

We might add here that the grounds on the eastern side were bounded by the little "Creso" stream and that not far from the entrance lodge there was a well with ornate steps leading down to it. Incidentally older residents remember a further well in the middle of Woodfield which was still in use in the early years of this century.

Many Occupants

The house had many occupants during its long existence and it may be that it was too large for some of the families concerned. In 1835 a Lt Col. Cator of the Royal Horse Artillery was in possession and Mr Edward Holohan as we have seen was there for the Parnell meeting in 1891.

The next occupant, about 1903, was the publican and member of Dublin Corporation, Patrick Murray, who at that time owned what is now the "Patriot's Inn". Mr Murray and his wife Ellen had seven sons, all of whom were subsequently to own their own pubs, and two daughters, both of whom became nuns. Four of these sons were renowned athletes and one of them, Denis, was the Irish 100 yards and 220 yards champion from 1901 to 1906. A grandson, also Patrick Murray, was up to a couple of years ago in business at the "Bow Bridge Bar" where the old pictures on the wall brought to mind the past athletic glories of this family.

The next occupants, the Cants, were to remain at the house for the next forty years. At a later stage, following their tenure, it sadly was allowed to go into decline and was finally demolished.

Chapter Twenty-Seven

Local Place Names

Kilmainham, Islandbridge and Goldenbridge

The dominant place name in the district for many centuries was Kilmainham which derived from Saint Maighnean who as we know had his monastery there. It was a name which was applied to a large area from Islandbridge to near Dolphins Barn and to some of what is now Inchicore.

Islandbridge as a place name only began to emerge about 1680 and up to then the bridge in question over the Liffey had been known as Kilmainham Bridge. As Islandbridge was never designated as a townland it could be said to be a name with undefined boundaries.

After Kilmainham the next most significant place name over the centuries was Golden Bridge, first mentioned in the *Extent of Kilmainham* and which later acquired status as the address of Richmond Barracks. Before the railway period the Black Lion was sometimes used as a name for the district in its vicinity and it is not unusual to see on an old birth certificate "Born at Black Lion, Golden Bridge".

As previously mentioned it was the advent of the railway works in 1846 which was responsible for bringing the then obscure name of Inchicore to the fore. Since that time it is a name which is applied to a much wider area including Goldenbridge. The latter name has gradually declined over the last sixty years and except for the relatively new industrial estate of that name is no longer used as a postal address.

The townland of Jamestown as a place name has also been superceded by neighbouring Inchicore. Originally it was one of the townlands of the old parish of Drimnagh. When the Earl of Shelbourne/Lansdowne bought Drimnagh Castle and its lands Jamestown also came into his possession. It is not an Irish name but as earlier noted may have derived from James Duke of York who had a land holding in the area.

Inchicore–Inse Chór

Patrick Joyce in his monumental *Irish Place Names* tells us that while Inis or Inse is the most common Irish word for an island it is also applied to the holm or low flat meadow alongside a river. We do not know whether our local Inse was a piece of ground originally surrounded by water or a riverside meadow but the Down Survey

Map of 1659 does indicate that it was adjacent to the Liffey rather than the Camac. In attempting to determine its exact location we have to take into consideration that other little stream, dubbed in modern times as the "Creso" stream which flows from the direction of the canal, through the railway works and is piped under Sarsfield Road. It used to then enter a pretty little glen before joining the Liffey opposite the boat houses. Unfortunately with modern developments this little glen has disappeared and the "Creso" stream has been culverted except for the last few yards. The stream was given that name because of the creosote (used for preserving sleepers) which seeped into it as it travelled beneath the railway works.

The Inse may well have referred to some of the area bounded by this stream and the Liffey, particularly the low ground below "The Ranch". We have also to remember that the land here alongside the Liffey presented a different terrain prior to the building of the large weir downstream at Islandbridge because up to then the river had been tidal nearly as far as Chapelizod. This probably gave rise to many creeks and half islands at some remove from the river and to all of them the word Inse would be appropriate. Further support for this location comes from an interesting reference in the Lodge Rolls of King Charles I in 1630 which refers to a six acre parcel of land near "The steep shrubby hill alias Nynescore alias Inchchore". The hill in question probably refers to the incline above the "Creso" stream and the Liffey and on the top of which Inchicore House was built.

The meaning of the second part of the name is uncertain. As stated earlier the problem is that the full place name is not mentioned at all in native sources and we have to rely totally on English documents which over the centuries have produced many variations e.g. Inchigore, Inseguore, Incycore, Inshecore, Inchycor and of course Inchicore itself which eventually was accepted as the official English version.

From the early days of the Irish Revival at the turn of this century and from the foundation of the State in 1922 the Irish form most commonly used was Inse Chaor which was taken to mean the river meadow of the berries. However the Irish Place Names Commission decided in 1956 that Inse Chór would be closer to the original name and from then on this became the official Irish version. They had not sufficient information to put forward a definite meaning for the second part of the name. We might speculate that it derives from Cora, the Irish word for a weir, particularly as the Inse was close to the Liffey, but this is only conjecture. Another possibility is that it referred to a personal name.

Whatever about the precise form of the original name the fact that it was mentioned even in an anglicised form in the *Extent* of 1541 means that it was well established when the Anglo Normans took control of the area in 1179. It is probably at least as old as that of seventh century Kilmainham itself. The mere fact that it endured as a place name both under Irish and foreign jurisdiction in spite of a very sparse population indicates that the location had an importance of its own for the early Irish inhabitants of the district.

The river Liffey near Islandbridge

Anna Liffey and Máigh Life

Basically it is not a river name by which our principal waterway is known. Rather is it the name of some of the district through which it flowed that is Máigh Life, the Plain of Life, the latter being the daughter of a local chieftain. From this we had Abhainn na Life which eventually entered the English language as Anna Liffey and finally just the Liffey.

However in earliest times the river was originally called Ruirtheach meaning something like a strong current.

Ballyfermot–Baile Formaid

The original Irish was Baile Thormaid which is an example of an Irish/Norse place name and points to a local association with those foreigners. The Anglo-Normans referred to it in a Latin document of 1212 as Villa Turmot. From the sixteenth century onwards the original Irish name had gradually altered from Baile Thormaid to Baile Formaid and this is now officially accepted.

There were numerous Anglicised versions before the present Ballyfermot became popular. However to my own knowledge quite a number of the old generation of

Inchicore people pronounced the name as "Ballyfarmot" and even still this can occasionally be heard.

Poll Buí

The Clondalkin historian Liam Ua Broin drew attention to an old forgotten place name originally known as Poll Buí (The Yellow Pool) which was close to the road near the old Ballyfermot graveyard and castle. Writing in 1944 he said that the name was by then known as Pulbee and referred to a roadside recess. He went on to say that sixty years earlier there had been stagnant water with a yellowish hue in this recess and hence the name.

Another historian Mr E. R. Dix who visited the graveyard and site of the castle in 1898 referred to "an oblong pond of moderate dimensions lined or faced on its south western side with regular blocks of hewn stone" which he speculated might have had a connection with the castle. Perhaps this pond was one and the same as the yellow pool.

Very recently Benny Connolly, who lived near this location, told me that a bend on the road along here was known in his young days as "Bowlbee" – a further corruption of the name. He is now probably the only person to remember this name.

Drimnagh–Droimeanach

The English form of the name used to be rendered as Drimna. In early times the area lay more to the west than at present and thus we had Drimna Lodge on the Naas Road opposite the junction with the Long Mile Road. Also the little oratory in Bluebell cemetery was referred to as the Parish Church of Drimna.

Droimeanach, the original Irish name meaning the sandy ridges, was a very apt description of the district before urbanisation. Apart from Kilmainham it is one of the few local place names to be mentioned in the Irish manuscripts. In one of these dealing with the Fenian tales it is recorded that the Ulster hero Conall Cearnach having left Áth Cliath behind him took the road through Droimeanach on his way to Naas. This is also a further indication that the ancient road to the south passed along here rather than through Kilmainham/Inchicore.

Portlester

This name, which has gone from public memory, referred to an area between Bluebell and Drimnagh Castle on the south side of the Naas Road. Sir Roland FitzEustace, Lord of Portlester, was a very powerful figure in the Anglo-Norman administration of Ireland who lived in County Kildare but took his title from the original Portlester which is near Trim in County Meath. He was connected through marriage with the Barnewalls of Drimnagh Castle and we can only assume that this accounts for the place name.

Sir Roland died in 1496 but a cloud hung over his latter years. One of his enemies alleged that while Lord Treasurer of Ireland for over thirty years he never accounted for one penny that he received.

A tablet in memory of this knight can be seen in old St Audeon's Church in High Street in what is known as the Portlester Chapel.

Glenranny and Knockgortagh

Local Irish names like Barnegyll, Stryffmore and Dromrathe mentioned in the *Extent of Kilmainham* as well as many more such names were lost with the urban development of the area.

Also from the mid-seventeenth century the tendency to name districts after inns or public houses such as Bluebell, Fox and Geese or Robinhood helped to obscure the original Irish names. Two such old forgotten names off the Long Mile Road on the outskirts of our district were Glenranny and Knockgortagh, derived respectively from the rushy glen and the hungry hill.

The names of places formed a very important element in our Celtic past and were indicative of a common culture from one end of Ireland to the other. It is a pity that more of these local names have not been used in new housing estates and apartment complexes.

Chapter Twenty-Eight

The Golden Bridge Area

Golden Bridge House

A Mr de Herries, fleeing from a plague in England, came to Ireland at the end of the seventeenth century. He bought a property at Golden Bridge on which he built a red-brick mansion and called it Golden Bridge House. This dwelling was of the King William or early Queen Anne period, which dates it to about 1710. At the same time for some unknown reason he changed his own name to Smith.

Several generations later one of Smith's descendants, a Miss Smith, married Major Wolseley of a well known Anglo-Irish family from Carlow. The Major took up residence with his wife, who was twenty-five years his junior, at Golden Bridge House and it was here on the 4th June 1833 that their son, Garnet, the future Lord Wolseley and luminary of the British Empire, was born.

In his biography, Lord Wolseley described his mother as being tall and stately and said that the poor and sorrowful of heart never came to her in vain for help and sympathy. Of his own boyhood at Golden Bridge, he has left no details other than his interest in athletics, rowing, shooting and all outdoor sports. He did comment on the house as being surrounded by an undulating and well watered park, eight acres in extent.

Given his military background, it was inevitable that the young Wolseley would make the army his career and soon he had left Golden Bridge behind for the Military Academy of Sandhurst. He rose to the heights of his profession and served widely in the many and distant territories of the Empire, notably in Egypt at the battle of Tel-El-Kebir. He was also responsible for a major reorganisation of the British Army. His military achievements were not appreciated, however, by the Nationalist members of Dublin Corporation who succeeded in preventing the Unionists from having the Freedom of the City conferred on him. On his death in 1913 he was buried at Westminster Abbey. In his favour it has to be said that he was opposed to slavery. He wrote: "It is always pleasant to me to remember that the year of my birth was that in which we abolished that greatest of all villainies, commonly called the Slave Trade."

Goldenbridge in the fifties

SISTERS OF MERCY

Some fourteen years after the death of their founder, Mother Catherine McAuley, the Sisters of Mercy bought Golden Bridge House as a convent. They came in 1855, which was the same year that the Oblate Fathers also first arrived in Inchicore. Their initial project was a rehabilitation centre for women who were about to be released from jail. They also established a day school for the children of the area which is still functioning and which was extended fifty years ago to provide free secondary education as well. In the early formative years, the person most prominently identified with the new foundation was Sister Ursula Rooney, who was also a talented artist.

Saint Vincent's Convict Refuge, as it was known, commenced on a small scale in April 1856 and an early report stated that the Sisters were proceeding carefully, cautiously and most successfully. It also mentioned that about seven acres of ground were attached to the Refuge and that an opportunity is afforded of teaching "the common branches of dairy work and washing, so far as they are required about an ordinary farm house". The final paragraph mentioned that "we were much amused to learn that an old woman who was a notorious fowl stealer is now a careful guardian of the hen house". In a further report two years later an inspector stated that:

> "The Refuge is intended for females of all ages selected from the prisons and for whose maintenance 5/- per week is paid. It contains forty inmates at present. Their sole employment just now except for house duties is washing for private families in Dublin and a small sum out of their earnings is laid aside for each woman to be given to her on her discharge. The grounds are unwalled and unguarded but there is no attempt at escape. The buildings are not sufficiently extensive for the number of inmates but everything is perfectly in order and clean. I have no doubt that when the new buildings are completed, this institution will under its excellent management become a model for all such establishments".

Because of a great lack of early records, we do not know how long the Refuge lasted, but it was later replaced by an orphanage and an industrial school. The latter received official recognition in July 1880 when it catered for 150 girls, but this number greatly increased over the years. Arising out of new educational attitudes, the orphanage, in common with similar institutions throughout the country, closed in 1966 and was replaced by family style childrens' homes. Since their first coming, the Sisters were also involved in the provision of varied social services for the poor of the area.

In recent years serious allegations have been made regarding the running of the orphanage in the 1950s.

A Second Golden Bridge House

From the time the Mercy Sisters took over Golden Bridge House, it has been known as Golden Bridge Convent. About twenty years later a large private residence was built on a site adjoining the convent grounds which was also called Golden Bridge House, by which name it is still known. This had been the location of a previous very old residence known as Rose Dale which a map of 1833 shows with very ornate gardens. In the early years of this century Mr Levins, who was one of a number of Jewish people who came from Eastern Europe to Dublin bought Golden Bridge House and resided there. The entrance to the house is from Tyrconnell Street, whose red-brick houses were built by this same man, as indeed were several of the houses on Tyrconnell Road and Inchicore Road.

Other Schools and Churches

For a good number of years before the arrival of the Mercy Sisters, there had been a cluster of small places of worship and schools in Vincent Street near the main entrance gate to Golden Bridge House. One of these, known as "The Golden Bridge General Male and Female Day and Evening Free Schools", was established in 1827 and was the first public school in the whole area but near it also according to a plan of the district was a 'R.C. School'. We presume that the former was mainly Protestant because it was used on Sundays for Church of Ireland services. It ceased to be used

The Chapel of Ease (Father Ryan's), Vincent Street. Old CBS school to the right

as a school in 1857, as the much larger Model School had been built some years earlier at Sarsfield Road.

The Golden Bridge School building was then enlarged to act as a full-time church for the Church of Ireland community. This in turn became too small and in 1864 was replaced by the fine Saint Jude's Church on Inchicore Road. The vacant church building was later acquired by the Catholic Archdiocese of Dublin and opened as a Chapel of Ease under the title of "Our Lady of Mercy" in 1885.

Next door to the school and church building just mentioned there had been a Methodist Meeting House from at least 1834. They moved to their picturesque red brick church on Tyrconnell Road in 1885 and their old building was bought by the Irish Christian Brothers who opened their first school in the district there.

THE IRISH CHRISTIAN ADVOCATE
14 AUG. 1885

NEW METHODIST CHAPEL
INCHICORE

It is proposed to erect a NEW METHODIST CHAPEL in the populous district which comprises Inchicore, Golden Bridge, Kilmainham and Richmond. The old building at Golden Bridge having been found unsuitable, it was thought advisable to build a New Chapel in a better locality. A most desirable site has been obtained and the Committee is anxious to complete the building, free of debt, within the next few months. The Chapel is specially intended for the use of the Military of the Richmond Barracks, the Employees of the G.S. and W. Railway, at Inchicore, and a large and flourishing Sunday School, having at present 120 on the roll. The cost of the proposed building is estimated at about £800, of which nearly £400 remains to be collected. In view of the urgent necessity which exists for the proposed Chapel, the Committee confidently appeals to your sympathy and liberality. Subscriptions will be thankfully received by any of the undersigned.

Rev. W.H. Quarry, Minister, 6 Blackhall Street, Dublin, Treasurer.
W.A. Davis, Golden Bridge House, Inchicore, Secretary

Golden Bridge "Village"

Golden Bridge was a hamlet with a mill nearby on the Camac River prior to the building in 1807 of Richmond Barracks. The proximity of the latter was to see it become a substantial village, although it was never known as such. It had its years of glory following the discovery of a spa there when stones were being quarried for the building of the Barracks. A map shows its location to the rere of Tram Terrace and it was called the Waterloo Spa in honour of the battle that had taken place a short time previously. According to a current street directory, it was noted for its medicinal qualities in bilious and liver complaints and other diseases. Shortly afterwards a second spa was discovered nearby which was called the Richmond Spa. For years crowds flocked out from the city to take the waters and a spa house was built for their comfort. A John Darcy is mentioned in 1835 as being a carpenter and "keeper of the original spa-house". In the end the fashion declined, leaving little record of its passing other than the name "Spa Road" which was formerly called Berry's Lane.

The opening of the cemetery in 1829 was for the next forty years to bring another type of clientele to the area i.e. the large numbers of mourners who accompanied the almost daily funeral processions.

Golden Bridge was a compact area with a large representation of small businesses and self-employed people. In 1834 it had seven boot and shoe makers, six huxter shops, numerous groceries and dairies, a billiard room keeper, a tailor and bonnet maker, several livery stables and carriers as well as an incredible nine vintners. Contributing to the local economy also was Bart Sullivan's paper mills when in use. In 1885 the area got a boost with the establishment there of the workshops and depot of the Tram Company who also built a row of small houses for their employees, which they called Tramway Terrace.

With the passing of the years, some of the area became dilapidated. Lord Wolseley in his memoirs said that a dirty slum had grown up in or about his old residence. In any event, like so many parts of Dublin at that time, it had its share of overcrowding and poverty and the presence there of unofficial army quarters did not help either.

The Puck

The "Puck" is a local place-name which is slowly going from public memory. It referred to that part of Golden Bridge which was west of Vincent Street, stretching by Tyrone Place towards Tram Terrace. Sometimes the Golden Bridge district in general was called by that name and years ago when the tram was starting from College Green the conductor might humorously shout out "First stop the Puck".

The Puck was a small area with streets and yards of white-washed cottages, some of which had hen runs and piggeries to the rear and also several dairies with adjoining cowsheds. Here and there were scattered huxter shops. However, the heart of the Puck was the little hollow with its circle of cottages overlooked by Tofts Amusements' winter quarters and Thompsons's Field which was a traditional halting site for travelling people with their Romany-style covered wagons. Back in the last century this hollow was officially called Cooper's Hollow from a nearby shop owner of that name.

Also in the locality were two very tall buildings known as the "Cambridge" and the "Eagle" respectively which up to the time of their demolition were in flats or tenements. From the very top floor residents had a fine view of the distant Vice-Regal Lodge now Áras an Uachtaráin in the Phoenix Park. Local tradition always maintained that Lord Wolseley lived in one of these houses. Whether this is correct we do not know, but he certainly was born in Golden Bridge House, now the Mercy Convent. Many people still remember the tunnel-opening at the back of these two houses which was believed to go under Vincent Street to connect with Richmond Barracks.

Another smaller olde worlde building was "Spa View House" with several steps going up to it and which was believed to have been used as some form of a dispensary over a hundred years ago, but this is not to be confused with the later dispensary at Haines's house at the bottom of Spa Road.

That the "Puck" was a well-established name is indicated by the fact that it was shown on a map entitled "Dublin and its Environs" in 1911. There are several stories regarding the origin of the name. One of these claims that when Richmond Barracks was being built, a regiment returned from India, but there was no room for them as the barracks was not completed. The story goes on to say that a temporary encampment was thrown up nearby to accommodate these soldiers who called it the "Puck", a name they had heard used in India for a similar type camp.

One or two older residents of that area have pointed out to me that in their young days there was another variation of the name when it was also known as the "She-Puck". They also recalled a tradition that soldiers' families were housed there and that their wives, many of them from all parts of the world, had a reputation for constant quarrelling.

The She-Barracks

For years historians had come across references to unofficial quarters for soldiers' wives known as a "She-Barracks" at some unidentified location on this side of Dublin. The following item, although it does not indicate its source, throws much interesting light on the subject. It first appeared in the Irish Times series "Times Past" in January 1932.

TIMES PAST

THE "SHE" BARRACKS

People who delight in old city landmarks may be interested in the following extract from an old work on Dublin:

When the Richmond Barracks were built at Golden Bridge they were intended to afford ample accommodation for more than an entire regiment. There was also a barracks at Island Bridge, and the distance between both was about half a mile. The former were generally occupied by infantry, and the latter by artillery. A person in the vicinity had a large building constructed through a speculative motive of a very extraordinary kind. He was aware that soldiers marrying without leave, or whose wives were dishonest, turbulent, quarrelsome, slovenly or habitually intemperate, were not allowed to bring such objectionable characters into the regimental quarters. He consequently calculated that he would find no difficulty in having his premises occupied by tenants, to whose habits he attached no importance provided that they paid the rent, and his expectations were not disappointed. His apartments were no sooner vacated by the incorrigible termagants of one regiment than a succession of vixens was supplied from another to fill the unedifying edifice. The proprietor had not appropriated any particular name to the building, but it became speedily known in the district under the designation of 'The She Barracks'"

The Irish Times,
January 4th, 1932.

However a British Army report on barrack accommodation makes it clear that the institution known as the "She-Barracks" was in fact located in Goldenbridge. In his evidence to an official committee on barrack accommodation in 1855, Colour-Sergeant Robert Reynolds of the 83rd Regiment gave the following replies:

Q. You think that one room is sufficient for a married private?
A. Quite sufficient.

Q. You would give him a fireplace in that room, in which his wife could cook his dinner?
A. Yes. I take my idea from the barracks, vulgarly called in Dublin the "She-Barracks", where the married soldiers lodged and paid a small weekly rent for the barrack utensils which were supplied by the

barrack-master, such as a wooden bedstead and table, and two, and in some cases three, ordinary-sized stools.

Q. In the barrack you speak of, what was the size of the rooms?
A. I cannot say the actual size, but they were small-sized rooms; they varied in size, and there was a trifling variation in the rent.

Q. What was the average rent paid for one of these rooms?
A. From 5d to 9d per week.

Q. Did that include furniture?
A. Everything.

Q. Fuel?
A. No, not fuel; they had to purchase their own fuel.

Q. That arrangement was found to work well?
A. It was considered an indulgence there. There was no other place, wherever I travelled, where we had that indulgence.

Q. Was that barrack any distance from the men's barrack?
A. Just across from the back gate of the men's barrack, about 40 or 50 yards.

Q. Across the street?
A. Across a narrow street.

Q. What barrack was that near to?
A. **Richmond Barracks.**

We can only speculate that the site of the original "Puck" or "She-Puck" was taken over by an entrepreneur who provided accommodation for married soldiers and their wives and that this led to it being known also as the "She-Barracks". The latter name has not been handed down locally and it is only "The Puck" and to a much lesser extent "The She-Puck" which have survived up to now.

A further place-name which has survived also is "The Orphanage" but which has nothing to do with Goldenbridge Orphanage. It referred to a substantial old tenement building which stood in the area between the end of Tram Terrace and the Camac and which housed twelve or thirteen large families up to about forty years ago when it was demolished. Older residents thought that the name may have indicated an old forgotten orphanage and one man believed it had been known as Mallon's Orphanage and that a fire had occurred there. Recently a new modern apartment complex block has been built nearby.

The Nobbs

Mrs Kathleen Shanahan (nee Brennan) remembered, along with other children in the early years of this century, looking through the window of the ground floor room of Lizzy Reid's house in Vincent Street where locals gathered for social evenings and which was known as "The Nobbs". Here they made their own amusement playing "house", the forerunner of bingo, during the week and dancing away at the weekends.

This lady also remembered Easter Monday 1916 very well. She and some of her young friends were getting ready to go on a hike when her father came in and said, "Be dad you won't be going anywhere today because there is a rebellion on and they are lying dead at the bottom of Mount Brown".

It is only a few years since the kindly Marie Lynch who for some reason seemed to me to represent the quintessential Goldenbridge person went to her reward. Marie in her young days was a barmaid in the family pub "McGrath's" of Vincent Street and remembered the Tans with Webleys strapped above their knee coming in to drink there.

Also remembered still is the Tailor Dunne, sometimes called the "Waltzy Man" and who in his spare time was well known as a bird fancier. Best remembered of all however was Father "Da" Ryan who spent such a long time as pastor in the area.

Old Families

Henry Beatley came from Cambridge to Inchicore as a member of a British Army band which was stationed at Richmond Barracks. He was later to be employed at the railway works in the drawing office and both he and his wife took up residence at Spa Cottage, which was close to the weir on the Camac River. Henry was a founder member of the Inchicore United Workmen's Club where he tutored their brass band which he may also have established. His grand-daughter Patty remembers as a child the white-washed two roomed cottage with its one door and two large windows and an extensive orchard alongside the little river. She herself was a seamstress in the carriage shop in the railway works as was her mother before her who also was amongst the first batch of tenants in Ring Street when the houses were built there.

One of Maura Brady's great-grandfathers was a stone mason. Having finished some work in Dun Laoghaire he found fresh employment in Inchicore at the building of the railway houses and settled down in Goldenbridge. Maura's aunt Kathleen Naylor told how her family kept a goat, which was not unusual at the time, and how as a young girl she had to bring it each morning to a grazing field near the Canal before she went to school. Her only fear was that it might follow her into the school. If the animal got sick at any time she brought it to an old woman in Goldenbridge who was very knowledgeable in such matters. Goats milk was sought after in those times because of the prevalence of TB.

This aunt was one of the older residents who used to mention the "She-Puck" and who believed that it referred to the houses where those army wives lived who were said at the time "not to be on the strength" and consequently not entitled to accommodation within the Barracks.

The other side of the Canal was officially known as Goldenbridge South and here was Condren's lockhouse, Parsons' Paint Factory, Brennan's farm, Franklin's orchards, Swift's nurseries and Cosy Cottage. At the turn of the century some of my own grand-aunts, the Doyles, lived as children in the latter which was the last thatched house in the entire area. They remembered seeing the British soldiers skating on the canal when it was frozen over during a very cold winter. It later passed to the Gartlan family who had a dairy alongside which was patronised by some of the first residents of the Bulfin Estate who used to cross over the lock to collect their milk.

Thatching In Dublin

John Duffy thatching the roof of "Cosy Cottage", 2nd Lock, the residence of Mr Larry Gartlan (on tractor) 1951

Difficult Times

Arthur Farrell was born and reared on Tram Terrace, his grandfather having been a supervisor with the old horse-trams. This terrace always had its own water supply, attributed to the fact that one of the Goldenbridge spas was situated to the rear long before the houses were built there. Pleasant memories of Arthur's young days were the good humour and banter of Moll Harte, the sight of Nanny Byrne's pet swan outside her house or the old lady who occasionally played her melodeon at the door with some of the neighbours doing a step or two.

However his most abiding memories are of the unemployment, poverty and even hunger which some people suffered from in the more deprived parts of the area in the 1920s and early 1930s. Some of them had to rely on food vouchers which were provided by the government of the day as well as assistance from the Saint Vincent de Paul Society and the Mercy Sisters. Additional hardship was caused one year by a coal and gas strike which saw young men looking for firewood along the canal and if a stray chicken came their way so much the better!

Men and women were glad to avail of seasonal work picking cabbages and potatoes from early morning until dusk for a modest wage. This was in the fields across the canal or out at Blackditch in Ballyfermot to where they travelled in a lorry from Emmet Road. Again across the canal other women found employment in the brickworks and Arthur says it wasn't unusual for them to get welts on their hands or knees because of the heavy physical work.

There were public toilets at the top of Spa Road as not all dwellings had such facilities. In at least one of the yards the tenants shared the use of an outdoor privy and the woman who took on the unpleasant task of cleaning this was rent-free in return.

As any form of insurance or even membership of a burial society was out of the question for some, the death of a relative created great financial problems. Occasionally a neighbour came to the rescue and allowed the bereaved family to make use of their own grave plot if a space was available. However from time to time unofficial use was made of a disused burial place out at the 11th Lock, then in the heart of the country. This in fact was part of the old monastic site of Killmahudrick. On payment of a few shillings to the crew of a passing canal barge, usually a "hack boat" drawn by horses, the coffin was taken on board and brought out to the 11th. The few mourners might be accompanied by a couple of neighbours who on several occasions included Arthur's uncles and these helped to dig the grave. On the way back they usually stopped for a drink in "Mary Theresa's" at the 7th Lock.

No account of Golden Bridge or the "Puck" would be complete without a reference to Willie Bermingham who, like Lord Wolseley, was born and reared in this locality, but at the other end of the social scale. Willie, who was a member of the Dublin Fire Brigade, was always interested in the old and the lonely and founded the organisation known as "Alone". He was also a nephew of local man, Joe Dalgarno, noted too for his concern for all living creatures. Willie died in 1991, aged forty-eight years.

Chapter Twenty-Nine

The Early Years of the Twentieth Century

Seldom in the history of the nation did so many events occur in such a short space of time as in the first quarter of this century, all of which were to be reflected in our own local story. While the land question had been largely settled and a considerable measure of local government achieved, the British were still putting Home Rule on the long finger. Following the disillusionment of the Parnell split, the dawning of the new century saw the beginning of a national resurgence through the inspiration of the Gaelic League and the Irish literary revival. This was followed by the foundation of Sinn Féin, the new political movement with its emphasis on national self-reliance and Irish manufacture.

Locally these early years of the new century were crowded with incidents, commencing with the long drawn out fitter's strike at the Railway Works in 1902. This was followed by the election of the workers' standard bearer, William Partridge, to Dublin Corporation in 1904 and Patrick O'Carroll for Sinn Féin in 1906. Also in the same year O'Carroll was prosecuted for using the Irish form only of his name on the side of a horse-cart.

In 1907 the first Dublin Corporation housing scheme in the area commenced at the "Bungalow".

In 1910 British soldiers were on the footplate during an engine drivers' strike. Also in the same year, the last hanging took place at Kilmainham Jail.

In 1912 the Irish Transport and General Workers' Union opened a premises known as the Emmet Hall. A year later this venue was to be the scene of disturbances during the 1913 lockout.

The year 1914 brought the Great War and 1916 the Easter Rising. The War of Independence and Civil War were to follow, leading to the establishment in 1922 of the Irish Free State.

The Fitters' Strike

The first significant event of the new century as far as Inchicore was concerned was the fitters' strike of 1902. These tradesmen were among the most highly skilled employees at the Railway Works and were the first to organise themselves as a strong

Islandbridge. Dublin

trade union some decades earlier when the majority of the workers were unorganised. The name of their union at that time was The Amalgamated Society of Engineers.

In 1902, against the better judgement of their union leaders, the fitters served strike notice when the Company refused to meet their demand for an increase of 3/- per week. Amongst those who had reservations about this course of action was William P. Partridge, but when the decision was made he played a very active part in the strike along with the Branch Secretary, Mr Billy Gaynor.

The strike commenced on 23rd May of that year and was to last for twenty-five weeks. As far as the Company was concerned, it was all out war and they immediately responded with the employment of about fifty-six "blacklegs" from across the water. It was this action which made it such a prolonged and bitter dispute. These workers were recruited by a Scotsman, Graeme Hunter, who specialised in this type of activity on behalf of large employers in the United Kingdom. The railway's records of the period indicate that £100 was paid to the "Graeme Hunter Society" for services rendered.

Right from the beginning these imported workers were under threat from the strikers. I well recall years ago hearing old timers from the Works telling of how some of the blacklegs were dragged off side-cars and the clothes torn off them as they travelled along the quays to Inchicore. The Company had to accommodate them in very large wooden huts specially constructed inside the Works premises. Here, although pastimes were provide for them as well, they had a rather confined existence

The Old Black Lion about 1903. Note the all-Irish signboard

The Old Black Lion following removal of small garden which was a traffic obstruction, 1906

and could only venture out in groups under police protection. This did not always save them and there were numerous incidents in the area. On some occasions the Company arranged to take them down by train to Kingsbridge, from where they were brought on day excursions to seaside resorts. Attempts were made by the Company to bring in further workers as the strike progressed. However these were met at Dún Laoire and other ports by union members who persuaded them to return to England.

Ernest Joynt, a draughtsman at the Works and of whom we shall be treating later, remembered Graeme Hunter as a big aggressive man who swaggered about the place in a tartan kilt. A much later employee, Tom Tighe, recalled how Hunter's chair was still in use in the office of the paintshop down to about twenty years ago. Mr Joynt also recollected that the skirl of pipes could be heard in the Works in the evening time as most of the blacklegs were from Scotland and they brought a bagpiper with them to keep up their morale.

An attempt was made to have eighteen strikers who lived in the Company's cottages evicted. While the courts granted the Company's application, they also allowed for an appeal which had not been heard by the time the strike ended.

By July it was clear that the strikers were not winning. The factors militating against them were that the other workers did not join them and the provincial workshops in Cork and Limerick kept open. Then of course Hunter's men were also playing a vital role by helping to keep the wheels rolling and the Company knew it only had to sit it out. Nevertheless the strikers persevered despite the hardship involved. Concerts and social functions were held to aid the strike fund and financial contributions were also made by other unions.

From start to finish strenuous efforts at mediation were made – but to no avail – by two local clergymen working in close harmony, the Church of Ireland minister, the Rev. Mr Nash and Father Daniel McIntyre, O.M.I.

In the end the workers had to capitulate and on 9th October the dispute came to a close on the Company's terms. No increase in wages was to be made except as earned under a piece-work scheme. The latter had been resisted for years by the union but now had to be accepted reluctantly. The vexed dispute regarding the differential between the railway rate and the down-town rate was not solved, however, and was an irritant between the two sides right up to the first hearings of the newly established Labour Court in the 1950s.

Notwithstanding their defeat, the union remained intact and the years that followed were to see an increase in their membership. The strike-breakers' huts were put to other uses and lasted for many years as a reminder of that bitter conflict.

Local Elections

What had been the New Kilmainham Urban District Council area became the New Kilmainham Ward of Dublin Corporation for election purposes from 1900 onwards.

In the January 1903 elections, Michael Lord of James's Street, a fitter at the Railway Works and a member of the recent strike committee, was elected as a councillor, replacing the outgoing Nationalist member. He was joined by the better known union activist, William P. Partridge, in 1904. In January 1906 Mr Patrick O'Carroll, a coal merchant near the Black Lion, was elected as a councillor for the new Sinn Féin Party, which had been founded only a few months earlier.

In 1912 one of the Murrays of Inchicore House, Mr John Murray, B.L., was elected as an Alderman. In 1913 a Mr Eager, interestingly described as a "Protestant Home Ruler", was elected. Other councillors in those early years of the century were James McCann, proprietor of both the Black Lion and Tyrconnell House, John Cooney of Inchicore Road and Thomas O'Hanlon of Emmet Road.

The Reverend G. D. Nash

The Reverend G. D. Nash came to the Church of Ireland parish of Saint Jude's in 1894 as an assistant to the vicar, the Reverend Thomas Mills. The latter, although he never actually lived in his parish, had been in charge for forty years until his death, both at the previous Goldenbridge church and Saint Jude's – surely a record for any denomination. He was a strong-willed and independent-minded man who was never inclined to give too much authority to his lay Select Vestry. However he was responsible for the building of St Jude's church in 1864 which was a major undertaking at that time.

Upon the death of the Reverend Mills in 1900, the Reverend Nash who had been living in rented accommodation at the spacious "Beaconsfield", took over as vicar. He was to bring about many improvements – the completion of a parish hall beside the church, the acquisition of "Fairfield", also beside the church, as a rectory and the clearing of parish debts.

Described as a very generous and kind natured man the Reverend Mr Nash had excellent relations with all sections of the public and from time to time dined with the Oblate Fathers. Unfortunately due to his wife's illness he had to retire in 1906.

Chapter Thirty

1913 AND THE EMMET HALL

The Irish Transport and General Workers Union was founded by Jim Larkin in 1909. The union opened a branch office with a small assembly hall and living accommodation overhead at 122 Emmet Road in 1912. This they called the Emmet Hall, but was sometimes referred to by older residents up to quite recently as Jim Larkin's Hall. The union were seeking to increase their membership locally, particularly amongst transport and general workers. However, they also sought to organise the farm labourers out in the county, some of whom were not much better off under their Irish employers than they had been under the old landlords. This was to result in an energetic campaign which brought about some improvement in their lot.

THE LOCK OUT

The premises at Emmet Road were mainly used for trade union administration, but the high point of its history was to occur during the protracted Lock Out of 1913. The demand of the tram workers to join the trade union of their choice sparked this conflict which commenced on 26th August. The company sought then to operate a skeleton service of trams manned by executives and some non-union members under police protection. Inevitably these "black" trams were attacked by strikers all over the city and when some of them were brought to the tram works at Spa Road, only a few hundred yards from the Emmet Hall, the workers there refused to repair them. In a statement to the press the Chairman of the Dublin United Tramway Company, Mr William Martin Murphy, confirmed that the works had been practically shut down:

> "We build, repair and paint the tram cars at Inchicore, but were unable to get our body-makers to repair the damaged cars. This of course could not be tolerated and a formal demand was made this morning on two of the men in succession. They both refused and were promptly dismissed. They were followed immediately by other body-makers and a little later by the painters."

Saturday 30th August was very tense, with disturbances in the city and some stone throwing at Spa Road. That night Councillor O'Hanlon and former Councillor

Patrick O'Carroll addressed a meeting from the upstairs windows of the hall. However, it was the next day, Sunday 31st August 1913, that the real action took place. It was on that morning that Larkin made his dramatic appearance in O'Connell Street, which was followed by the memorable baton charge.

Later that afternoon considerable rioting took place all along the tramway line between College Green and Inchicore and particularly at High Street, Cornmarket and Thomas Street. Two trams were seriously damaged and many police were injured. At Kilmainham a Sergeant of the D.M.P. was felled to the ground by a brick and had to be taken to hospital. A third tram succeeded in making its way under a heavy escort of police with batons drawn to Inchicore. By then a large meeting being addressed by Patrick O'Carroll was in progress outside the Emmet Hall. The police and crowd came into collision and soon a general fight was in progress. A baton charge followed and some of the crowd sought refuge in the hall. The police broke into the hall and it was there that O'Carroll received a severe head wound. The fighting continued up and down Emmet Road and in the lanes behind. All of this was luridly reported by an unfriendly newspaper:

> "To the accompaniment of shrieks from the rioters, the combined police force charged up towards Tyrone Place but had to withdraw owing to the hail of bottles and stones. Each time the police drew back the howling rabble followed them and made havoc in their ranks with the shower of missiles which followed them from all directions. The little barefoot urchins, boys and girls, more daring than their elders, dashed out every now and then gathering up fresh "ammo" for the mob. Women with dishevelled hair and looking like maniacs were even more persistent than the men in belabouring the police."

In the meantime a further tram had arrived and it too was greeted with stones. The police had no alternative by now but to call on the assistance of the military at Richmond Barracks who provided a detachment of the West Kent Regiment. The soldiers helped to restore order and to escort the two beleaguered trams to their sheds at Spa Road. This brought the proceedings to a close.

The strike was to go on for the next five or six months and during that time the Emmet Hall was a hive of activity, a mini-Liberty Hall in fact. Some of the food supplies donated by the English trade union movement were brought out from the city by any and every means of transport including coal carts. They included pots of jam, bread and bully beef, which was stored and distributed at the hall to needy strikers. Strangely enough, during those difficult days another source of supply was the grub which in some mysterious fashion made its way out from the canteens of Richmond Barracks!

In January 1914 the conflict came to an end. The employers had won but things would never be the same again.

Trade union activity at the Hall was to decline for several years and the branch funds were at a low ebb.

It was during the strike that both the Citizen Army and the Irish Volunteers came into existence and the local units of these two groups were to use the Hall for training and drilling in the years leading up to the 1916 Rising.

Michael Mallin

Partridge was the first Manager of the Hall, but when he became National Organiser for the Union, he was replaced by Michael Mallin, the Citizen Army leader. The latter, with his wife and five young children, took up residence above the Hall in May 1915. Only one of these children now survives – Father Mallin, a Jesuit priest in Hong Kong. Michael Mallin himself was a silk weaver who was born in the Liberties and had served with the British Army in India. It so happened that when he came to Inchicore his mother was already living at Kearn's Place, Old Kilmainham, and there is at least one person, Maisie Houlihan, who remembers her well. As the financial position of the union was not too good at that stage, a small shop was opened and on a very old picture of the premises the name Micheál Ó Mealláin appears on the sign board.

The caretaker of the hall was the one-armed Mr McLoughlin, who had met with an accident in the Bobbin Mill and who was known on occasion to conceal bullets in his artificial arm.

Social and Cultural Centre

From the beginning the little assembly hall, apart from being used for union meetings, was also a popular venue for concerts, socials, ceilithe, Irish classes and pipe band practices, as well as accommodating a local branch of the Irish National Foresters. In the years before the Hall closed in the late 1920s, a gymnastic team which was then a popular pastime practiced there, coached by local man, Johnny Hodgins, who later continued in another very small premises beside the Patriots Inn.

At the rere of the hall there was a fairly large garden, bounded somewhat incongruously by the wall of Richmond Barracks. Here on fine Sunday afternoons outdoor concerts were organised by the branch committee of the union. In the *Irish Worker* there is special mention of one such event held on Sunday 22nd June 1913, several months before the Lock Out and described as an "Aeriocht Mor" at which Jim Larkin was present. The programme included singing, dancing, recitations and a recital by the Transport Union Band. Local dance teacher, Harry Donnelly, who lived on the High Road, came in for much praise. "By common consent Harry is given the most credit for the success of the Aeriocht – his figure dancers are the talk of the place." Mention is also made of that well known old timer from the Ranch, Daisy O'Neill.

Very recently Mr Bill Butterly, who lived across the road from the Hall, told me that he remembers as a small boy in 1919 going there to see one of the first silent film performances in Inchicore. It was the classic "Birth of a Nation" concerning the American Civil War.

Men of Vision

Today one can pass this unpretentious building, long used for commercial purposes, and not be aware of its historic past or the exciting scenes it once witnessed. Under its roof high-minded men often discussed late into the night their vision of a better Ireland. Through its doors passed such notables of the national and labour movement as Councillors Partridge and O'Carroll, "Big Jim" and the executed 1916 leaders, Michael Mallin and Con Colbert. Let us hope that in the not too distant future a plaque will be erected – it is the least that can be done.

Chapter Thirty-One

Councillor Patrick O'Carroll — Coal Merchant and Patriot

Councillor Patrick O'Carroll, known locally as Paddy Carroll, was born in 1866 in Dublin, but where exactly we do not know. It was probably in the Thomas Street area as at the time of his marriage to Mary Kelly of Francis Street he was residing at 136 Thomas Street.

The O'Carrolls came with their four children to Inchicore early in this century and took up residence at 209 Emmet Road, now the premises of Messrs A. C. Boles, which at that time was a private dwelling alongside the Black Lion. He built up a successful coal business with a number of men employed and had an office at his house.

Pádraig Ó Cearbhaill was very committed to the Irish language and all things Irish. That he had a good knowledge of the language is shown by the fact that he completed the census form of 1911 totally in Irish. We have no details of his family background and neither do we know what influences inspired his national outlook. He was a founder member and first treasurer of the original Sinn Féin movement established in 1905 by Arthur Griffith. He was amongst the first small group of Sinn Féin candidates to be elected to Dublin Corporation in January 1906 and represented the New Kilmainham Ward. He was re-elected at subsequent elections, playing an active part in Corporation sub-committees, but did not go forward in 1912 because of the death of his wife.

Irish Language Campaign

In the same year that he was first elected as a member of Dublin Corporation, Councillor O'Carroll was prosecuted for his part in the country-wide campaign to obtain official recognition for the Irish language. He inscribed his name and address on the side of his coal carts in Irish only, as had many of his fellow activists, but this was not acceptable to the authorities. He was charged in June 1906 for allowing a dray, his property, to be used in James's Street "without having his name and residence properly painted thereon". Found guilty he was fined 10/-, which he refused to pay.

Some weeks later the newspapers reported that a horse and cart conveying coal, the property of O'Carroll, had been seized in the city by the police and brought to the Bridewell. Here a ton of coal was removed and the driver, with his horse and cart, was then allowed to go free. A letter from the police followed which stated that unless the fine was paid before 1.00 p.m. on 16th June the coal would be auctioned at Bachelor's Walk. The Councillor ignored the letter and together with a large crowd of supporters from all parts of the city went down to the auction rooms to make a protest. Anticipating trouble, the police were already on duty inside the premises and after a short time the auctioneer announced that the ton of coal was going to an unknown party, from whom he said he had received a bid of 1/-. This led to further uproar, at which a police inspector approached O'Carroll and ordered him off the premises. The situation was very tense now and he decided to leave in order to avoid a complete riot. Immediately he was outside the auction rooms his supporters chaired him shoulder high along the quays, feeling very satisfied that they had gained a moral victory. Following this incident Councillor O'Carroll issued a statement to the press:

> "I am determined to keep my name in Irish on the carts. All my billheads, memoranda and business and private cards are printed in Irish. I find no difficulty in doing business with either Englishmen or Scotchmen. The Post Office accepts postal orders sent to me written exclusively in Irish. 'Coal Office' are the only words in English characters that are to be seen on my premises. I shall have them immediately replaced by Irish".

Some months later, the Nationalist Councillors got Dublin Corporation to agree to have the lettering on all of their many carts changed from English to Irish. This was a turning point in the campaign and the authorities did not press the matter further.

The 1913 Lock Out

Patrick O'Carroll was not on Dublin Corporation when the 1913 Lock Out commenced. Immediately, however, he took the part of the workers, which was unusual for a self-employed man and which gives some idea of his character. As previously noted, he was prominent at the Emmet Hall meeting where he received a severe blow on the head from a police baton. This may have contributed to his relatively early death less than a year and a half later. He was in at the formation of the Irish Volunteers in 1914 and acted as trustee of "F" Company under Con Colbert. He died, however, within a few months at his home at Emmet Road on 13th December 1914, aged forty-six.

I met his niece, Mrs Richardson, then an elderly lady, a good number of years ago. Her mother was a sister of Patrick O'Carroll. She remembered as a young girl helping him in some of his election campaigns, distributing leaflets and taking part in processions during those exciting years. She recalled him as a good natured man, popular with his customers, and as an Irish speaker. She also remembered him attending the four o'clock devotions on Sunday afternoons in the little chapel in Vincent Street. She was of the opinion that the police had it in for him since the incident of the coal cart in 1906.

Mrs Richardson could not shed any further light on her uncle Paddy's background but remembered his funeral, headed by Father O'Ryan and the pipers' band.

Chapter Thirty-Two

COUNCILLOR WILLIAM P. PARTRIDGE — LABOUR LEADER

William Partridge, a remarkable man by any standard, was the most significant political figure in the district in the years before 1916. Born in Sligo in 1874 he had, like Padraig Pearse, an English father. A fitter by trade he was active with his union the A.S.E.S. from an early age and came to the Inchicore Railway Works from the Broadstone in 1899. As already mentioned he played a full part in the long fitters' strike of 1902 and was elected two years later to Dublin Corporation representing the New Kilmainham Ward. He was in "digs" with my grand-aunt Mrs Bruton (nee Byrne) at Number 11 South Terrace where I myself was to live later and where I first heard the name of Bill Partridge mentioned. This also was the address he gave when he first offered himself for election. He later lived at Patriotic Terrace, Brookfield Road, and married again following the death at an early age of his first wife. As a councillor he was much to the fore in all that concerned the rights of workers and the betterment of the area, particularly in the matter of housing. As a result of his efforts and those of like minded councillors new housing was eventually provided at "The Bungalow."

In 1912 Partridge was dismissed from his post as a charge-hand fitter at the Works when he alleged religious discrimination in the matter of promotions. In his well known pamphlet "My Crime" he explained how he was summarily dismissed and given only a week's wages in lieu of notice notwithstanding his thirteen years' service. He went on:

> "Last week I drew the attention of the Board to the appointment of non-Catholics in these works over the heads of Catholics who were more competent and in every way better qualified for such positions. My letter was dictated as much in the interest of the Company and the travelling public as it was in the interest of any individual in the shop.
>
> Fair play demands that service and ability alone be made the only test of promotion in the Works or on the railroad. The religion of the candidate should in no way influence his selection."

He subsequently obtained employment elsewhere but unfortunately suffered an injury to his finger which prevented him from continuing with his trade. Jim Larkin then appointed him as manager of the Irish Transport and General Workers' Hall at Emmet Road from where he helped to organise the farm labourers of County Dublin. Shortly after this he became national organiser for the union, setting up new branches throughout the country and finding time also to contribute a pungent column to the weekly *Irish Worker.*

The 1913 Lock Out found him travelling extensively through England mustering support for the workers at home. Partridge was a notable public speaker and a trade union activist of the period had this to say about him:

> "Of all the speakers I have heard and I have listened to a great many in Ireland, England and Scotland I consider Partridge to possess the finest and most powerful voice for outdoor meetings. No matter how large the meeting or how strong the wind his voice would carry to the outmost limits and vigorous indeed must be the opposition and uproar before he could be shouted down."

Partridge was both a nationalist and a socialist and was in the Citizen Army from the start. His philosophy was very much in the James Connolly mould of "Ireland apart from her people means nothing to me". Even when a member of his craft union he showed as much interest in the general worker as the skilled operative.

In Holy Week 1916 he was entrusted with a message in connection with the unloading of the arms consignment on board the *Aud* which was due at Fenit, County Kerry but was intercepted off the coast. He returned to Liberty Hall with the news and late on Saturday night called to Peadar Doyle's house at Emmet Road where they had a long discussion on these latest developments.

Easter Monday found him as part of the garrison in the College of Surgeons with Mallin and the Countess Markievicz. She later described how he brought under fire a wounded woman soldier of the Citizen Army from outside the Russell Hotel into the safety of the College. All his life Partridge was strongly attached to his religion, a part of his character which is often overlooked, and during the week of fighting when circumstances permitted he led the rosary at night in the barricaded College of Surgeons. The Countess, who in part attributed her conversion to Catholicism to his example, was moved to write the poem which included the lines:

"Your silvery voice soft as a dying breath
Was answered by a hundred strong and clear
Craving a grace from her whom all hold dear"

Letter from Richmond

c/o Officer i/c Prisoners
Block L, Room 6
Richmond Barracks
Inchicore
3/5/1916

Dear Mr. Bruton

I await trial in above barracks and in this crisis of my life I write to thank both yourself and Mrs. Bruton for the great kindness you ever extended to me during my residence beneath your roof. I have forgotten everything except the kindness of Mrs. Bruton and yourself and trust you both will forgive me the unpleasantness I unwillingly and unconsciously caused in your household.

I pray God may bless you both and asking a place in your prayers as one who ever sought to act up to his honest convictions

I beg to remain
Faithfully Yours

W. P. Partridge

Mr Jas. Bruton,
11 South Terrace,
Inchicore.

The "unpleasantness" mentioned may have been a reference to the threat to evict employees from the railway houses during the 1902 fitters' strike.

The date on this letter shows that it was written on the day of the first executions and understandably Partridge was concerned about his own fate. In the event he was sentenced to ten years penal servitude. However by now he was rather ill and following his release from an English jail a year later he deteriorated further and died on the 26th July 1917 at the age of forty-four.

A terrace of houses in the "Bungalow" bears the name of the patriot. I understand he will be further remembered by a full-length biography at present in preparation by a former employee of the railway works.

Chapter Thirty-Three

The Irish Volunteers and the Outbreak of War

In October 1912 the Unionists of Northern Ireland armed themselves and founded the Ulster Volunteers in order to oppose the British Government's proposals to introduce some form of Home Rule for Ireland. One year later Irish Nationalists responded by setting up the Irish Volunteers. This new movement spread rapidly throughout the country, but came very much under the influence of the Irish Parliamentary Party.

A local unit was to be launched in Inchicore on Sunday 25th July 1914 by means of a public meeting. Nearly 2,000 people, some of whom had marched in from Clondalkin, assembled by four o'clock with two bands at the corner of Vincent Street. However, the guest speakers were unable to attend because on that very day Erskine Childers' yacht, the *Asgard*, had arrived at Howth with a consignment of arms. Father O Ryan of Goldenbridge stepped into the breach and presided at the meeting, the platform for which was an empty brake. The lot of addressing the crowd fell on the local organiser of the meeting, Mr Peadar Doyle, who was making his first public speech. However after a few minutes a message was passed to him that, following the Howth gun running, a confrontation with the British Army had taken place at Bachelors Walk in the city and that there had been civilian casualties. He realised the seriousness of having in the circumstances such a large crowd in close proximity to Richmond Barracks and accordingly took steps to bring the meeting to a close. Before doing so, he invited all who wished to join the Irish Volunteers to attend at a field in the district whose location we do not know, on the following Tuesday. Over 1,000 men attended this second gathering at which companies were formed and drill instructors appointed.

Outbreak of the Great War

In the weeks following this initial meeting, marching and drilling – very often with only hurley sticks – took place. One of the venues for the drilling was on the open space behind the Workmens' Club. However, the outbreak of the Great War between England and Germany on 4th August 1914 brought about a fundamental change in the whole Irish political situation. The Irish Parliamentary Party under its leader, John Redmond, had already achieved considerable influence in the leadership of the Irish Volunteers and had a different agenda from the founders of that movement. On 23rd September 1914 Redmond committed the Irish Volunteers to supporting England in return for a promise of Home Rule when the war was over. This immediately split the Volunteer movement, both nationally and locally. The majority supported Redmond and they became known as the Irish National Volunteers, with many of their members taking part in the war.

The minority continued as the Irish Volunteers, taking the traditional separatist view that England's difficulty was Ireland's opportunity. Locally they were organised as "F" Company of the 4th Battalion, which stretched from Rathfarnham to Chapelizod. The split saw their members drastically reduced from about 1,000 to forty-nine within a month. They were given the use of the Emmet Hall two nights per week free of charge and a miniature rifle range was set up in the back garden. The smaller Irish Citizen Army were also using these premises, but both groups kept their separate identity. The Company Captain was the young Limerick man, Con Colbert, with local man Peadar Doyle as Quarter Master and former Councillor Patrick O'Carroll as trustee of their funds. For the next two years they trained and endeavoured to procure arms as best they could. Most of the members made a small weekly contribution to an arms fund. By the time the rising came around, they appear to have been fairly well armed, having also received a share of the Howth guns, and with a considerable supply of ammunition.

The outbreak of hostilities saw reservists being called up and Richmond Barracks being put on a war footing. Horses were commandeered from private firms for army use. Emmet Road was to witness much activity with the constant coming and going of soldiers. All of this was good for the local economy, with shops and pubs benefiting. Furthermore, some of the families of army personnel found accommodation with local residents. Saint Judes' Parochial Hall was put into use as a recreation hall for the troops and here regular concerts were provided and teas served throughout the week. A fund was set up to make additional comforts available for soldiers on active service. The general consensus at the time was that the war would only last for six months and few realised that it would go on for more than four years.

The Government carried out a very energetic recruiting campaign, leaving no stone unturned to obtain more recruits. They even put on a special tram decorated with bunting and posters which traversed the city. It often made its appearance in Inchicore on a Saturday night as men were leaving the Black Lion at closing time and with the recruiting sergeant and his aides urging them to join up and fight for small nations. Those who "took the shilling" were conveyed on the tram down to Ship Street Barracks at Dublin Castle, where they enlisted.

As of now we do not know how many joined in this district. Some joined in response to Redmond's call and felt they were doing so in the best interests of Ireland

TO THE GLORY OF GOD.
AND IN PROUD AND LOVING MEMORY OF
THOSE MEMBERS OF OUR CONGREGATION
WHO NOBLY GAVE THEIR VALUED LIVES
IN THE GREAT WAR 1914-1918.

ATOCK,A G: MC: 2ND LT RE.
BAKER,W A: L CPL RIFLE BRIGADE.
BARSBY,C W: TROOPER S I H.
BURNS,P F T: 2ND LT KINGS L POOL REGT.
BURNS,W: SERGT R I RIFLES.
CAMPBELL,C W: C DE GUERRE. C Q M S. R D F.
CANT,RJ: CQMS RI REGT.
COMBIE,H A: PTE MIDDLESEX REGT.
GOODEVE,T E: MAJOR R E.
GRJFFIN,J: PTE R INNIS FUS.
HARBORNE,G F: M M & BAR L CPL R INNIS FUS.
HENDERSON,R C: PTE M T, R A S C.
HUMPHREYS,JWH: CPL R D F.
KIRBY,J: DRIVER R F A.
MC. CONNELL,W: M M: CPL IRISH GUARDS.
MC CONNELL,C: PTE IRISH GUARDS.
MOORE,C: PTE R D F
NOBLE,J T: PTE IRISH GUARDS.
PLOWMAN,J: M C: CAPT. LEINSTER REGT.
PRESTAGE,R: M M & BAR SERGT R D F.
RIGGS,J T: GUNNER R F A.
SMITH,R J: PTE MACHINE GUN CORPS.
SUTTON,F: PTE LEINSTER REGT.
WHARTON,H: S B A R NAVY.
ADAMS S D: PTE R I RIFLES.

"THE STRIFE IS O'ER, THE BATTLE WON."
"BLESSED ARE THE DEAD WHICH DIE IN THE LORD THAT THEY MAY REST FROM THEIR LABOURS AND THEIR WORKS DO FOLLOW THEM."

1914 War Memorial tablet formerly in Saint Jude's Church

but many others did so because of the chronic unemployment position. A typical example of the times was the Ryan family from Carrickfoyle Terrace in Old Kilmainham. Here in one of these small little houses the eleven children of this family, seven brothers and four girls, were reared. All of the seven brothers joined and one of them, Thomas, was killed at the Dardanelles while serving with the Dublin Fusiliers.

With regard to the members of the Protestant community, the motivation because of their mostly English background was understandably loyalty to the Crown. In their case we do know that twenty-five young men of the local parish of Saint Jude were killed in the war, something which was in the long term to have implications for the future of their community. One of these was Arthur George Atock, the only son of Dr Atock, the railway doctor who lived at "Hampton", a fine red brick residence in its own grounds on Tyrconnell Road.

This house in the 1930s was occupied by another doctor and his family, one of whom, Dermot Ryan, was to be Archbishop of Dublin and later a Cardinal in Rome before his untimely death. This house has been replaced by apartments in recent years and the name changed to "Hamden Court" for some reason.

Chapter Thirty-Four

Francis Ledwidge at Richmond Barracks

On the 24th October 1914 a young Meath man presented himself at Richmond Barracks and enlisted in the Royal Inniskilling Fusiliers. His name was Francis Ledwidge, the gentle poet of the Meath countryside.

His choice of unit was coloured by the fact that it was an Irish regiment, but more importantly to him it had within its ranks as an officer his literary mentor, Lord Dunsany. However the latter was rather annoyed when he found that Ledwidge had joined and would have preferred if he had stayed at home to devote himself to his blossoming literary career. Notwithstanding this he continued to guide and take an interest in the young poet, eventually arranging to have his first book of poetry published during the height of the war.

Another boon companion and fellow spirit of Ledwidge while at the barracks was Sergeant Robert Christie, a Belfast man who had a play accepted by the Abbey Theatre. Both of them during their time off frequented literary gatherings in the city, while on other evenings they joined Dunsany in his quarters to discuss poetry, their abiding passion. On one particular Saturday night Ledwidge gave a poetry reading in the recreation room of the barracks.

But it was not to be all poetry for him or anything like it. The work of preparing for war continued all that winter which was a particularly severe one and involved battalion training, musketry, field days, night operations, skirmishing in the Phoenix Park, and that which was most detested of all by the soldiers – the long route marches.

A soldier's pay at that time was seven shillings per week, but from time to time Ledwidge was engaged in clerical work in the Orderly Room, for which the pay was increased to ten shillings per week. In a letter to a friend dated 31st March 1915 he wrote:

> "From the desk where I am writing this I see through a window across the recreation ground spire on spire of Dublin and hear the bells of trams and the shout of all its worry and woe, but my thoughts are in Wilkinstown."

In a further letter he wrote:

> "I look forward to poetry and fame after the war and feel that by joining I am helping to bring about peace and the old sublimity of which the world has been robbed."

The Inniskillings left Richmond Barracks for the war at the end of April 1915. A fellow soldier described their going:

> "I will never forget that afternoon. As we marched out of the barracks the gates were packed with people and from that until we arrived at the boat we marched through solid cheering crowds all waving to us and wishing us good luck and a safe return. Not only that but they pressed into our hands and stuffed into our pockets as we passed packets of cigarettes and biscuits, sweets and even bottles of stout. What a send off they gave us!"

Ledwidge saw active service in several of the theatres of war before his death.

Following the work of Alice Curtayne in this field local poet Liam O'Meara, who lives at Saint Michael's Estate where Richmond Barracks once stood, has after much research gathered together more of the scattered poems of the soldier-poet, some of them previously unpublished. This has resulted in the recent publication of *Francis Ledwidge, the Complete Poems*, which has been compiled and edited by Liam.

Chapter Thirty-Five

The Easter Rising

The Easter Rising was a very much on-off-on affair. The failure to land a large consignment of German arms on the south coast caused Eoin MacNeill, the Chief of Staff of the Irish Volunteers, to cancel at the last moment the general mobilisation which was arranged for Easter Sunday, 23rd April 1916, and which was to be a cover for a widespread rising. A few nights previously, on Good Friday to be exact, the local "F" company in preparation for this mobilisation had met at a disused quarry near the 3rd Lock Bridge where several thousand rounds of ammunition were distributed following a roll call.

In the event McNeill was over-ruled by the secret Irish Republican Brotherhood who, although they knew it could not be a military success, decided to go ahead with the Rising on the next day, Easter Monday, 24th April. The ensuing confusion led to a lesser turnout than might otherwise have occurred and also to the Rising being in the main confined to Dublin.

Early on Easter Monday morning, Captain Con Colbert visited Inchicore and conveyed the news of the new arrangements. As a result approximately forty-two out of the forty-nine members of the company turned out, the bulk of them making their way in small groups to Emerald Square off Cork Street, which was the mobilisation point. The remainder, because of the confusion, attached themselves to other units in the city. At Emerald Square they joined with their other colleagues of the 4th Battalion under Comdt Éamonn Ceannt and Vice-Comdt Cathal Brugha. Amongst those present also were William T. Cosgrave and Joseph McGrath, later to be one of the founders of the Irish Hospitals Sweepstakes.

The combined group, accompanied by about fourteen young women of Cumann na mBan, who were also to brave the hazards of the week, and a horse drawn dray carrying boxes of ammunition, then moved off. By mid-day they had occupied the South Dublin Union in James's Street, the Marrowbone Lane Distillery and Roes Malt House at Mount Brown.

At the same time other Volunteers had occupied the G.P.O. and many public buildings throughout the city. Whether the rank and file were aware that morning if this was the real thing or just another further general manoeuvres is a question which is still debated.

The small Inchicore group which belonged to the Irish Citizen Army reported directly to Liberty Hall. Amongst these were Comdt Michael Mallin, William

The Easter Rising 1916. British soldiers near James's Street

Partridge and Willoughby Scott, a County Fermanagh Methodist who resided at New Road in the "Bungalow". All three were very much involved in the fighting at the College of Surgeons, Stephen's Green, where Mallin was in charge.

South Dublin Union

Within an hour of the occupation of the various buildings the fight was on. The authorities had responded immediately by sending out all available troops from the various city barracks, including Richmond. The latter, consisting initially of 200 men from the Royal Irish Regiment, were ordered to come to the assistance of Dublin Castle. They had marched along Old Kilmainham when their advance party of thirty men came under fire at 12.40 p.m. from a group of Volunteers posted in the sloping fields of McCaffrey's Estate, now the housing area known as Ceannt's Fort. The British suffered casualties at this close range, retreated temporarily and then came on the offensive. In the ensuing engagement three of the Volunteers were shot dead and the remainder withdrew within the shelter of the walls of the South Dublin Union. Roe's Malt House on the other side of the road, where a small number of the Volunteers were posted, now came under fire from machine guns which the British had mounted on the roofs of buildings in the Royal Hospital and in the course of the next few days the Volunteers were forced to evacuate.

Later on that Monday afternoon more soldiers from Richmond Barracks made their way up Brookfield Road and along the canal. Following a very heavy exchange of fire they succeeded in breaking into the Union grounds at the Rialto gate. In the course of this battle, a Dublin man serving with the Royal Irish Regiment, Lieutenant Alan Ramsay, was fatally wounded. For the rest of the evening action was limited to sniping on both sides. Peadar Doyle recalled that it seemed quite evident that the sniping and roar of the Howth Mauser rifles left the military unsure of their own position.

Éamonn Ceannt had made his H.Q. in the Nurses Home, not too far from the main gate in James's Street, which had been securely barricaded, as indeed had many of the buildings in the extensive grounds. Snipers were posted at various vantage points at overhead windows. Later in the week a large tricolour flag was attached to a top window of the west wing.

While the rest of the Inchicore men were detailed to the Marrowbone Lane area, Peadar Doyle acted as A.D.C. to Ceannt at the Union as well as being Quarter Master in charge of rations and distribution of ammunition.

Also on that first day of the Rising, the British lost no time in calling up reinforcements from the provinces. The first of these, 1,600 troops from the Curragh, passed through Inchicore in special trains and by 5.00 p.m. had arrived at Kingsbridge Station from where they were immediately deployed to various parts of the city.

As already mentioned, the Old Marrowbone Lane Distillery Building was also occupied and barricaded by the Volunteers on Easter Monday. They had a strong position here with plenty of provisions. Con Colbert was one of the officers in charge in this district. Also occupied in the same locality were some small outposts. I remember many years ago an old Inchicore man telling me that he was stationed in one of these and that they were not called upon to fire a single shot during the week!

However, the distillery building itself was to see plenty of action, with the occupants exchanging heavy fire with the soldiers throughout the week. Inchicore men were mostly involved in this garrison, with names like Sergeant Ned Neill, Mick Liston and Mick Reardon coming to mind. By Thursday they were hemmed in by the British, who now bided their time rather than attempting to storm the building.

General Maxwell

The British Government decided to send over General Sir John Maxwell, K.C.B., K.C.M.G., C.V.O., D.S.O., to take complete charge of operations against the insurgents. He arrived at the North Wall at 2.30 a.m. on Tuesday, by which time many of the buildings in O'Connell Street were in flames. He said that he proceeded immediately with some staff officers to the Royal Hospital, but this would not appear to be correct, as British Military Headquarters in Ireland had been transferred from there to Infirmary Road in 1913.

British army at the Inchicore Railway works during the 1916 Rising

However during the Rising the Royal Hospital became a strong point, with a very large amount of soldiers being accommodated in every available space. Also of course it was from the tops of some of the buildings there that continuous machine gun fire was directed against the South Dublin Union buildings for most of the week.

In his memoirs Ernest Joynt tells us that during the Rising, Inchicore was completely isolated from the rest of Dublin:

> "We could only guess what was happening from the distant rattle of rifle fire and machine guns, the booming of cannon and the reflection of gigantic conflagrations in the night sky."

When he had crushed the Rising, General Maxwell sent a comprehensive report to the British Government in the course of which the following item of local interest occurs:

> "During the Wednesday afternoon the Reserve Cavalry Regiment which had been escorting ammunition and rifles from the docks was held up on Ormond Quay by enemy fire. It was relieved by armoured motor lorries which had been placed at my disposal by Messrs. Arthur Guinness and roughly armoured with boiler plates at the Inchicore Railway Works."

South Dublin Union Again

On Tuesday morning the troops who had penetrated the Rialto gate made a determined attack in the direction of the Nurses Home but were repulsed. However it was later that morning that Frank Burke, a half-brother of William T. Cosgrave, was killed by a sniper.

On Wednesday afternoon a heavy volume of fire was directed against all the occupied buildings, but the expected attack did not materialise. It was postponed until Thursday and again preceded by a similar volume of fire. From the top windows the occupiers could see a large number of troops advancing in extended order in the fields between Mount Brown and the South Circular Road. The ensuing battle lasted for seven hours until nightfall. The soldiers succeeded in occupying part of the Nurses Home, also making use of small hand grenades which they lobbed into part of the building. It was in this situation that the Vice-Commandant, Cathal Brugha, although seriously wounded, single-handedly fought off the enemy, giving his men a chance to rally around again. In the end the British were forced to retreat from the building.

It was during this engagement that Peadar Doyle and a colleague were endeavouring to make their way back from the other strong point at the main gate. They had to throw themselves down in a valley between two roofs to escape machine gun fire from the Royal Hospital and a sniper who was operating from the top of a private house on the South Circular Road. They were pinned down in that position until dusk when they finally got clear.

The Beginning of the End

As in the case of Marrowbone, the British did not proceed with a further assault on the Union, knowing that they had isolated these areas. By now they had also closed in on the centre of the city using artillery to shell the Volunteer Headquarters at the G.P.O. By Saturday Padraig Pearse and his colleagues had no alternative but to surrender unconditionally.

On Sunday afternoon Thomas McDonagh, accompanied by Father Augustine O.F.M. Cap., arrived at the Union to inform Comdt Ceannt of the position. The latter then addressed the men, explaining the position, and it was agreed that they would surrender as a group. However, there were a few who did not adhere to this and managed by some manner or means to make their escape from the Union grounds.

Here we must mention the bravery of the hospital chaplains, Father Gerard O.C.C. and Father Dillon, who attended to the wounded throughout the week, and also the tragic death of Nurse Keogh who was caught in crossfire. With regard to the hundreds of inmates of the Union they had, along with the staff, moved to buildings in a relatively safer part of the fifty-acre complex. Red flags were displayed from the windows of these buildings and provisions were allowed through. Nevertheless it must have been quite an ordeal for those concerned during that week of fighting.

Before three o'clock Ceannt, accompanied by a British officer, led out his men and proceeded towards the city along James's Street, where they were joined by the men and women of the Marrowbone Lane Garrison. They were still carrying their weapons and as they marched along they broke into the Soldier's Song. In sharp contrast to the reception they were to get later that evening, they were greeted by cheers, particularly in the poorer parts of the city. The surrender took place at Saint Patrick's Park in Bride Street. Then, together with their colleagues from Jacobs', they were placed under a very heavy escort of soldiers and marched back out to Richmond Barracks, which had been designated as a holding centre by the authorities.

Chapter Thirty-Six

THE AFTERMATH OF THE RISING

AT RICHMOND BARRACKS

Following the surrender, the British military moved swiftly to deal with the situation. First of all they selected Richmond Barracks as a holding centre and at the same time reopened the nearby Kilmainham Jail, then in a state of disrepair, having been closed since 1910. They had also decided that the leaders of the Rising and other officers would be held at the barracks for trial, while the rest would be deported to England as soon as possible.

On Sunday morning the first large batch of prisoners arrived. These were from the G.P.O. and Four Courts garrisons and included most of the leaders, with the exception of Pearse and Connolly. The former was apparently brought by motor vehicle while the wounded Connolly was detained at a hospital in Dublin Castle. Later in the day the Citizen Army contingent who had been in the College of Surgeons arrived. They were led by Michael Mallin and Countess Markievicz, the former passing his home at the Emmet Hall. The last to arrive in the afternoon was the 4th Battalion, which included most of the Inchicore men led by Éamonn Ceannt.

All of them were subjected to a barrage of abuse and threats at Kilmainham and Emmet Road by people whose relatives were fighting with the British Army in France. The Citizen Army man and later Trade Union leader, Frank Robbins, has left us with the following account:

> "There was cheering and waving of hats and Union Jacks for the Staffordshire Regiment, particularly at Inchicore, as they marched us into the barracks. The shouts of "Good old Staffs" and "Shoot the traitors" seem now almost incredible. A very small section of those assembled did spread a ray of hope amongst us by raising their voices in our support. They were indeed blest with stout hearts, though considerably in the minority."

Because of overcrowding at Richmond Barracks, the only remaining garrison, that of Boland's Mills, were detained at Ballsbridge for a week and not brought out to Inchicore until 6th May. It was this delay which helped to save the life of their Commandant, Éamonn de Valera.

As soon as the prisoners began to arrive, they were carefully scrutinised in the gymnasium by the Detective Branch of the D.M.P. All of those who were recognised as signatories of the Proclamation or of having played a prominent part as leaders in

Wexford prisoners being escorted from Richmond barracks to Kilmainham jail, May 1916

the Rising were detained in that building. They were to spend the night sleeping as best they could on blankets laid on the floor.

With regard to the rank and file, the first 500 of these were that very evening on the march once more, this time on the first leg of their journey to England. They were not accompanied by their female colleagues who were brought over to Kilmainham Jail. Before leaving, the men were allocated a ration of bully beef and biscuits. Dusk saw them proceeding under a very heavy escort and headed by a mounted officer through the grounds of the Royal Hospital and then down the quays to the docks where they were put on board ship.

In the days and weeks that followed, similar procedures were adopted and in all fourteen separate contingents passed down Emmet Road, the last of them on 16th June. The numbers of detainees at Richmond had been augmented by hundreds of suspects and sympathisers who were brought there from all parts of Ireland following a widespread police round-up and many of these were also deported to England. In all, over 3,000 people passed through the barracks and of these about 1,000 were released following investigation. All of this led to very crowded conditions with every available room being crammed with prisoners. Some distance inside the main gate, a barbed wire fence was erected over which relatives were permitted to converse with prisoners twice a week under the watchful eyes of armed guards.

Interestingly one of the officers dealing with prisoners at Richmond Barracks was an Irishman, Lieutenant Robert Barton. Later on he was to become a prominent member of Sinn Féin and eventually was one of the signatories of the Treaty in 1921.

The Court Martials

The first court martial at which Padraig Pearse, Thomas MacDonagh and Thomas Clarke were tried took place on Tuesday 2nd May. The court sat in a three-storey block directly opposite the gymnasium on the east side of the square. We get some idea of the proceedings there from the recollections of Herbert Shaw, one of the prosecutors:

> "In a bare room the three officers of the court sat at a table covered with a military blanket. There were the necessary papers, two bibles and a volume of military law. At another small table I sat as prosecutor. Prisoners were brought in one by one to stand their trial. They were charged with taking part in armed rebellion and waging war against His Majesty, the King.

Prisoners at Richmond barracks, May 1916, Emmet Road in the background

A room in Richmond barracks, June 1916. From their appearance most of the group seem to be detainees rather than actual participants in the Rising

"In no single case with which I dealt was there a shadow of doubt as to the guilt of the accused and neither did any of them attempt to dispute the facts against them. In several cases they were in the officers uniforms of the Irish Volunteers in which they were captured. The work was far from pleasant. However strongly I felt about the gravity of their crime, I could not forget that I had fought them according to the rules of war. Moreover, the accused behaved with great calmness and dignity and in the grave and patient atmosphere of the court, it was hard to realise that they stood on trial for their lives."

As was customary with court martials, no verdict was announced at the close of proceedings and the three men were brought back to the nearby gymnasium. Later that evening an officer called to them and informed them that they had been found guilty and sentenced to death. They were then escorted on foot to Kilmainham Jail and shot there the next morning, Wednesday 3rd May.

The notes of Padraig Pearse's statement to the court did not come to light until 1946 when the widow of a retired British Army records sergeant who had received them from Pearse while in Kilmainham, presented them to Margaret Pearse.

The trials continued, followed by further executions:

Thursday, 4th May
Joseph Mary Plunkett, Willie Pearse, Edward Daly and Michael O'Hanrahan

Friday, 5th May
John McBride

Monday, 8th May
Éamonn Ceannt, Con Colbert, Michael Mallin and Seán Heuston

Friday, 12th May
James Connolly and Seán MacDiarmada

The wounded Connolly had been tried at Dublin Castle and brought to Kilmainham by ambulance. Inchicore had lost the two leaders, Colbert and Mallin, who had been associated with the area prior to the Rising, while Partridge died one year later. Both Partridge and Peadar Doyle had been sentenced to ten years' penal servitude.

On hearing of the Easter Rising in Dublin Francis Ledwidge was deeply moved and mourned for his friend and fellow poet Thomas McDonagh who similarly found himself in Richmond Barracks, but under different circumstances:

"He shall not hear the bittern cry
In the wild sky where he is lain,
Nor voices of the sweeter birds
Above the wailing of the rain.

Nor shall he know when loud March blows
Thro' slanting snows her fanfare shrill,
Blowing to flame the golden cup
Of many an upset daffodil.

But when the Dark Cow leaves the moor,
And pastures poor with greedy weeds,
Perhaps he'll hear her low at morn
Lifting her horn in pleasant meads."

One year later in 1917 Francis Ledwidge, at thirty years of age, was killed on the Western Front following a short but eventful life.

Change of Outlook

As the executions proceeded, the outlook of the Irish people in relation to the Rising was changing from disapproval to sympathy and soon "all was changed, changed utterly". Many more of those who had been sentenced to death at Richmond

Barracks would have been executed were it not for this change of mood which was expressed very forcibly in the House of Commons by the members of the Irish Parliamentary Party and particularly by their leader, John Dillon. Also Irish-American opinion played a crucial role in the course of events as Britain was very much dependent on American aid during the war with Germany. Such was the concern in London that the British Prime Minister, Mr Asquith, travelled over to Dublin to gauge public opinion and on 14th May he visited Richmond Barracks, where he spoke to some of the prisoners.

Amongst those who were reprieved and had their sentences commuted to penal servitude for life were Countess Markievicz, Éamonn de Valera and William Cosgrave.

Two further trials took place at Richmond, this time of British Army personnel. On 6th and 7th June, Captain Bowen-Colthurst was charged with the murder of the pacifist, Francis Sheehy-Skeffington, and two other men at Portobello Barracks. He was deemed to be guilty but insane.

On 12th June, a Sergeant of the Dublin Fusiliers was charged with having had two men shot in Guinness Brewery. He was acquitted and this brought to an end the long list of court martials at the barracks.

By 16th June 1916, Richmond Barracks had seen off the last of its unexpected guests to England and it now resumed its war-time role, for Great Britain and Germany were still in conflict. It had also, like Kilmainham Jail, entered the pages of Irish history.

Chapter Thirty-Seven

Guerilla Days (1)

Release of Prisoners

With the outcome of the Great War still very much in doubt, at a time when there had been a fall-off in recruitment since the Rising, and in order to assuage Irish-American opinion further, the British government had released all Irish prisoners unconditionally by June 1917. Soon after their arrival back in Ireland preparations were put in hand to reorganise the Irish Volunteers with a view to resuming the struggle on a guerrilla basis.

In line with this policy the local "F" Company was reformed with Christopher Byrne of Bow Bridge who had been "out" in the Rising as captain. Most of those who had participated in the Rising continued their membership, but some did not remain as active members, mainly because of employment and economic difficulties. However, their places were taken by new members who tended to be somewhat younger men. One of these, Michael Dwyer of Old Kilmainham, told me he witnessed the volunteers coming out in surrender from the South Dublin Union in James's Street. Michael later became transport officer in view of his background in the motor trade.

Here it should be acknowledged in fairness that the Inchicore Railway Works accepted back those employees who had been involved in the Rising or interned.

A notable addition to the volunteers at this time was Jim ("Tyers") Donnelly, an Armagh man who had earlier emigrated with his family to Liverpool and, having served with the Royal Engineers in France, now came to reside with his sister Mrs Monks at Ring Street. He was later elected as captain of "F" Company in succession to Kit Byrne following the latter's promotion.

Training

At this stage the company was about fifty strong and paraded regularly at Landsdowne Valley and the disused brickworks on Jamestown Road. Their area stretched from Old Kilmainham through Inchicore to Bluebell and Chapelizod. Headquarters was at Portlester House, Bluebell, the home of the Flood sisters.

From the beginning the force was very poorly armed, only having a few Mauser rifles, relics of the Rising, some shotguns, as well as miniature rifles. With the latter they carried out target practice in the outlying areas such as the sandhills of the Long Mile Road known as Cavanagh's Banks and even in Bluebell Cemetery. During 1918 the company was actively engaged in raiding for shotguns and cartridges, particularly from landowners with pro-British backgrounds in Crumlin, Newlands and Bluebell. Another source of supply was arranged by Section Officer George Dwyer of Turvey Avenue, who with some of his colleagues became friendly with British soldiers from Richmond Barracks who frequented the "Horse and Jockey" across the road and who were anxious to supplement their meagre pay. As a result the soldiers carried out three revolvers in their pockets and handed them over at 50/- a piece. Other guns were brought out while hidden under the contents of a slop car owned by a local piggery man. By degrees arms and ammunition were acquired from a variety of sources, but at no stage had the company an adequate supply.

Dumps were established at the Jamestown Road brickworks, at Portlester House, and also out at Ballyknockan in the Dublin/Wicklow hills. At this time, military exercises were carried out also in conjunction with other units of the Dublin Brigade, again in the Dublin hills.

Later in 1918, war games had to be put aside temporarily on two occasions. The first was during the attempt by the British government to impose conscription on Ireland and local volunteers took an active part in the anti-conscription campaign. This involved the obstruction of recruiting meetings in James's Street and elsewhere. During this period there was a big influx of new members bringing the company strength up to 120. However when the crisis passed over, many of these newcomers left.

With the ending of World War I on 11th November 1918 and the defeat of Germany, pro-British supporters took to the streets in the city in celebration and clashes with nationalists occurred. In Inchicore stones were thrown at the Emmet Hall by soldiers and some Union Jacks were displayed.

1919 – The First Dáil Éireann

Following the success of the anti-conscription campaign, the local volunteers then had to involve themselves in the General Election campaign of December 1918, when they carried out a very active and enthusiastic campaign. Their election headquarters was the little shop at Grattan Crescent at the corner of Larkin's Lane and older residents remember the celebrations here with lighted torches and banners when the results came in. The overall outcome of that election was a sweeping victory for Sinn Féin, culminating in the establishment of Dáil Éireann on 21st January 1919 – a turning point in Irish history indeed. The room over the shop continued to be used for some years as a Sinn Féin social club with billiard table and sing-songs.

At that first meeting of the Dáil in the Mansion House, the Inchicore company supplied some members for protective duties. They were part of a specially selected group, fully armed, whose function was to prevent any of the delegates, the first

Teachtaí Dála, from being arrested by the British authorities. Happily their services were not called upon.

It was at this time that the guerilla campaign commenced in the southern counties, but Dublin was relatively inactive until the second half of 1920. Insofar as Inchicore was concerned the training, drilling and preparations continued. A minor confrontation with British personnel had taken place on Tyrconnell Road late in 1919.

No opportunity was lost in acquiring arms. For example when an army car broke down near the Black Lion and the two occupants of the car made their way on foot to seek assistance, they were overpowered and relieved of their side-arms in the process.

Empty army lorries were held up and burned on the Naas Road on several occasions, as were R.A.F. vehicles near Baldonnell aerodrome. A supply lorry containing food and rations was taken over near the 3rd Lock Bridge and the contents distributed in the "Bungalow" area.

1920 – Munitions

Early in 1920 a new development commenced at the Inchicore Railway Works with the secret manufacture there of hand grenades by volunteers who were employed at the Works. This was at the special request of headquarters who urgently required them for use against British lorries in the city. The man who organised this venture was Mick Morrissey of New Road, a foreman in the stores department. Amongst his aids were two other "Bungalow" men, Johnny Gargan and Jack Gough, the latter still remembered in the area as a very talented singer. Eight men in all were lined up in key jobs in the Works and within three weeks the "assembly lines" were rolling. The cases were made at lunch breaks and following casting were hidden among axle boxes. In addition guns were being constantly repaired and bullets cut down to suit various models. Seán Ó Conchubhair of Nash Street, who was also employed at the Works and who with nearly all of his family were involved in the War of Independence, was kept busy making the necessary arrangements for this repair operation.

It is difficult to understand how all these activities went on undetected, particularly in view of the pro-British outlook of the management. The Works was raided on several occasions but nothing was found. A story is told that during one of these raids a wanted activist got into an empty boiler and had one of his mates weld up the entrance until such time as the danger passed over.

Also in the railway context, a number of train crew personnel played a vital role in the transmission of messages and dispatches on behalf of the underground movement. Furthermore as the conflict progressed some of them also refused to transport British military or munitions and which resulted in their dismissal.

Rates and Income Tax

In furtherance of a campaign to hamper British civil administration, it was decided to destroy all income tax records in the neighbourhood of Dublin on the night of 3rd April 1920. As part of this operation, a group of Inchicore men on that night took possession of all the books and income tax records for this area, which were held at the home of an official in Lucan. Because of British patrols they had to cross many fields with the bulky ledgers and files before reaching Bluebell, where they were burned.

This was followed by the seizure from the homes of rate collectors of all the monies collected for rates, which were then handed over to Dáil Éireann.

An attempt to destroy the unoccupied Crumlin Police Barracks was only partially successful, due to an accident in which one of the attackers was himself badly injured in the ensuing fire. An attempt to burn Chapelizod Barracks did not succeed either due to the intervention of a party of soldiers who opened fire.

Death of Seán Doyle

Volunteer Seán Doyle, the nineteen-year-old son of Peadar Doyle, was shot dead at Kilmashogue Mountain on 19th September 1920 under dubious circumstances while on a training weekend with his unit, the 5th Engineers. An official statement was issued from Dublin Castle that night:

> "A company of the Irish Republican Army which is alleged to have been in the habit of meeting on Sunday mornings on the slopes of the Dublin Mountains for rifle, revolver and bombing practice, was this morning surrounded by forces of the Crown in plain clothes numbering thirty five men.
>
> "In the course of the round-up, two men were shot while attempting to escape, one of them fatally. Bombs were found in his possession.
>
> "Forty men were arrested. Rifle, bomb and revolver munitions as well as a tent were seized."

At the inquest it was strenuously denied that he was carrying bombs. The men in plain clothes were in fact the first elements of the new Black and Tan force which had just arrived in Ireland. It is clear that they had received a tip-off and that the Irish side was caught off guard.

At the removal, the funeral procession was headed by the Saint James's Band. "On arrival at Inchicore the scene was especially impressive. The tolling of the church bell at intervals as dusk was falling, the strains of the Dead March and the steady tramp of the Volunteers on Tyrconnell Road provided a scene of intense solemnity."

There was a great wave of genuine sympathy for the Doyle family and the funeral on the next day to Esker was of enormous proportions.

The funeral of Volunteer Seán Doyle passing Richmond barracks, September 1920

Seán Treacy

The Tipperary leader, Seán Treacy, within forty-eight hours of the gun battle with British forces in Drumcondra, arrived in a very dishevelled condition on 13 October 1920 at the home of the Holland family at Silverdale Terrace on Inchicore Road. Here he first had a meeting with some members of the G.H.Q. Squad and then spent the night there. The next morning Mrs Holland, who was distressed at his condition, did what she could for him. After breakfast he left on his bicycle for the city, where spotters soon picked up his trail and he was killed later that afternoon following a shoot-out in Talbot Street.

Search for Spies

On Saturday 21st November, fourteen newly arrived British agents were shot in various hotels in the city. As part of this operation all units were requested to supply a number of volunteers. The Inchicore group of about eight or ten men were allocated to a hotel in Leeson Street. They took over the building but failed to find the person they sought, a lieutenant colonel, and after some hours they withdrew.

The next day the Black and Tans fired on the crowd at a football match in Croke Park by way of reprisal. One of those killed on that occasion was the nineteen-year-old Joseph Traynor of Ballymount who as it happened was a member of the local company. He was also captain of the Fox and Geese minor football club and went to Croke Park on that Sunday with a number of companions from the club of whom one was the athlete Paddy Ryan. The Traynor family originally lived in Drimnagh Castle before moving to Bluebell and then to Ballymount.

At a later stage in the company's own area a soldier charged with espionage was abducted and shot.

Chapter Thirty-Eight

Mná na h-Éireann

Mary Jo's Memories

While Cumann na mBan may not have been formally organised in the area, individual members of that organisation, as well as other women who were not affiliated, played a significant role in the War of Independence. One of these, Mary Jo O'Connor, belonged to a Limerick family, who came to reside in Nash Street in April 1916 as it so happened. She has left a valuable account of her involvement during the ensuing years of which the following is a summary.

"I was a member of Cumann na mBan from 1917 until December 1921 when I went to France. My father and two brothers were members of "F" Company. It is not too much to claim that during the Black and Tan War I was constantly on duty. I was employed in carrying arms and dispatches as well as caring for the wounded, preparing meals for men on the run and looking after prisoners. House to house collections were made for a prisoners' dependent fund and friends donated food and clothing, the latter being washed and mended by my mother.

"I also helped to look after the guns in the dump at the Brick Works on Jamestown Road. The weapons were placed in a long box which was lowered by ropes into a deep hole. It was raided on one occasion by the military from Richmond Barracks, but we had got word beforehand and they only found an empty box. Every week the guns had to be thoroughly cleaned and the rusty ones cleaned with nitric acid. I burned my hand when the bottle overturned and the marks stay to this day.

"As the need arose to find an additional hiding place for homemade bombs, guns and ammunition, we decided to store them in the space between the roof and the ceiling of our own house in Nash Street. The only way to get in was through a small ventilator in the middle of the ceiling and my young brother, Holly, was the only one who could fit through. We had to put a chair on a table and he hoisted himself up. We then handed the items to him through the hole and he stocked them around inside. The same method had to be used to get them out. As a certain amount of ammunition had to be on hand for the men who called for supplies, I kept an old hat full at all times. During a raid one night, the hat remained on a table but luckily no notice was taken of it.

"The raids continued on our house, sometimes three or four times a week, but nothing was ever found, although the place was a veritable arsenal. Then there was a house to house search in our locality. Our house was the only one without a man in it, as it was not considered safe and none of them stayed there at night, but were billeted out amongst the neighbours. Some had as many as sixteen men in their house when the house to house search came and of course most of them were arrested.

"In 1921 we had the Teeling escape from Kilmainham Jail. In order to escape notice, I went in by the back of the Jail with Capt. Jim Donnelly. We spoke to the prisoners who were waiting and tried to get a rope ladder over the wall, but this failed. The British soldiers and their girls, who were in the side alley at the time, had to be arrested, as they witnessed the whole performance. They were kept in a hut overnight and later brought blindfolded along the canal to a country house some miles away. They were detained there until finally the escape was effected nearly a week later by means of bolt-cutters.

"The Truce was signed in July and in November my mother died. My father, who was still in the Curragh, came home on parole. We had great difficulty getting him home and it was through Michael Collins, then in London for the Peace Talks, that he was allowed out on parole for ten days. He was released on the general release of prisoners after the signing of the Treaty. Then another period of war started."

Nellie Bushell

Nellie Bushell, the daughter of a silk weaver, was born in Newmarket Street in the Liberties and was to become one of the Abbey Theatre's most famous employees. An eager dedicated young woman, she took up her duties as an usherette on the very first night that the Abbey opened its doors on 27th December 1904. She was to serve that theatre faithfully for the next forty-three years until her retirement. In those early years, she only received a very small wage, but to Nellie it was the cause that mattered. She supplemented her income by weaving poplin on a loom in her own home, a skill which had been brought to that area by her Huguenot ancestors.

Over her long years she built up an unrivalled knowledge of the many famous Abbey personages: Lady Gregory, Yeats, O'Casey and all the other talented actors and actresses. Old theatre-goers remembered her as a dignified figure courteously showing patrons to their seats or perhaps on occasion in earnest conversation with some of the critics, for she had a deep-rooted love and knowledge of the drama. She was also present when drama really came alive on the night of the "Playboy" riots in 1910 and she was pressed against an exit door by the crowd.

Nellie was an ardent nationalist associated with the many patriotic causes of the period. The 1916 Rising found her as a member of the Jacob's Garrison and engaged in the hazardous task of bringing dispatches to and from the G.P.O. and Marrowbone Lane.

Following the Rising, she came to reside at number 2 New Road, Inchicore, where she remained for the rest of her life. During the War of Independence, she was involved with intelligence work and at the same time her house at New Road was a constant haven for men on the run. It was during that period that Michael Collins attended a performance at the Abbey during which word was conveyed to Nellie that the Black and Tans were about to enter the theatre. She walked calmly down to where he was seated and whispered in his ear, following which he quietly accompanied her to a door at the rere of the stage and down a lane to safety.

Nellie Bushell died in August 1948 and was buried in Mount Jerome Cemetery with military honours.

The Flood Sisters

Portlester House was situated on a bend of the old Naas Road at Bluebell known as Flood's Corner from the name of the family who resided there. It was a substantial two storey slated house with six top windows and an iron railing to the front. Alongside was a small ten acre dairy holding which the family operated.

The name Flood is fairly common between Inchicore and Clondalkin, with several of that name being prominent in the public life of the area during the last century. Amongst these were Councillor Michael Flood of Stone House and Joseph Flood of Portlester House, a member of the board of Poor Law Guardians. It was the latter's three daughters Lily, Josey and Annie, well known figures coming down to the Oblate Church in their pony and trap who were to play an important role in the War of Independence.

The house was used for meetings and as a refuge for men on the run while guns and ammunition were hidden in the out-buildings. It is possible that the soldiers and their girls who were detained during the Kilmainham Jail escape were held in this house also.

The sisters took enormous risks, being on the side of the main road which was busy with constant military traffic. During the subsequent Civil War they helped the anti-Treaty side and until the house was demolished for road widening a bullet hole in the fanlight remained as a reminder of that time.

Other Participants

Amongst other participants were Kathleen and Angela Doyle of Ring Street, Bridie Dwyer (nee Nolan) of Turvey Avenue, Lena Byrne (nee Holohan) of South Terrace, Lucy Fleming and Myra Geoghegan, both of the "Ranch", and on the intelligence side Tilla O'Reilly (nee Cregan) of North Terrace. There were others still whose names are not available as of now.

Another enthusiastic nationalist was the draper Lizzie Mulhall who had a shop on Emmet Road directly opposite Richmond Barracks and who in defiance put a tricolour on the roof of her premises from time to time. In 1916 immediately after the Rising she had been arrested and held for several days in Richmond and it was said that she insisted on bringing her parrot with her!

Chapter Thirty-Nine

Guerilla Days (2)

Active Service Units

From January 1921 the struggle intensified both nationally and locally. Later Capt. Jim Donnelly wrote:

> "During the years 1920/21 it might be said that "F" Company was in complete control of the Naas Road from the 3rd Lock Bridge to the Red Cow and the country on either side. Picked men were out even by day sniping at enemy vehicles while at night the full company frequently went out on armed patrol. Some of the men were only armed with shotguns and weapons of different patterns, the best of our rifles having been sent to the south on the orders of Michael Collins."

An important development had been the formation of Active Service Units in Dublin composed of selected men who were available for full time duties and who were paid a weekly allowance. These units moved from area to area seeking to engage British forces whenever an opportunity presented itself. They operated both independently or in co-operation with local companies as the circumstances required. But even before this departure "F" Company had two or three men including Padraig O'Connor and George Dwyer who were on twenty-four hour call and these became part of the new unit.

Kilmainham Jail Escape

The main factor in the escape from Kilmainham Jail in February 1921 was the co-operation of several friendly soldiers who were on duty there. These men brought out a sketch of the cell blocks and then smuggled in a bolt cutter as well as a loaded revolver. At that time there were no warders in the jail which was totally under the control of the army.

At a secret meeting in Dolphin's Barn Oscar Traynor, O/C of the Dublin Brigade, gave details to local officers of the plan to rescue amongst others Frank Teeling who was under sentence of death arising out of the shooting of the British agents in November. He also explained the role they were expected to play which involved meeting the prisoners and escorting them to safety. They were also asked to provide a rope ladder in case there was any hitch with the bolt cutter.

It was not possible to set an exact date for the breakout with the result that the small outside party were in attendance near the jail morning and evening for a whole week without any results. These men stayed overnight at Floods of Portlester and Mary Theresa's 7th Lock Pub before walking down the railway line in the morning to avoid curfew. Two others who were road sweepers with Dublin Corporation arranged their rosters so that they could act as general lookouts in the vicinity of the jail.

Finally, word was received that Sunday 13th February was definitely the big night and a van was put in position near the Laundry on Inchicore Road to get the prisoners away. However, it was first necessary to detain three soldiers and their girl friends who were at the side of the jail as already mentioned by Mary Joe O'Connor and this was done with the assistance of the two Cumann na mBan members. They were initially held at Grattan Crescent and later moved out to Bluebell.

In the meantime the prisoners were attempting to cut the heavy bolt on the side gate but were unable to make any impression on it. At this stage an attempt by those outside to throw over the rope ladders also failed and the prisoners had no alternative but to return crestfallen to their cells. They did not give up hope however. A few days later Teeling, with the assistance of one of the soldiers, succeeded during the daytime in cutting the bolt which had been greased with margarine saved by the prisoners from their meals. They waited until that night to make their bid for freedom.

After dark the three men, Frank Teeling, Ernie O'Malley and Simon Donnelly crossed the yard and approached the heavy gate. Slowly one half of it swung open on its rusty hinges and they were outside without interruption. It had not been possible to send out word of the new circumstances so that they had to make their way themselves on foot along Inchicore Road. Ernie O'Malley later wrote:

> "Gas lamps beamed out of the blackness, front porches shone on to small evergreen shrubs in tiny gardens."

It was in one of these gardens that he hid the gun he was carrying. Then they proceeded up Tyrconnell Road miraculously not meeting any troops. At the 3rd Lock Bridge they walked down the far side of the canal until they reached Rialto from where they took a tram into town.

A Welshman belonging to the Royal Irish Fusiliers who was on duty at Kilmainham and who may have played some part in the episode later settled down in Inchicore having married a local girl. He had first met her when he used to call to her mother's house to collect the washing for his superior officer in Richmond Barracks.

The major role was played by two soldiers who were members of the Welsh Regiment and who following court-martial received eight years' penal servitude. An official inquiry found that there was grave negligence on the part of the officers in charge of the jail.

Railway Works Raided

Delivery had been taken at the Works on behalf of the British Army of a consignment of steel plating to be used in the protection of army lorries. When the company got wind of this they decided to destroy the material before it could be used. On the night of 6th March the whole company of about fifty men turned out and took over the entire Works. They were there from 10.00 p.m. until early the next morning. All the gates were secured and night staff were not allowed to leave. The plating was loaded on to two lorries and driven at 6.30 a.m. when curfew ended up to Ballyfermot. Some of the material was taken to Clondalkin and dumped. However the second lorry broke down at the 7th Lock Bridge and its contents had to be thrown into the canal. Consternation reigned next day not only amongst the military but also amongst the railway management.

Ambush Near 7th Lock

The most serious local incident of the whole period occurred on 30th March 1921 when a pedal cycle patrol of four armed R.I.C. policemen from Lucan station was ambushed on the road from Fox and Geese to Chapelizod. According to the Dublin Brigade Review they were induced to visit the area by the burning of cars and lorries by an active group of Inchicore juveniles. Fire was opened on the patrol on the Ballyfermot side of the 7th Lock Bridge and two of the R.I.C. were killed and one injured. At this stage an armoured car approached from the Naas Road, forcing the attackers to withdraw from the scene.

Morgan Frazer told me that he was in the Brass Shop when the Tans, later that day, came down through the fields and into the Works. They made him and others present show the soles of their boots to see if there was any grass on them. These were anxious moments as it so happened that there were several revolvers in the locker nearby awaiting repair but no search was made.

People were very frightened when houses in Bluebell and along the Naas Road were raided and threatened by the military but in the event nobody was arrested. A number of the juveniles mentioned were relatives of older activists and a few of them had received some arms training.

Long Mile Road Attack and Other Incidents

R.A.F. personnel from Baldonnell and Tallaght aerodromes going on local leave in the city had to be heavily escorted. When one of the escort vehicles protected by body armour and containing a complement of soldiers was returning to Baldonnell it was attacked on the Long Mile Road near the Half Way House some weeks after the 7th Lock ambush. Heavy fire and grenades were directed at the vehicle which almost turned over but the driver managed to right it again and, although wounded, kept on going. Two of the attackers were injured, one of them seriously, when a grenade bounced off the side of the vehicle and exploded on the road. Later that evening the Auxiliaries arrived and set fire to the Half Way House in reprisal. The blaze could be seen from the 3rd Lock Bridge.

The Dublin Brigade Review tells us that the Inchicore juveniles previously mentioned now pointed out a spot from which it would be possible to fire at Richmond Barracks. It was in fact a tree at the back of Inchicore Road. From here revolver fire was directed at army personnel inside the front gate as the morning guard was being changed at the various sentry posts. Casualties were claimed.

Many years later a local man, Desmond McNamara, was travelling across England by train when he got into conversation with another passenger who was very interested on hearing that he was from Inchicore. He went on to explain that he was a bugle boy at Richmond in 1921 when the above incident took place and said that he would have been killed or seriously injured were it not for the fact that one of the bullets ricocheted off the bugle he was carrying.

A small group entered the Railway Works and dismantled the phone and telegraph system while some days later several wagons carrying military stores were burned at Kingsbridge Station.

For some reason the Metropolitan Laundry on Inchicore Road was raided but the manager was able to raise the alarm and three men were arrested.

House to House Search

On a Sunday morning the British initiated a house to house search in the "Bungalow" area which they first surrounded with a cordon of troops. When residents of Railway Avenue awakened that morning they found soldiers sitting on the boundary wall at the rear of their houses. The entrance to Ring Street was blocked off and soldiers were also placed at the back of that street in the Oblate grounds. Many old residents remember that morning well and Mrs O'Connell recalls that the officers went from door to door with a list of names and had many of the houses searched. She also recalled all the men being asked to stand outside the front doors, some of them in their shirt sleeves.

Mick Byrne remembered the army lorries being parked on the green and the twenty or so men who were arrested being marched under escort down Tyrconnell Road to either Richmond Barracks or Kilmainham Jail. Many of these had been very active and were quite a loss to the Irish side.

Whether it was at this stage or at some other period of the conflict we do not know but according to another resident three youths were given "one-way" tickets out of the country because of loose talk.

Ambushes at Grattan Crescent and Red Cow

On 17th May 1921 a military lorry which had turned into Grattan Crescent from Emmet Road was attacked and one soldier was killed. The lorry kept going with the other soldiers returning the fire.

The well known Jim Nolan of the Pipers' Club in Thomas Street had reason to remember that Monday morning. He had just taken up his first job as a conductor with the Tower Bus Company (Inchicore/Clondalkin) and was standing beside his bus when he heard the shots ring out around the corner of the Black Lion.

Later that month an elaborate plan to attack army lorries coming down the Naas Road near the Red Cow went awry. The purpose of the attack was to capture rifles and ammunition. This was a combined operation between the A.S.U. and the local company and a larger number of men than usual was involved. It was intended to block the road with farm carts but due to a timing error the lorries swept past earlier than anticipated and only random shots were exchanged with them.

Anglo-Irish Truce

One of the last major incidents in the Dublin area took place in June when a train carrying soldiers was attacked at Ballyfermot Railway Bridge.

Secret negotiations between the Irish and British sides had been taking place for some time (the British having first set up the Northern statelet) resulting in a ceasefire with effect from mid-day on 11th July 1921. On that morning members of the local company were once more in the Railway Works, this time procuring coke for munitions purposes. They were still on the premises when word came through that a truce had been agreed.

Chapter Forty

The War of Recent Comrades

The Truce Period

Peace had returned for the time being and negotiations continued right through to January 1922 when the Anglo-Irish Treaty was accepted by a small majority of Dáil Éireann. The British commenced to withdraw on a gradual basis from the twenty-six counties and to hand over some of their barracks to the newly formed Irish Free State Army. Locally however they remained in occupation of Richmond and Islandbridge Barracks as well as the Royal Hospital and Kilmainham Jail. With regard to the latter they only kept a handful of soldiers there as it was now empty of prisoners from the previous December.

Civil War

Relations between the new Irish Provisional Government and those opposed to the Treaty gradually deteriorated, coming to a head with the occupation by the latter of the Four Courts on 13th April 1922. Amongst other buildings occupied on the same day was Kilmainham Jail, from which the small number of British soldiers there were ejected. One of the great tragedies of Irish history was about to unfold when all too often the high ideals of the 1916 Proclamation would be forgotten by both sides.

As might be expected, the local company was as deeply divided as their colleagues elsewhere. The group opposed to the Treaty continued to use the old designation of "F" Company, 4th Battalion, Irish Republican Army and as well as holding Kilmainham Jail under their Captain Jim Donnelly they maintained a presence at the brick works at Jamestown Road. It was there that Cecil Cregan (North Terrace) was killed in a shooting accident while on guard duty. We now had a situation in Inchicore where the British were still in Richmond and the Republicans in the two locations mentioned.

Others of the company who favoured the Treaty joined the Irish Free State Army and one of these, Pádraig O'Connor, later a colonel, played a very prominent role in the ensuing civil war. A third group did not take sides and discontinued their activities. Both of the rival parties were far better equipped than during the War of Independence as a large amount of armaments came into the country both officially and unofficially during the long truce period.

The forces of the Provisional Government attacked the Four Courts on 28th June 1922 and used several eighteen-pounder field guns which were provided by the British Army. On the night before, these guns were handed over under cover of darkness to a group of Irish Free State officers either in the grounds of the Royal Hospital or the Phoenix Park and drawn by lorries down to the quays. General fighting had now taken place in the city and the local Republican group decided to assist their colleagues there. They vacated Kilmainham Jail and, coming together for the last time at the Brickworks, boarded two lorries which they drove down Emmet Road, passing Richmond Barracks on the way. They joined the other anti-Treaty forces at the Stanley Street outpost.

The main fighting in Dublin ended on 5th July when the Free State side had gained the upper hand. Locally Sean Monks (Nash Street) of the Republican side was killed nearly opposite the Red Cow during an exchange of fire with Free State troops in June 1922 while in July a colleague, Patrick Hickey (South Terrace), died of gunshot wounds in Portlaoise Jail. Many other local Republican activists including Jim Donnelly were at this stage rounded up and either jailed or interned.

Kilmainham Jail was put into use once more and a large number of women prisoners were detained there.

The disillusionment felt by many at that time is reflected in the words of Mary Jo O'Connor towards the end of her memoir:

> "It seemed that the fine men who died that Ireland might be free had died in vain. I always say that our happiest times were during the Black and Tan terror for all that time we worked together for one cause."

The Railway Protection Repair and Maintenance Corps

Having been defeated in the city the Republican side, also known as the Irregulars, continued the fight on a mainly guerrilla basis. In the course of this campaign they attacked the railway system, particularly in the south where their support was strongest, with a view to hampering the movements of their Free State opponents. Very serious and costly damage was caused to trains, bridges, signal cabins and to the railway lines themselves. In order to counter this, the Provisional Government set up within their army "The Railway Protection Repair and Maintenance Corps" and a key unit of this new corps was based at Inchicore Railway Works. Here armoured cars were converted so that they could run on the railway tracks and engines and wagons were armour-plated as well. Also army lorries were provided with steel protection. Small armoured trains were used to provide cover, while repairs were being carried out and also to transport troops.

On two occasions action against the corps was carried out within the Works. In the first instance the cylinder of an engine was damaged, but a second incident was much more serious as an official account reported:

The Railway protection corps

"On the night of the 22nd December 1922 an engine with steam up was allowed to run off the Shed Yard at Inchicore right through one of the carriage stock gates, smashing into the armoured lorries therein, scattering them in all directions and putting a hand crane entirely out of action. The armoured motor lorries were badly wrecked and the company believes that the damage was malicious."

The corps continued in action until the end of the Civil War.

Tragic Events

Guerrilla tactics by the Republican side continued in the Dublin area and at Bluebell army lorries came under fire on several occasions.

In September 1922 a Fermanagh Republican, John Stephens, who had been abducted in the city, was shot dead early in the morning on the side of the road a short distance above the 3rd Lock Bridge. This was part of a pattern in which five men in all of the same persuasion were killed in similar circumstances on the Naas Road between Inchicore and Clondalkin. Nobody was brought to account for these road-side killings.

As the conflict became more bitter the Provisional Government issued an ultimatum in October that anyone found in illegal possession of arms would face the

Óglaigh na h-Éireann

VOLUNTEER RESERVE

Railway Protection, Repair and Maintenance Corps

I .... (name in full)

of .... (address in full)

in the County of .... hereby agree :—

1. To serve in the Volunteer Reserve (Railway Protection, Repair and Maintenance Corps) for a period of six months, or such longer period as the Army Council may determine in accordance with the provisions aud conditions hereinafter set forth.

2. In full discharge of my service to accept pay calculated in accordance with the rates specified in the Schedule hereto and the particulars given by me in my Enrolment Form.

3. To obey all orders of my Superior Officers.

4. To be subject to such code of discipline or regulations as to discipline applying to the Volunteer Reserve as may from time to time be in force.

5. Should I commit any breach of discipline, or any offence against such code of discipline, or such Regulations as to discipline applying to the Volunteer Reserve as may from time to time be in force, to accept and undergo such punishment as may, in accordance with such code or Regulations, be awarded me.

6. This agreement is subject to the following conditions and provisions:

   1. The Railway Protection, Repair and Maintenance Corps shall not be employed save for the purpose of protecting, repairing and maintaining the Railways within the area of the Irish Free State.

   2. The Railway Protection, Repair and Maintenance Corps shall not be disbanded until such time as the Army Council shall consider it advisable, having due regard to the safety of the members thereof.

(Signature of Recruit) ....

Date ....

death penalty, but offered an opportunity of surrendering weapons before that date. The first group to be executed under this policy were four young men from the inner city, James Fisher, Peter Cassidy, John Gaffney and Richard Twohig, who were shot in Kilmainham Jail on 17th November.

The next night, Saturday 18th November, Inchicore was shaken by a very loud explosion about 9.00 p.m. It was in fact a land mine which had accidentally exploded while being handled by some men in a field sloping down from the Naas Road to the Camac River, just beyond the canal bridge. Four men were killed and it was a miracle that the only two houses nearby, Magees in the little Camac glen and Warrens on the side of the Naas Road, were not destroyed. A woman who must have lived in the latter told of how she had noticed after eight o'clock about five or six men coming out of the field in answer to a whistle from the roadway where there were about three further men. The group coming out were all bunched together as if they were carrying something, but because of the darkness she could not see what it was.

> "I was gazing down the road, trying to make out the shadows of the men. Then suddenly as I stood at the door a terrible big flare of light burst up from the ground into the air with a red flame and spread out like a great fire. Almost at once there was a horrible noise like a sudden crash of thunder. I felt pains in my head and ears and I was bashed back against the door. I was half stunned, but managed to reel into the house."

Having been alerted, a priest from the House of Retreat rushed to the scene of carnage where he gave the Last Rites. In the meantime two lorry loads of soldiers, on their way back from Baldonnell, arrived about ten minutes after the explosion which they heard some distance away. It is surmised that they were the intended targets, presumably in reprisal for the executions of the day before.

The survivors had made good their escape and a number of rifles and ammunition were found in the ditch nearby. The four men who were killed were Bernard Curtis, Thomas Whelan, Patrick Egan and Thomas Maguire. Both Bernard Curtis and Thomas Whelan were engine cleaners at the Running Shed. The former lived at Canal Cottages, Bluebell, while the latter, a County Limerick man, was a boarder at number 1, St Mary's Terrace, The Ranch.

The Takeover

During all of these bloody events the British Army was still in occupation of Richmond and Islandbridge, but with their troops confined to barracks. However, by December the British government had decided that the Provisional government had obtained sufficient control of the new Irish Free State and that they could now complete their withdrawal. Both Richmond and Islandbridge were evacuated and handed over on 15th December 1922 to the Irish Free State Army and the Royal Hospital a few days later, although some of the pensioners were to remain on.

As the battalions of the Shropshire Light Infantry, the Welsh Regiment and the King's Own Regiment left Richmond Barracks, a detachment of the new army drawn up outside the Guard House presented arms. The British troops then wheeled right and followed by a number of well wishers marched down Emmet Road for the last time on their way to the North Wall.

The Civil War was not fully over and lingering hostilities were to continue for nearly another six months. Sniper fire was directed at Richmond Barracks, now renamed Keogh Barracks, in March 1923 and again on 25th May. On the second occasion rifle and revolver fire came from three points and one soldier was wounded.

The takeover of Richmond Barracks, 16th December 1922

The fire was answered and patrols were sent out, both from the barracks and the Railway Protection Corps at the Railway Works.

This was the last action of the Civil War in this district. On the day before, 24t May 1923, the Republican leadership, realising that they could not sustain the conflict any longer, called a "Ceasefire" and instructed their members to dump arms.

Kilmainham Jail was finally closed in 1924 when the last remaining prisoner there, Éamonn de Valera, who had been arrested after the Civil War ended, was transferred to Arbour Hill Prison.

The Post Civil War Period

Notwithstanding the ending of the Civil War, sporadic incidents of shootings, raids and robberies were to continue all over the country for nearly the next ten years. Locally Frank Warren of Holybrook House, the only house then between the 3rd Lock Bridge and Lamb's, had been fatally injured in February 1923 when he came upon intruders.

Members of the Anti-Treaty side in possession of Kilmainham Jail, May 1922

The last sign of English rule in the area came to an end in 1927 when the remaining pensioners at the Royal Hospital were transferred to Chelsea. The final Church of Ireland service at the hospital chapel was held on Sunday 23rd January 1927.

The twenty-two-year old Republican activist Timothy Coughlan from Ring Street was killed in a shooting affray in Terenure in 1928. The roof of the British Legion Hall at Granite Terrace was blown off on the eve of Armistice Day in November 1929. A man staying in the area was abducted and shot by the I.R.A. in Crumlin in 1931.

These were the last echoes of the Civil War. While the bitterness would last for many years, it is remarkable how quickly the democratic process had already begun to function. But then the public at large had not been enthusiastic about the Civil War or a resumption of hostilities against the British.

Chapter Forty-One

THEY SAW HISTORY IN THE MAKING

JOSEPH DOYLE, VINTNER

Joseph Doyle, proprietor of the licensed premises at 12 Inchicore Road, retired from business in 1964. The premises, along with other houses nearby, were all subsequently demolished to make way for the expansion of Rowntree's factory. He had been born here where he was to work all his life and had taken over on the death of his father. Being right opposite Kilmainham Jail, he had many memories of events there:

> "My first recollection of death in the Jail was the final hanging there in 1910, of Joseph Heffernan. He was executed for the murder of a girl and the affair was known as the "Mullingar Murder". I saw Heffernan getting out of the Black Maria with his hands in his pockets. He seemed completely unconcerned - as if he was lost in a dream.
>
> "In the weeks following the 1916 Rising, I was regularly wakened at 6.00 am by the volleys from the Jail.
>
> "During those times my family used to have constant visits from Father Eugene McCarthy of St James's Church, in which parish the Jail was then situated. Many a time I saw the unfortunate man heartbroken.
>
> "He used to come over to our place for breakfast after he had heard the last confessions and accompanied the condemned men to their executions. Breakfast is an exaggeration. All he was ever able to take was a cup of tea. But the worst state of distress I saw him in was the day he married Joseph Mary Plunkett to Grace Gifford; that was just prior to Plunkett's execution. The usual cup of tea was placed before Father McCarthy, but he was too choked with emotion to swallow it.
>
> "I also remembered some of the prisoners being marched from Richmond Barracks to the Jail and later others being marched through the grounds of the Royal Hospital on the first stage of their journey to English prisons.
>
> "During the War of Independence which followed, our premises were extensively used by Michael Collins's intelligence men to glean information from the British military who drank there. They used to pretend to be overjoyed at the sight of British uniforms and play up to them by criticising the Irish gangsters who had taken to arms. They used to create the impression that they could really let their hair down while basking in the protection of His

Majesty's forces. Soon they would all be great friends and the Irish lads would leave at closing time minus a few pounds but plus valuable information."

Finally Mr Doyle recalled the last of "those hectic years" when during the Civil War the Republican women prisoners were held in the Jail. Their women colleagues would stand outside the prison all day, shouting out words of encouragement to their friends inside. Then at night-time they set up beds outside the wall to show that they were giving their full support to their imprisoned friends.

MÁIRE NÍ CHEARÚILL, SAWMILL COTTAGE

"I was born in Inchicore and lived adjacent to Brassington's Sawmills. My father, who was a sawyer, worked there and was responsible in no small way for the buying of trees in the neighbouring counties. Some of these trees were transported by canal barge to their destination and were lifted by gantry onto the banks just below the Third Lock Bridge at the canal entrance. They were then taken down to the Mill on bogeys run on rails. I remember as a child often getting a jaunt on them. Trees were also brought in on horse-drawn drays through the front entrance on Tyrconnell Road opposite the Oblate Church, by men who were contracted for the job. My father worked on a horizontal saw, which cut planks of all sizes. I remember seeing him sharpening the saw with special files used for the purpose. Various other items were also cut – clog-soles which were paired together by a strip of leather tacked to the back of the heels, staves, bungs, bobbins, spiles, top-shives, which were used in the making of barrels by Messrs A. Guinness & Sons.

"Great devotion to Our Lady was apparent in the numbers coming to pray at the newly opened grotto. The Torchlight Processions held every year on 11 February will always live in my memory. I was very glad to embroider altar cloths for use on the Grotto altar. Inchicore was famous for the May Processions held every year in the Oblate grounds. People came from all parts to attend and walked around singing hymns, accompanied by the St James's Brass and Reed Band, which remained afterwards to entertain the people on the Square in front of the Church and everyone remained on until the recital was over.

"On Easter Monday 1916, our next-door neighbour asked my mother to let myself and sisters go for a walk. She brought us down the canal to Rialto Bridge, which to our surprise was manned by the British Army. We were ordered by a British Officer to go back immediately, as it was dangerous there, for fighting was going on in the South Dublin Union. We did not take long to obey him when we saw a stretcher being handed over the wall to the Bridge. On it was a wounded British soldier. On our way home bullets were whizzing through the trees on the canal. We were glad to get home safely.

"Another 1916 memory I have is when, on the occasion of the transfer of prisoners who took part in the Rebellion – some of whom belonged to Inchicore (Paddy Byrne, Ned O'Neill, Mick O'Neill and others) – to Richmond Barracks before being sent to England, my mother brought us down to Emmet Road to see the men being marched to the Barracks. We were near a spot known as "Murray's Lane" where there were women and children waving Union Jacks and jeering the prisoners as they passed by. These were people who had fathers, brothers and husbands serving in the British Army and naturally resented the marching men. I also remember my mother, when food was then scarce, going to look for flour and bread as far as Kilmainham, carrying a white pillow case to carry the goods."

Methodist Memories by Mrs Charlotte Brooks

"My family lived in number 8 Tyrconnell Road from 1914 to 1933, the first house on the road beside the Methodist Church. My father, Ernest Joynt, was chief draughtsman in the Inchicore Railway Works, where he had served his apprenticeship.

"Nearly everyone in Inchicore lived, moved and had their being by virtue of the Works. The great stone wall of the Works bounded our garden and the Works' horn summoned the community to work and sent them home again to their dinner and tea – carpenters, boilermen, cabinet-makers, gaffers, office-workers and draughtsmen – no shortage of skilled workmen in Inchicore. I had a row of wooden dolls which one of the cabinet-makers carved for me out of pieces of odd bits of wood and a box of oak bricks which my grandchildren play with now.

"I became aware of the politics of my native country very early. I cannot have been more than five years old. The dreaded Black and Tans were the preoccupying subject of conversation and although our parents did not intend to infect us with their anxiety, fear is catching and we felt the uneasiness in the house. At night the great lorries roared up Tyrconnell Road directing their blazing searchlights into our windows. We wondered whose house might be searched and feared it would be ours, because my father was an old Gaelic Leaguer and a writer in Irish and the house was full of Irish books – quite enough to have him carted off to Kilmainham and God alone knew what would happen to him there. My mother would hang an old photograph of Queen Victoria in the hall every night, but my father would take it down again. He was a quiet man and a firm Home Ruler, but he had his principles. Actually, our house was never searched because it was believed that, living next door to the Methodist Church, he would be the Methodist minister, and therefore loyal to the Crown. He was a Methodist certainly, but not a minister, and certainly not loyal to the Crown.

"Other childhood memories include: British Army tents pitched on the lawn of the Methodist Church – why I do not know; crying myself to sleep because our beloved maid (a native speaker of Scots Gaelic from Glencoe) got caught in the curfew in town on her day off.

"When I was seven years of age, the tram in which my mother and I were returning from town was held up at the old Richmond Barracks on Emmet Road to allow the British soldiers to march out and away forever, very smart and orderly, and the bedraggled-looking Irish Army to take their place. My mother, who had little love for the National Movement, drew my attention, with acid comments, to the difference between the two battalions, but my father, when we came home, told me that I had witnessed history. I did not know what he meant, but if I had, I would have realised that I had been witnessing history for most of my young life. However, I learned in a more immediate way what the departure of the British soldiers meant on the following Sunday at church service. The six back pews of the church had always been filled with an impressive body of these smart soldiers, but now their hearty bellowing of the hymns was greatly missed, and as Methodists are very much given to enthusiastic hymn-singing, their loss was sad indeed. I was inclined to think the change had been rather for the worse.

"As children we attended the Methodist National School next door. Previously as an infant I went to a dame school run by Miss Mai Connell who lived at Grattan Crescent. Miss Connell was also a music teacher for the children of the district, and a very nice woman she was too.

"The principal of the Inchicore Methodist School was a Miss Taylor, an Englishwoman, who was also the organist of the church. Her real genius lay in her ability to produce musicals for the annual church party called the Tea-meeting, which took place on the Monday following the Harvest Thanksgiving Service in the Church in October, for which the church was decorated with flowers, fruit and sheaves of wheat. For weeks before the Tea-meeting, afternoon school was devoted entirely to singing and rehearsals, which we all loved. "Nix" had to be kept for the arrival of an inspector. The tea on this great occasion was organised and largely paid for by the ladies of the congregation. Each of the long trestle tables was in the charge of one of the ladies and was spread with her best linen and lace cloths, her vases filled with flowers and plates of her home-made cakes and scones, although large bracks and fruit cakes were provided from central funds. After that all would help with clearing away and there would be a concert organised by Miss Isabel Joughin. (The Joughins were a family of Manx extraction who lived in number 12 Tyrconnell Road). The same musicians usually performed the same items every year, but that bothered nobody. The last item would be Miss Taylor's operetta. Then the men would clear up the schoolroom to be ready for school the next morning and mothers would hurry their excited children off to bed, leaving Miss Taylor to receive her well-earned congratulations.

"The Brays, Peates and Kirkhams were some of the prominent Methodist families. My father's first wife was a Miss Ethel Bray and Mr. Peate worked in the Clearing House in Kingsbridge. One of the Kirkhams built the Inchicore Cinema, as well as what was considered to be a very modern house in Grattan Crescent. His daughter was a friend of mine and we had free seats for the shows. There we saw all the films of the old silent cinema, now solemnly discussed by film enthusiasts and of course Charlie Chaplin was the favourite, although Tom Mix, Mary Pickford and Rudolph Valentino were the serious stars.

"The Methodist community in Inchicore was small, consisting of not more than fifteen families, as far as I can recall. They were simple people, but upright and humane and believed in living in charity with their neighbours, bound together by a sincere faith. As children, we were strictly brought up and we had few luxuries, but the security of this small community and its moral values had a lasting effect on my life."

William Booker, in an Interview (1994)

153 Inchicore Road (formerly number 8 Silverdale Terrace).

Born in Edinburgh in 1904, where his father was a cooper in Youngers, the family came to Dublin when the father got work in Guinness's Brewery. They took up residence on Saint Patrick's Day 1910 at the above address, where Billy has been residing ever since. His wife died some years ago. He has nothing but happy memories of all the old neighbours on this terrace, all of whom helped each other in times of difficulties and sickness. Neither was it necessary in those times to lock or bolt their doors.

He attended the Model School and as a youth commenced to work at the Metropolitan Laundry, Inchicore Road, only a short distance away and here he remained for fifty-four years. About 200 people, mostly women, were employed at the Laundry. The hours were long – 8.00 a.m. to 6.00 p.m. and up to 1.00 p.m. on Saturdays. As was customary at the time, there were no holidays except on Christmas Day and Bank Holidays. It took a general laundry strike in 1945 which lasted fifteen weeks to have the one week's annual leave granted in 1932 extended to two weeks.

In his young days he remembers seeing the old veterans with their red tunics, blue trousers and three-cornered hats in the grounds of the Royal Hospital. He also witnessed one of their funerals when their comrades hauled the carriage carrying the coffin with ropes, and then fired the customary three volleys at the graveside. Another frequent sight in those years was the route marches of the British soldiers through the district with their bands. By way of contrast, Billy and his family saw their near neighbours, the three Holland brothers, Frank, Bob and Dan, leaving with their guns and equipment on Easter Monday 1916 to take part in the Rising.

He remembers "Churchill House" on Inchicore Road being used during World War I as a convalescent home for injured officers and the horse-drawn ambulances arriving there. Billy also mentioned the tall brick "spite-wall" between "Beaconsfield" and "Churchill House" which arose out of a dispute between the two owners many years earlier. In his time "Beaconsfield" was owned by Captain Haycock, who was in charge of the horses in Guinness's Brewery. He wore a monocle and in his old age came out at night to talk to the birds in the trees. He also recollects the Inchicore Co-Operative Store which had a large shop on Inchicore Road and paid a dividend to its members at Christmas. It went out of business during World War I.

Billy worked at many and varied tasks, starting as yard man and looking after the horses. Also he worked the sluice gates at the Laundry Pond and mill race to control the flow of water as required. The laundry horses were brought to be shod at a long forgotten forge in Egan's Yard on Grattan Crescent near the Black Lion. Billy is now the only person in Inchicore to remember this forge.

Along here also at Grattan Crescent was Flood's (later Connell's) provision shop, O'Reilly's paper shop, Muddiman's shoe repairs, the Brush Yard and barber O'Connor's.

Billy also recalled another colourful character, "Granny" Tyrell, who lived across the road in Woodfield. She was an enthusiastic nationalist who on occasion would open her window and sing a few verses of the "Peeler and the Goat" as a couple of D.M.P. men were passing by. Funnily enough she herself kept a few goats in her back garden which she had to bring in and out through the front door.

Billy himself later progressed to delivery man. The Laundry had sixteen horses stabled alongside and half of these were used on alternate days. Collections and deliveries were made in a wide area of the city and even as far as the Curragh Camp, where they had a contract. For the latter run two horses had to be used with the van. They worked in all weathers with a tarpaulin sheet thrown up on bad days.

He remembered another incident in 1920 when fire was directed at Richmond Barracks. He brought me out to the back garden and showed me where the attackers had a view of the entrance to the Barracks between the gap in the houses on Emmet Road leading to Saint Pat's Football Ground. From here they fired at soldiers within the Barracks and then made good their escape. Following this a party of soldiers came in pursuit, crossing over the Camac and entering the houses on Silverdale Terrace by the back doors. One of these told him that a soldier had been shot dead.

Finally he remembers the Dynamo Room at the laundry, where up to the establishment of the E.S.B. electricity was generated from the waters of the Camac River as provided by the mill race. This supplemented the coal fire boilers and during the emergency years of World War II turf was also used in the latter. The electricity generated also provided a certain amount of lighting, but this was not so satisfactory in the summer months when the water level was low.

Notwithstanding the long hours and the inclemency of the weather Billy, a cheerful soul by nature, has very happy memories of his fifty-four years at the laundry.

Mr Billy Goggins – Tyrconnell Park

"I was born at Emmet Road in 1908 and our family lived at Ardmore Terrace within a few doors of the Emmet Hall where we often played as children. I still remember the small stage there on the ground floor and the then young children of Michael Mallin, the 1916 leader, and his wife, all of whom resided for a period over the Hall. From our back window we had a view of the "Barrack Field", that large expanse of ground attached to Richmond Barracks and on which the later Bulfin housing estate was built. Here we saw the soldiers playing their war games, some of them in trenches, which had been specially dug in the fields, before they went off to the real thing.

"Troops frequently paraded with their band past our door. I also remember as a child attending band performances on the main square in Richmond Barracks which were open to the public before the outbreak of World War I. Another memory is that of army supply wagons being drawn by mules.

"Across the road from us was the Richmond Cafe, owned by Mrs. Moses, which was patronised by the young soldiers. She in fact later opened a second cafe nearby.

"My only memory of the 1913 Lock Out is of "black-leg" trams being escorted by D.M.P. policemen.

Mr Goggins as a young boy beside Mr McDowell's motor car. The Garrison church (now Saint Michaels) in the background

"I do remember Murray's Lane opposite, many of whose residents were at the Front, being festooned with Union Jacks during the war.

"On Armistice night, the 11th November 1918, I heard the crash of glass when the windows of the Emmet Hall were smashed by soldiers.

"I was an altar server in Fr. Ryan's Church in Goldenbridge and from the gallery of this little church we could in 1916 see the prisoners in Richmond Barracks exercising behind the rolls of barbed wire.

"Two final memories, both concerning 1921: the first that of my mother and myself peeping out at night between the curtains at patrols of soldiers on both sides of Emmet Road enforcing the curfew. The other nearly had more serious consequences for me. As I passed Richmond Barracks one morning on my way to the Christian Brothers School in Goldenbridge, fire was directed at the Barracks from somewhere in the area of Richmond Park. I heard a shot and a bullet grazed my cheek. Apart from the fright, I was not injured and continued to school. I didn't even get a half-day out of it!"

Mrs Lily Mackin

Mrs Mackin of number 3 Madeleine Terrace, now 165 Emmet Road, remembered hearing the bugle calls twice a day in Richmond Barracks across the road – reveille at 6.30 a.m. and lights out at 10.00 p.m.

It was at this house that the well known writer and scholar Standish O'Grady used to stay for short periods over a number of years. He often commented on the pleasant sight of the swans at Egan's Pond which could be seen from the rear of the house.

Mrs Mackin in the evenings enjoyed the harmony singing of local young men sitting on the steps of the Emmet House. She also recalled the travelling "Hurdie-Gurdie" which put on shows at the ground at the back of the Workman's Club. One special occasion was the performance by a troupe of dwarfs who were accommodated by people along the terrace during the week of the show.

Chapter Forty-Two

Sagart Aroon

There is no doubt that among the older generation, the best remembered priest, indeed the best remembered person in the area, was Father Thomas W. O'Ryan, affectionately known to one and all in his day as "Da" Ryan. A priest of the Dublin Dioceses, he was born in Youghal and was in charge of the Church of Ease in Vincent Street, Goldenbridge, for twenty-eight years from 1896 to 1924. At that time Inchicore was part of the Parish of James's Street. He was also Chaplain to Goldenbridge Convent and lived in the red brick house beside the canal known as Saint Anne's which was provided by the Sisters of Mercy. This house is now used by the Oblate Fathers. The small Church of Ease, often referred to as "Father Ryan's" stood near the Convent gate beside the old C.B.S. school and right opposite the wall of Richmond Barracks.

Before going on for the Church, Father O'Ryan was a medical student for some years and he often put the knowledge he acquired then at the disposal of his flock. Widely travelled and a studious reader, he was a man of great general knowledge. He was a keen ornithologist and antiquarian and had acquired a wide collection of curios and books. However it was for his charity and concern for the poor and the sick in an era of much poverty and no social welfare that he is best remembered. He was known to give everything he had – even to the blankets off his bed – to the less fortunate. He was a total abstainer all his life and practiced a simple lifestyle. In addition he found time to become involved with the Mendicity Institute on the quays, one of Dublin's old charities.

He strongly believed in education for the youth, realising that without it they had no hope of improving their lot. As a result he was indefatigable in his pursuit of school mitchers, usually on his bicycle, and when he caught them, lost no time in depositing them in their respective schools. In fact, he acted as an unofficial school attendance officer and it is also in this role that the old residents have a keen recollection of him.

Prison Chaplain

What is not so well known about Father O'Ryan is that in addition to his many priestly duties he was also a chaplain at Kilmainham Jail. Here he was one of the priests who attended Joseph Heffernan, the last person to be hanged in the Jail. The Freeman's Journal of the 5th Jan 1910 gives the following report of that event:

> "Yesterday morning at 8 o'clock in Kilmainham Jail, Joseph Heffernan was executed for the murder of Miss Mary Walker, a telegraphist at the Mullingar Post Office.
>
> "The only persons present at the execution were the Governor of the Jail, Mr. Michael McGann, the High Sheriff of County Westmeath, Mr. Hyde, the Chaplain, Father O'Ryan of Goldenbridge, Father Flood of James's Street, the medical officer and the warders.
>
> "It appears that the man was very repentant and attended to the ministrations of the clergy with deep devotion. He was attended also each day by the Sisters of Charity, Basin Lane, who prayed fervently for him to the end. At 7 am yesterday morning he attended Mass in the Prison Chapel and received the last rites of the Church. At 5 minutes to 8 he was taken in charge by Pierpoint and his assistant and led to the place of execution. He was perfectly calm and delivered the responses to the Litany with much fervour.
>
> "The morning was very cold and foggy and a crowd of about three hundred people gathered in front of the Jail. A heavy mist shrouded the whole place while the solemn tolling of the prison bell conveyed to those who were near that all was over and gradually the people went away."

This experience had quite an effect on Father O'Ryan for obvious reasons, but also because he strongly believed that Heffernan was of unsound mind and should not have been put to death. Some years ago Mrs Nano O'Reilly of Emmet Road told me that she remembered being a schoolgirl in Goldenbridge Convent at the time and how Father O'Ryan used to call in frequently to ask them to pray for the condemned man.

The 1916 Rising and Countess Markievicz

Father O'Ryan was a nationally minded man and had been present, as mentioned earlier, at the formation of the Irish Volunteers in Inchicore in 1914.

Following the 1916 Rising when all the prisoners and other detainees were brought to Richmond Barracks, he was able to obtain entry to look after their spiritual needs. During these weeks crowds gathered on Emmet Road outside the Barracks to make enquiries regarding the whereabouts of relatives and friends and indeed to ascertain if they were dead or alive. Fr O'Ryan did what he could to assist these people whenever he came out from the Barracks.

At this time also Father O'Ryan found himself back again at Kilmainham Jail as a Chaplain. Here he met some of the prisoners, notably Countess Markievicz, who was expecting the death penalty following her court martial. She declared her intention of becoming a Catholic and asked him to be with her at the end. In the event, she was sentenced to death but reprieved. "The court recommends the prisoner to mercy solely and only on account of her sex."

When she died eleven years later in 1927 her funeral, which was of enormous proportions, was not without its drama, as the approaches to Glasnevin Cemetery were surrounded by armed soldiers of the Irish Free State Army in order to prevent volleys being fired. Tensions were understandably high on the Government side as the Minister for Justice, Mr Kevin O'Higgins, had been assassinated only a few days previously. Following the saying of the De Profundis by a Franciscan priest, Father O'Ryan was on hand to recite the prayers in Irish. He may or may not have still agreed with her politics, for the Civil War had brought much divided opinions, but he subsequently told Mrs Hannah Sheehy-Skeffington that he was there to fulfill his promise to the Countess to be with her at the end.

"Da" Ryan left Goldenbridge in December 1924 when he was appointed Parish Priest of the rural parish of Rolestown in North County Dublin. On his leaving, a representative committee was formed which presented him with a motor car. It was felt that this would be of use to him in a country parish and also that if he received a money present he would give it away.

Father O'Ryan's long ministry in Inchicore was an eventful one, coinciding with many of the great episodes which shaped our modern history and to which he was so close. These also included the great strikes and there is a story told that during the fitters' strike of 1902 he saved a black-leg from being strung up on a lamp-post at Woodfield. Finally he was here for the transfer of power from English to Irish hands and for the tragedies of the Civil War.

In 1931 Father O'Ryan came back to the city as Parish Priest of Saint Audeon's, High Street, where he died in 1943.

Chapter Forty-Three

Ernest Joynt – Locomotive Draughtsman and Gaelic Scholar

Ernest Joynt, chief draughtsman at the Railway Works, resided at number 8 Tyrconnell Road and was one of the most interesting and intellectual people who ever lived in the area. This chapter is based on a summary of some of his journal and railway recollections which his daughter Mrs Brooks kindly placed at my disposal a good number of years ago. She herself as we have already seen provided her own valuable recollections of the area as well.

Mr Joynt, who was born in Ballina in the Methodist faith, came to Inchicore at eighteen years of age in 1892 to serve a pupilship in mechanical engineering. He recalled that the horse trams were still on the road providing a good service. The cars on the different routes bore distinctively coloured panels and lights at night. "The horses had bells on their collars and the tinkle tinkle as they trotted along was rather pleasant to hear." The canal with its locks, culverts and barges he found to be full of interest and he noted that a short walk across the bridge brought one into the open countryside.

He attended Kevin Street Tech. three nights a week and walked in and out not finding that the long day from 6.30 a.m. to 9.30 p.m. did him any harm. Having completed his apprenticeship he was appointed as an assistant in the Loco Department. Shortly after this in 1896 he accompanied his father on a month's tour of the northern capitals of Europe and was present in Moscow for the coronation of Czar Nicholas II.

He was not long at the Railway Works when a charge hand in the Brass Finishing Department was pointed out to him as one of the Crown witnesses in the Phoenix Park murder trials of 1882. He went on to say that this man had been under police protection for some years but eventually the hostility to his person faded. Likewise he was told that the man's fellow employee who was with him in the Phoenix Park had "fled to America precipitately".

Ernest Joynt showed a remarkable affection for the Irish language and the people of the Gaeltacht. Although not of the majority religion he was much influenced as a young boy by the scenes of poverty, the wholesale emigration and the tyranny of the landlords which he witnessed in his native county. In 1896 he was invited by a member of the clerical staff at the Works, Mr James Casey (Séamus Ó Cathasaigh), who was also honorary secretary of the infant Gaelic League, to join that organisation. He did so and attended the classes of the Central Branch (later the Árd Craobh) in Sackville Place. He was soon to achieve a tremendous fluency and accuracy in Irish and went on to become a writer in that language under the pen-name "An Buachaillín Buidhe."

A great traveller, he toured much of Europe, particularly Brittany where he became a firm friend of the Breton nationalist writer Louise Le Rou. "I developed a European outlook which soon led to a distaste for the narrow British nationalism which formed so much a part of my early education."

On the Road

As part of his apprenticeship and before entering the Drawing Office the young Ernest had to spend several years obtaining practical experience in the various departments such as the pattern shop, the foundry, the running shed and even on the footplate out on the road.

> "The old engine shed at Inchicore was the most remarkable looking building in the premises. It was built of stone with buttresses and ornamental stonework and had a crenellated parapet and handsome turret. There was nothing in its appearance as viewed from a passing train to suggest that behind its ivy-clad wall locomotives were housed and grease-stained men were busy. It was a credit not only to the founders of the railway but also to the aesthetic taste of the architects and builders of the period.
>
> "For some months during the summer of 1894 this was my working headquarters and where much was to be learnt in connection with the firing, driving and general running of locomotives. The foreman was an Italian named Mr. Pizani who spoke with a continental accent. He was very clever, devoted to scientific hobbies and a wonderful photographer.
>
> "The principal trains were the day mails and expresses between Dublin and Queenstown (Cobh) and people at the country stations set their timepieces by these trains. The largest engines, those of the "60" class, were employed on these services and the most experienced men were put in charge. These were the famous "mailmen", the crack engine drivers of the last decade of the 19th century.
>
> "I did most of my "firing", that is shovelling the coal into the firebox, on the night goods trains.
>
> "There was the sleeping countryside; the dark and deserted stations; the long train of wagons moving like a huge snake round the curves; the glare of the fire periodically lighting up the clouds of steam from the chimney; the shunting at the stopping stations directed by a single man with a lamp; the other trains passing in the dark; the dawning of the early summer morning."

The Foundry

"I started work in the foundry in the middle of autumn and remained there during an exceptionally cold winter until the new year. The atmosphere was dense with smoke and reeking with pungent gases. Twinkling flames came from every moulding box and from castings in the sand on the floor. Portions of hot solidifying metal lay all over the place. Boys with skimming irons, shading their faces from the livid glare and burning heat, were busy at each crucible as the metal was poured into the moulds.

"Foundry work was certainly laborious and physically exhausting, more so in some respects than in other trades. The shop at that time had the reputation of being the hardest worked in Dublin. The foundry men at Inchicore did not earn their money easily."

The Drawing Office

Following his two years of practical experience he then joined the Drawing Office as a draughtsman. Here over the years he was involved not only in the designing of locomotives but also coaches of all kinds together with wagons, cranes and gas plants. The work also entailed travelling to England to visit the great railway establishments at Crewe, Derby and Swindon. Finally he was appointed chief draughtsman in 1908. He has left an account of the high point of the Inchicore Works, from 1896 to 1914:

> "During this period it enjoyed an unprecedented era of prosperity and progress. Successive types of locomotives were designed and built to cope with the ever growing demands of the traffic. Wagons of all types and sizes were turned out in their hundreds.
>
> "The absorption of the small railways in the south and south east also caused a great increase in the amount of work to be done at Inchicore. The size of the boiler shop was doubled and a new power house was completed for the electrification of the works. The former wagon shop was converted into a running shed large enough to house all the locomotives operating from Inchicore. The period of Mr. Coey's and Mr. Maunsell's tenure of office is looked back upon as the busiest and brightest in the history of the works."

He also tells us that it was at that time that the hooter was installed in place of the works bell. One wonders how the latter could be heard above the din of the workshops.

The Great War

With war looming in 1914 the Drawing Office was instructed to design a complete ambulance train. This they did and when hostilities commenced in August of that year it was possible to assemble it within a very short time. "Subsequently it transported many a load of maimed and shattered humanity from the southern seaports to the hospitals in Dublin and other Irish towns."

During the war there was a fairly continuous building programme of coaches and wagons but the works were also engaged in the turning out of military equipment of one kind or another. Amongst these was a large number of army service carts, but it was mainly shell fuses which were extensively manufactured. For most of those years there was a military presence to a lesser or greater degree at the works.

Inevitably the war years and the Irish struggle which followed had an adverse effect on the railways. There was also a change of management which he maintained had broken with the traditions of the past when the works had flourished and prospered. Furthermore he found the prevalent tone of the administration of the G.S. & W. Railways to be extremely West British and that length of service, efficiency and fidelity scarcely counted as qualifications for promotion. This reminds me that the well known athlete and physio Paddy Ryan who lived well into his nineties and spent all his life as a fitter in the Works told me that up to World War I a number of the managers used to retire for a celebration each year on the eve of 12th July. That other great old timer Barney Farrell also remembered the last gaffer to wear an orange lily.

Ernest Joynt became discouraged and left the railway in 1919 after twenty-seven years' service to take up a position with Bolton Street Technical School where he later became principal. He had been chief draughtsman for the last eleven years of his career at Inchicore and said that he looked back with pride on the fine Irish locomotives and coaches for the design of which he was responsible. It is clear from reading through his papers that not only was he a scholar but a gentleman as well.

Denis MacNamara – Man of Genius

One of Ernest Joynt's friends was Denis MacNamara who also worked in the Drawing Office.

> "His character was attractive by virtue of its simplicity and goodness. He was an extraordinarily clever man, an inventive and painstaking genius and a great amateur of the sciences. He was a pioneer experimenter in photography, phonography and wireless telegraphy. Before the Great War he used to set the time office clocks by the Eiffel Tower time signals. He made the model locomotive which stands in the hall of the Institute of Mechanical

Special train conveying delegates from Cobh to Dublin for international conference of loco engineers 1926

Engineers in Westminster and a model dining car which was featured in the Paris Exhibition.

"His talents and knowledge were freely made use of by the Railway Company but very badly rewarded. Dinny had travelled far in Europe – to Rome, Milan, Paris, Brussels and Lourdes. I myself had two holidays with him on the Continent and a brighter or more interesting travelling companion it would be difficult to find. Had his lot been cast in a country different to ours he would have achieved great worldly success."

Across a Century, the Oblate centenary number, supplies us with the additional information that he invented a phonograph or talking machine about 1900, the rights of which he sold to Edison, the famous American inventor. We can see as well from an old programme that he took part in the fund-raising fetes where he put on a telescope/astronomy exhibition. Also longtime railway employee Tom Tighe, formerly of South Terrace, and a distinguished model maker in his own right, tells me that Denis MacNamara originally lived on Abercorn Terrace and that on the outbreak of World War I British military personnel called to his house and took away his wireless receiving apparatus.

This gifted man then living at 64 Tyrconnell Road died on 31st December 1926 and was buried in his native Cappamore, County Limerick.

Chapter Forty-Four

The First Years of Self-Government

Apart from the political uncertainty the new state got off to a very shaky start, given the poor state of the economy, high unemployment and a world depression to follow.

Within two years of its take-over from the British, Keogh Barracks was found to be surplus to the Irish army's needs and was closed in 1924, with consequent loss to local business. However before the end of the decade Inchicore had benefited from two major housing developments which brought about a substantial increase in the population. In order to alleviate somewhat the dreadful housing conditions in the city, the new government decided in 1925 to convert the disused barracks into working class flats. This task was completed rapidly, providing much needed employment in the process and within a year the old army blocks were filled with hundreds of families, mainly from the inner city. In addition a number of small one-storey dwellings were built within the barrack boundaries and also two or three buildings were converted into shops. The whole complex was renamed Keogh Square, but the new residents were soon to be known to the locals as the "Barrackers".

Although the three-roomed flats might be viewed as somewhat spartan by today's standards, they were luxury compared to the overcrowded city slums (which were amongst the worst in Europe) and many great families were reared there.

When the new residents had settled in they were eventually able to produce two football teams, Emmet Rangers and Emmet United, some of whom contributed players to the early Saint Pat's. They also, in the 1930s, threw up their own community leader in the person of Tom Trundle. While mostly unemployed Tom made use of his time to help his fellow tenants who in the main were also out of work and he was sometimes called the Lord Mayor of Keogh Square. He canvassed the business people and Dublin Corporation for funds to bring the families on excursions to the sea-side and the kids to the matinees in the "Core", where they also got bags of sweets. Occasionally they were brought into town to Bewleys.

In those years also John Fortune, the well remembered resident manager of the Emmet House, organised regular visits for the children of the Goldenbridge Orphanage to that same cinema where the owner, Mr Kirkham, made the balcony available to them.

Tom Trundle was also an able man with the pen, as a former resident Willie Hillick, remarked. He remembers him wearing a long coat and with a somewhat professional air about him. Willie said that Tom was often called upon to negotiate with the Corporation regarding rent arrears and other such disputes and when required would write the necessary letters.

Another former resident, Mrs Brophy, remembered Tom as being the heart and soul of all the social activities in the barracks. She has a special memory of one New Year's Eve when he organised a party on the bandstand in the middle of the square with singing and dancing, and when some of the youths made their way up to the clock-tower above the archway and rang the old bell which was there from British times to welcome in the New Year.

The second major development occurred in 1929, when Dublin Corporation built the extensive Bulfin Housing Estate on the former fourteen-acre Barrack Field. This was one of the earliest tenant purchase schemes in Dublin and helped also to bring a new dynamism to the area.

Churches, Schools and a Curate's Memories

To cater for the influx of new residents, the garrison church of Richmond Barracks was bought by the Catholic authorities and the small Chapel of Ease in Vincent Street was taken over by Golden Bridge Convent as an infants' school. The larger church now dedicated to Saint Michael was opened and blessed by Archbishop Byrne on Sunday 25th April 1926. The first pastor there was Father Eugene Traynor, who had served as a chaplain in the British Army. The whole area was still part of the Parish of Saint James, but in 1933 was constituted as the separate Parish of Saint Michael. The first parish priest was Father (later Canon) James Doyle and the first assistant priest was Father John O'Sullivan. The latter has left a valuable account of his experiences in various Dublin parishes including Saint Michael's, of which the following is a résumé:

> "In December 1933 I was transferred to St Michael's Parish which had a population then of about 17,000 and later around 21,000. Down the centre of the Parish was the tramline carrying the well-known number 21 tram, which brought many visitors to the Lourdes Grotto and at Christmas time to the Oblate Crib.
>
> "My house was a small stone-built one near the church, primitive and lacking many amenities. In the former military days this house was that of the Sergeant Farrier and two of the anvils were still in an outhouse.
>
> "When the third priest was appointed, the parish priest succeeded in buying a larger house on Emmet Road, to which I transferred and shared with the newcomer, Father "Flash" Kavanagh.
>
> "St Michael's was a busy parish. There were also calls to accidents in the Railway Works and on the Line. Furthermore the growing volume of motor

traffic from the country entering the busy city caused another problem. The traffic was developing faster than people's awareness and there were many accidents. But there is one feature of the many calls that I vividly remember. It was the very large number of young people having haemorrhages because of TB, which was then rampant. What sad and unforgettable sights they were! Thank God that scourge was dealt with effectively in later years.

"For some reasons I do not know I seemed to have received more converts into the Church in those years in Inchicore than anywhere else.

"St Michael's Church was still not big enough and had to be enlarged in 1934. A welcome visitor on the day that the extended church was blessed was Father "Da" Ryan, former pastor of Golden Bridge. Such was his popularity that when he was about to be transferred, the people at first contemplated blocking the roads".

Here we might mention that the church was further enhanced in the 1940s by the installation of some magnificent stained glass windows from the Harry Clarke studios.

It should be pointed out also that this first parish of Saint Michael covered the whole area from South Circular Road to the 3rd Lock Bridge, although strangely the south side of Jamestown Road was still left in the Parish of Clondalkin.

The Christian Brothers' School in Vincent Street proved to be too small also and they acquired a considerable site within the old barracks which included two of the one storey recreational blocks, the historic gymnasium and a sportsfield. The first classes commenced on 15th February 1929.

At that time also Dublin Corporation acquired a small building which was formerly the band room and opened it as "St Brigid's Child Welfare Centre". This soon became known locally as the "Baby Club" and was of great benefit to the young children of the area.

The "Core"

It was during the Anglo-Irish Truce period that the Inchicore Cinema – to be henceforth popularly known as the "Core" – opened for the first time on 25th November 1921 at 7.00 p.m. The main film was "The Breed of the Treshams" starring Martin Harvey and the supporting programme consisted of the first Dublin run of the "Great Haig Serial".

The promoter of this venture was "Daddy" Kirkham, an early pioneer of Dublin cinemas who lived on Tyrconnell Road. These were the days of the silent screen and occasionally a local singer contributed from the wings where appropriate during the showing and a pianist always played at the interval. From time to time a variety show or a local talent competition was included in the programme but this came to an end with the advent of the talkies in 1929.

Tyrconnell Road with Inchicore Cinema and Doctor O'Sullivan's car on right, about 1932

Some early films of the silent screen shown at this cinema were *In Old Arizona, Doctor Fu Man Chu* and *In a Monastery Garden.*

With the coming of television the "Core", like so many other suburban cinemas, came to the end of its run and no more would queues of patrons be seen on Tyrconnell Road patiently awaiting their turn, sometimes on wet and windy nights.

KILMAINHAM POLICE BARRACKS

The original two storey Kilmainham Police Barracks at the bottom of Emmet Road which dates from at least 1850 was under the control of the old Dublin Metropolitan Police, an unarmed body whose jurisdiction extended out as far as the 3rd Lock Bridge where the armed Royal Irish Constabulary took over. In 1922 the barracks came under the control of the newly established Garda Síochána and a few years later its strength was shown as one inspector, three station sergeants, four sergeants and thirty gardaí, with fifteen of the latter living in the barracks.

The building however was not in good condition as this report of 1926 shows:

> "The barracks is very old and badly situated. There is very poor accommodation for the gardai living there and the space does not permit of a recreation room or a sergeants' mess-room. The ground at the back is almost on a level with the roof of the barracks which prevents the sun from shining on the rooms until the afternoon."

Keogh Square in 1967

Keogh Square

It was strongly advocated that a new police barracks should be established instead in Keogh Square, specifically in some of the buildings which later were acquired by the Christian Brothers as a school, but this proposal was turned down.

Nine years later in the course of a report to headquarters dated 23rd October 1935 the superintendent for the area wrote:

> "I have again carefully considered the defects which render Kilmainham Station entirely unsuitable as a structure both for the housing of men and for the carrying out of ordinary Police administration.
>
> "In my opinion the primary consideration should be in respect of the health and comfort of the men who reside in Barracks, and the existing accommodation allows them only a place in which to eat and sleep. They have no recreation room or place for active physical exertion and there is no inducement for single men to remain in Barracks when off duty. Again, owing to the construction and situation of the building the ventilation, especially in the bed rooms, is poor and is scarcely adequate to maintain the high standard of health required for police work.
>
> "The Station office is so small and the ceiling so low that a strain is imposed on Station Sergeants who must perform their tour of eight hours in what must be a vitiated atmosphere.
>
> "There is also another handicap in that there is no proper ground on which to hold a parade and on my monthly inspections there is no opportunity for drilling the men properly."

It was finally decided to establish a new barracks or a station as it was now being called at Kilmainham Lane on part of the grounds of the Royal Hospital. Here was located several buildings which were formerly used as coach-houses for the Master of the Royal Hospital. These included five big coach-houses as well as two large stables with stalls for four horses in each and with lofts overhead. All of these were renovated and reconstructed and although the work was not by any means completed the gardaí moved there from the old barracks in March 1938. By now the number of men living in the premises was down to seven and eventually this practice would cease altogether.

Their days of hardship were not over however, due to dampness and inadequate heating and even difficulty at times in drying wet clothes. It was to be years before these matters were put right but in that era it could certainly be said that "a policeman's lot was not a happy one."

Railway Amalgamation

Due to the difficulties brought about by World War I, the War of Independence and particularly the Civil War, the railways were now in a very run-down state. They suffered also from a loss of business due to increasing road competition and workers had to accept cuts in their wages. Morale was so low that the G.S. & W.R. contemplated closing down. However the government did not wish this to happen and in 1925 they amalgamated all the railway companies within the Irish Free State into one company to be known as the G.S.R. This involved transferring a considerable portion of the mechanical operations of the Midland Great Western Railway Company from Broadstone to Inchicore and to provide for this the large erecting shop behind Railway Avenue was built.

Saint Patrick's Athletic

One of the first soccer teams in Inchicore which was for boys under eighteen years of age was known as Saint Patrick's and dated back to 1898. It was drawn from young apprentices in the Railway Works and organised by the late Dick Neville, also an apprentice at that time, and who went on to spend a lifetime in football administration. A later junior team also known as Saint Patrick's which emerged in 1919 was mostly composed of players from the Ranch and they played in the grounds of Inchicore House nearby.

The present Saint Patrick's Athletic was formed as a junior side in 1929 and amongst the founders were Paddy Morgan, Paddy Dunphy and Martin Dunne. The new team played in several local grounds including Flood's field in Bluebell but commenced their association with Richmond Park, then owned by the McDowell family, in the early1930s. Richmond Park as earlier mentioned was the ground where the old G.A.A. Saint Patrick's team played in the last century.

Saint Pat's won their first major victory when they took the junior F.A.I. cup in 1940/'41. Then after years of trying to gain membership of the League of Ireland they were finally admitted in 1951/'52. They were in fact to take the League by storm in winning the title in that very first season, something which they repeated in 1954 and 1955. The F.A.I. Cup came their way in 1959 and 1961 and the League again in 1990.

The Saints were in exile on several occasions in places such as Chapelizod, Glenmalure Park and Harold's Cross, but always retained the loyalty of the fans. In December 1993 they returned to their true home at Richmond Park which by then had been very much upgraded and this was followed by their becoming League of Ireland Champions once more in 1996 and now again in 1998 and 1999.

Other old teams in the area were Inchicore United, based in the Bungalow, and then later on, Bulfin United.

E.S.B. Transformer Station

A major achievement of that first Irish government was the establishment of the Shannon hydro-electric scheme in 1929. Shortly after this a site for the Dublin transformer station was selected on part of the grounds of Jamestown House which was known as Kane's Field. This family were the last occupants of that very large house which was one of the oldest in the district and had some years previously been destroyed by fire.

German technicians were involved in the construction of this station and were accommodated locally while the work was in progress.

Chapter Forty-Five

Oblate Developments

Father M. Sweeney O.M.I.

Father Michael Sweeney O.M.I., who was described as a man who thought big and acted accordingly had taken over as Superior in 1925. He brought about the final completion of the Church of the Immaculate Conception with the erection of the twin spires and the addition of the two transepts. He followed this up with a more ambitious project still when he set in train the building of a replica of the Lourdes Grotto in the church grounds. As in the case of the old wooden church, this grotto was built by the voluntary labour of local men. Hundreds of these volunteers worked for several years under the direction of "Clerk of Works" Brother McIntyre O.M.I., who had travelled to Lourdes to study the formation of the Massabieille Rock. The task of digging for the foundations which had to be eleven feet deep to bear the heavy structure was very laborious indeed. Some of the bricks from the discarded brick works at Jamestown Road were used in these foundations.

When completed the "Irish Lourdes" was solemnly blessed and opened on Sunday 11th May 1930 before a massive crowd estimated at between 80,000 and 100,000 who came from all parts of the city. The whole district was decorated for the occasion with arches of flowers spanning the streets and flags fluttering from many windows. The newspapers reported that all the roads leading to Inchicore were for a solid two hours black with people despite a downpour of rain. A massed choir of 1,000 children sang the Lourdes hymns. The ceremony was preceded by a procession of 5,000 members of all the city confraternities in their colourful regalia and "even the rain could not dim the brilliance of the scene".

It was Father Sweeney who on taking up office declared publicly that it was time to take the crucifixes and religious emblems out of the school presses and he arranged to have them permanently displayed in the classrooms from then on.

The next Superior Father Daniel Collier O.M.I., well known Gaelic scholar, gifted preacher and amateur film maker was responsible for further major developments. These included the building in 1936 of the large and imposing Scoil Mhuire Gan Smál, together with the spacious community hall "Áras Mhuire". The latter necessitated the demolition of the old church building which had housed the crib. The crib itself was then transferred to the now almost forgotten "Leo Hall." This was a single storey annexe attached to the House of Retreat which for the previous fifty or sixty years had been used for social functions such as concerts, plays and

Army participation in ceremonies at the Inchicore grotto

Railway workers marching to Mass during the Holy Year, 1950

meetings. It was destroyed in the disastrous crib fire of 1948. The new Áras Mhuire would become the ballroom of romance for the area for many years to come.

Father Collier's film shows for children with a tea party afterwards are remembered by many who were young in those more innocent times.

Fund Raising Fêtes and Carnivals

It could be said that right from the beginning the Oblate Fathers were of necessity involved in continuous fund raising. There was never a lack of voluntary workers and the local business community were very much involved as well. The fêtes held in the grounds in the 1920s and 1930s were very ambitious indeed. The fête of 1923 shortly after the ending of the Civil War lasted a whole week with a tremendous variety of stalls and a different band performance every evening.

The annual inter-shop football tournament organised by the railway workers were held on summer evenings in the 1940s at their sports ground in "The Pond Field" in aid of the foreign missions. The Blue Bell Fife & Drum Band always paraded down on the final night when the trophies were presented.

The fund raisers in the new parish of Saint Michael's were no slouches either and their speciality in the 1930s and 1940s were the monster carnivals at Cassell's field and Richmond Park. Mr William Toft, the well known amusement proprietor who had come to live in Goldenbridge, provided top line performers. The best remembered of these were the daring German couple who circled on a wheel at the top of 100-foot pole, and of course the "Wall of Death."

Chapter Forty-Six

1930–1950

Change of Government

The first change of government took place in 1932 when Mr Éamonn de Valera came to power. One of the public representatives for the area, the young Seán Lemass, was appointed as Minister for Industry and Commerce and was to take a lively interest in the future of the railways. He relaunched the Irish Sugar Company, which brought more business to the G.S.R. as the sugar beet was transported by rail. In turn this resulted in a wagon building programme at the Inchicore Railway Works which gave a great boost to employment there. Bus and lorry building was also undertaken. This period of renewal at the Works culminated in the building of the last great steam locomotives, "Maedhbh", "Macha" and "Tailte".

During the election campaign of 1937 Mr Lemass was met by his supporters at the 3rd Lock Bridge following his arrival at Baldonnell Aerodrome from Geneva. They then marched in a large procession to Saint Catherine's Church in Thomas Street, where a meeting was held. There was also that famous occasion when he was addressing a public meeting at the corner of Vincent Street and an over-excited chairman introduced him as Mr Molass – much to the merriment of the crowd.

At the end of World War II Seán Lemass, hoping to promote heavy industry, had a chassis factory built at the top of Jamestown Road. Unfortunately an incoming government did not proceed with this venture and the premises were given to the Board of Works as a maintenance depot.

From Small Beginnings

The Roche family came to Inchicore in the early thirties and established a bakery and confectionery on Tyrconnell Road where today a similar type shop, "The Bread Bin" is in business. In the very old days this had been a butchers' stall. In 1932 they bought from M. Kirkham a small coal and concrete block business across the road at McCann's Yard officially known as Saint James's Place. Included in the sale was a Model T Ford truck, a hand block machine and a tiny office.

They concentrated on the sand and gravel haulage business and it was from these small beginnings that the young and hard working Roche brothers, Tom and Donal, with other associates were later able to form the Castle Sand Company. This was the forerunner of Roadstone in 1949 when they left McCann's Yard and moved to a five acre site in Bluebell where they built a new depot and workshops. In 1970 Roadstone merged with Cement Limited to form the giant Cement Roadstone Holdings.

It was in 1934 also that the next major housing development in the area took place with the building of the Tyrconnell Park scheme by the Dublin Utility Society. As the entrance from Tyrconnell Road was by means only of a narrow passageway between the houses on that road, number 46 (Pikes) had to be demolished.

Far Foreign Fields

The short-lived Blue Shirt Movement had a local representation of both men and women in 1934. At the other extreme, some young men were attracted to left-wing politics and a group of these fought in the Spanish Civil War (1935-37) as members of the International Brigade. Amongst these were Joe Monks, Paddy McElroy, Bill Scott Jnr, Liam McGregor, Michael May and Tony Fox. The last three lost their lives in that conflict while one of the survivors, the late Joe Monks, has recorded his experiences in a booklet entitled *Along the Ebro.*

Meanwhile back home, Irish ex-servicemen who had fought in World War I continued their annual Armistice Day commemoration. They assembled on the morning of 11th November each year at their hall at Granite Terrace which had been previously damaged and was under Garda protection for some years. Then, wearing their medals and poppies and accompanied by a group of ladies carrying large wreaths, they marched down South Terrace, headed by the British Legion band.

The parade stopped at Kingsbridge Station, where honours were rendered at the plaque which bore the names of railway personnel who had died in the War. Staff at the station were instructed that no shunting was to take place that morning. Following this they proceeded to the Wellington Monument in the Phoenix Park where the main ceremony took place. When the new War Memorial Park was completed, the ceremony was held there instead.

Work on the National War Memorial and a surrounding park to honour the 49,400 Irishmen who had died in World War I commenced at Longmeadows/Inchicore North on 28th December 1931. These lands along the Liffey were already in public ownership from British times and were known as the Phoenix Park Extension. The Cosgrave government had agreed to make them available in response to a British Legion request for a memorial site somewhere in Dublin. The scheme took five years to complete and gave employment to 300 men, all of whom had served in either the British or Irish armies, but mostly the former. It was during this work that the Viking finds came to light.

The impressive memorial was designed by Sir Edward Lutyens, and all the granite came from the quarries of Ballyknockan and Barnaculla. Copies of the illuminated

Inchicore United
Back row: John Enright, Tom Christian, Frank Burton, Michael Kavanagh, Martin Downes, Tom Wall, Michael Penrose, Jimmy Reilly.
Centre row:Willie Graham, Pat Delemere, Tome Coffey, Fred Murphy, Willie Hartnett, Dessie Harwood*
Front row: John Bergin, Willie Hartnett, Jimmy Enright*
** First cousins*

volumes which contain the names of the fallen soldiers are housed in the memorial area. Also housed there is the Celtic memorial cross which was brought back from the trenches in Flanders.

When the War Memorial was completed it was not officially opened because of residual political tensions.

Alderman Peadar S. Doyle T.D. (1874–1956)

The longest serving local representative, Peadar Doyle, was orphaned as a young boy and reared by his aunts at Old Kilmainham. He attended the Christian Brothers School in Goldenbridge and served his time as a fitter in Guinness's Brewery. Following this he was employed at the Inchicore Railway Works. As a nationally minded young man he was involved in all the Irish Ireland movements, such as the Gaelic League and G.A.A. and played football with the local team, the Henry Grattans. He took part in the elaborate 1798 centenary march through Dublin city in 1898.

As we have seen, Peadar was a moving spirit in the formation of the Irish Volunteers in Inchicore and left his wife and young family to play an active part in the 1916 Rising. During his twelve months' imprisonment in England he was held in several jails such as Lewis and Portland, where he often engaged in mechanical drawings in order to pass the time. On his release in 1917 he was presented with a very artistic illuminated address totally in the Irish language by the Workmen's Club of which he was secretary.

During the War of Independence, as already mentioned, his son Seán was killed. Peadar was first elected to Dublin Corporation in 1920 and following the Treaty which he supported he was elected as a Cumann na nGael (Later Fine Gael) T.D. in 1923. He retained this seat in many subsequent elections until his death in 1956 and in the meantime had been elected Lord Mayor of Dublin on three occasions, in 1941, 1942 and 1945. In more modern times two other local T.D.'s the brothers Jim and Gay Mitchell were also to hold this office.

Peadar Doyle originally lived at 193 Emmet Road and later at "Avondale", 25 Tyrconnell Road.

The Tram Terminus

The tram tracks from the city terminated in the middle of the road opposite the Black Lion at the junction of Emmet Road and Tyrconnell Road and this was the focal point of Inchicore in those years. Here before making the return journey to College Green the conductor alighted and transferred by means of a long cable the overhead trolley from one end of the tram to the other.

From the twenties the district had a variety of public transport as apart from the trams there were at least six private operators running small buses to and from the city. On the route from College Street to The Bungalow were the Red & White Line as well as the Sarsfield operated by the local Foley brothers. The Savoy & Saint Christopher Lines catered for the new Bulfin Estate with a service from O'Connell Bridge via the quays while the Saint Augustine Line ran from O'Connell Bridge to the Ranch. A further service still, owned by Mr McEvoy the then proprietor of the Black Lion, linked Inchicore with Clondalkin.

Under new legislation, nearly all of these lines were taken over in 1934 by the D.U.T.C. who by then were operating buses as well as trams. Locally, for a number of years up to 1939, they also put on a very useful service from The Ranch to Sandymount via Sarsfield Road, Grattan Crescent and Emmet Road.

In 1931 the last trams ever to be completed at Spa Road, where a great tradition of coach building had evolved over the years, went on the road. These were a fleet of fifty-seven vehicles of the Luxury class, some of them capable of carrying seventy-six passengers and all remarkable for their speed, comfort and smooth running. They were mainly used on the Dun Laoghaire and Dalkey routes and were acclaimed all over Europe.

The "Sarsfield" bus at Ring Street, 1932, with Dan and Jim Foley

On the curve of the road near the tram terminus the boot and shoe maker Sam Bond had his shop where he also kept a few cage birds. Sometimes he used to hang on the wall outside, a cage in which a lark would sing to its heart's content, oblivious to the passing traffic. A few doors away was the butchers' shop, remembered for the two lifelike reindeer heads complete with antlers above the window. Across the road with its spicy aroma of pork products was Mr Stumpf's shop, while next door children bought their comics and fishing nets in the novelty shop owned by two elderly sisters. Along here too Mr O'Malley with round tweed hat and brown shop coat might be seen on occasion inside the door of his small provision shop expertly skinning a rabbit for a customer.

At the corner of Spa Road stood that very old house with many chimneys which used to accommodate several families, the last of these being the Haines family. Up to the 1930s part of it was used as the local dispensary and the Vincent de Paul Society also had the use of a room there. It has been said that in days gone by farmers on the way to the Dublin market with their produce stayed there overnight. Others claim that it was an old public house and point to the cellars which extended some distance under the footpath outside. Perhaps, but this is only conjecture, the vintner Patrick Berry, earlier mentioned, and who gave his name to Berry's Lane which later became Spa Road had his business there.

A few years ago this old house, by then unoccupied, was used as a film location where scenes from *The Devil's Own* were shot.

The Emergency Years (1939–1945)

Notwithstanding our neutrality, the outbreak of World War II in September 1939 had a devastating effect on the fledgling Irish state. Fuel and many foodstuffs were in short supply, causing much hardship and resulting in rationing. Large numbers of workers were laid off and "many young men of twenty went away", mainly to England, where there was an abundance of work due to the war. Others joined the Irish defence forces which had to be greatly expanded. A number of Inchicore men found employment in the six counties, chiefly in the Belfast shipyards and some of them were there during the German air raids on that city. Boiler-maker George Wilson told me how on the occasion of the first attack he had, along with the other residents of the house where they were staying, to take refuge under the stairs. On subsequent nights they remained in air raid shelters nearby.

In spite of the looming fuel crisis, most of the Dublin electric trams were taken off the road within six months of the outbreak of war and replaced by double-deck buses which only operated until 9.30 p.m.. The last tram on the Inchicore route – the 21 route – finished quietly and without any fuss on Saturday night 3rd February 1940.

With the shortage of coal and other materials the Railway Works were particularly hard hit and it was a tremendous effort to keep the wheels moving. One of the many improvisations was the assembly of a briquette plant which had been procured in Wales. Used as a substitute for coal, the briquettes were made from a mixture of hot pitch and anthracite dust, leaving the operatives like miners at the end of their stint. The plant operated day and night on a shift basis for seven days a week and the need for it remained until 1947. Old timers still have fond memories of one of the stalwarts of the plant, "Villager" Nolan from Crumlin.

Old passenger coaches were converted into wagons and whole trains of these went down the country to collect turf which was brought back and stored in huge clamps along the main road of the Phoenix Park. Once more a certain amount of military work was undertaken for the Irish Army, which involved the making of hand grenade cases and the fitting of pneumatic tyres to field guns.

For the six years of the Emergency Ireland was in constant danger of invasion from both sides. Inchicore had its local air raid precautions group of both men and women who distributed gasmasks to every house in the district. An air raid warning siren was placed on the roof of Scoil Mhuire Gan Smál and tested every Saturday morning. A number of surface air raid shelters were also erected. Concrete pill boxes were constructed at a low level on the side of all the approach roads to the city.

Local units of the Local Defence Force and the Local Security Force were formed and one group of the former met and trained at Camac House, Bluebell. The power station at Jamestown was placed under an armed guard. An anti-aircraft battery was sited at Ballyfermot hill which on several occasions fired at unidentified planes and at night the sky was criss-crossed with the beams of search-lights. The outskirts of Inchicore and Ballyfermot saw very realistic and large scale manoeuvres by the army in 1944 following their long march from the south.

Vegetable growing in front and back gardens which had always been a feature (indeed a necessity) of the area was now redoubled. Allotments were made available in the Memorial Park, the grounds of Inchicore House and indeed wherever space could be found. Sometimes young boys collected fallen leaves from gardens in small push carts and these were later used as fertiliser in the plots. Men, some of whom had never seen a bog before, cut turf on the Featherbed and Glasamucky.

Brassington's Sawmills sold sawdust at 1/- a bag, which was used as fuel in an improvised stove for cooking purposes. It was in these years also that many of the great trees still remaining along the banks of the canal were felled.

Electricity was rationed and in order to supplement his supply Dan Wall installed a wind-charger on the top of the flat roof of his billiard saloon at Grattan Crescent. This when connected to motor car batteries provided some additional current and although Europe might be tearing itself apart his clients were thus enabled to continue with their favourite pastime.

The use of gas was also very much restricted and a sharp lookout had to be kept for the greatest menace of the emergency years – the nefarious "Glimmer Man"!

Crusade of Prayer

Throughout the Emergency years prayers were constantly offered for peace and the protection of Ireland in the local churches. Week after week Masses were offered for these intentions at the request of the employees of local firms such as Lambs and the Metropolitan Laundry and also the residents of different streets. Highlight of this crusade of prayer was the uninterrupted Rosary Novena of 1941 at the Inchicore Grotto. It began at 6.00 a.m. on 2nd February and in spite of severe weather continued without a break, day or night, until 11th February, Feast of Our Lady of Lourdes. Rosaries were said throughout Ireland in association with those gathered at Inchicore and the number of people all told was put at 300,000. The concluding torchlight procession on the 11th was of enormous proportions, giving an impression of a river of light as it wound its way through the grounds. An observer wrote: "Rarely in a lifetime does one have such a profound spiritual experience."

After all those years there are a few residents who still remember also the neatly dressed young man who stood each night on Tyrconnell Road selling prayer leaflets as he called out "Prayer for peace one penny!"

The prayers at the grotto were heard and Ireland with determined political leadership escaped the ravages of World War II which ended in 1945. However, the

An Inchicore Railway Works Tug-O-War team, about 1931
Back row: W Heffernan, C Delaney, Simon Quigley(3rd from left), D Morrissey, Theo Foley (2nd from right).
Other names not known as of now
Front row: Tommy Lawlor and his father

hardships of the Emergency period were to last for years afterwards and normal supplies were slow in coming back. All of this was compounded by the disastrous harvest of 1946 when city workers transported by army lorries went out to help the farmers in the surrounding countryside. This was followed by the blizzard of 1947 with snow falling intermittently from February to May and people queuing for fuel, sometimes having to make do with wet turf. The Liffey was frozen over between Chapelizod and Islandbridge.

Transport was nationalised by the government in 1947, bringing bus and rail operations together under the new entity known as Coras Iompair Éireann. This was to result in major changes in the management structure at the Inchicore Railway Works.

Saint Jospeh's Youth Club

It was during those emergency years, on 25th April 1944 to be exact, that Saint Joseph's Boys' Club, the first of its kind in the district, was established at Ring Terrace by the Conference of Mary Immaculate of the Saint Vincent de Paul Society with the active encouragement of Father William Devine O.M.I., well known for his concern for youth welfare. Some years later it was transferred to its present location at "Grotto House" on Tyrconnell Road where a wider range of activities was undertaken and where eventually it became Saint Joseph's Youth Club. The good work initiated in those difficult times has been carried on ever since by successive generations of dedicated voluntary workers.

Here we should mention that the conference in question is probably the oldest voluntary group in the district dating back to at least 1890.

Chapter Forty-Seven

FROM DOOR TO DOOR

THE MILKMEN

Before the advent of bottled milk the liquid was delivered to the door by milkmen who mainly came in from the surrounding countryside in their horse-drawn cars, complete with churns and cans. These included Connors from Baldonnell, Mastersons from Robin Hood, Haines and Powers from Bluebell, the Harelawn from Ballyfermot, Spendloves from Chapelizod, Tierneys of Violet Vale, Tommy Merryman from the "Ranch", Paddy Denton of Ballymount, Finnegan's "New Ross" Dairy from Goldenbridge, Dobbels "Hermitage" Dairy, Ardiffs from Old Kilmainhan and the more commercialised Lucan Dairy from Parkgate Street, their man being the popular "Joe the Lucan" (Hayes).

For long distance however, pride of place must go to Connors of Baldonnell who hail, rain or snow delivered milk twice a day involving a total of twenty-four miles. John Connor lived on the edge of the airfield with his brother, father and grandfather, his mother having died when he was four years old. He remembers how the cows were milked at 3.00 a.m. and the tackling of one of their two ponies for the six mile run to Inchicore which was reached at 6.30 a.m. As well as delivering the milk they often acted as a clock by calling people for their work. In some cases at the end of the week the milk money was left under a jug inside the door.

After the morning delivery they made their way home. At three o'clock in the afternoon the second pony was tackled, sometimes proving difficult to catch in the field, and they set off for Inchicore for the second time. Nightfall saw them on the way home and John recalls the terrible weather conditions and how very often on an icebound road they had to lead the pony half on the road and half on the path.

Very old residents still recall his father, Bill Connor, on his rounds – soft hat, leggings, black moustache, always a joke and a laugh with his customers and well known for his generosity during those days of economic stress. Another member of the Connor family was employed as a timber feller in Brassingtons and John recalls this uncle bringing in large trees on a long bogey to the mill.

OTHER ROUNDSMEN AND WOMEN

Apart from the milkmen there were up to the 1960's numerous other services to the door as well. These included many bread firms such as Kennedys, Johnston Mooney and O'Brien's, Monks, Halligans, Thompsons; as well as laundries – the Metropolitan, Dunlop's, Swastika and Whiter Heather. The laundrymen had uniforms and caps as well as the mineral water man who called once a week on Saturday afternoons. The latter had a long four wheel horse drawn car with a selection of mineral waters, both in siphons and in bottles.

All the big city coal firms were represented – Doherty's, Donnelly's and Heiton's, not to mention the local bell-men who were constantly to be heard on the road. Also on Saturday mornings, up to World War II, men from the bogs of Kildare with broadleafed black hats, not unlike their Connemara counterparts, sold turf from door to door.

Vegetable cars as well as fish women made their rounds a few days per week. Many local shops employed messenger boys who delivered vegetables and groceries to the houses with heavy carrier bicycles. Some shops had small ponies and cars for this purpose. Newspapers were delivered morning and evening, usually by schoolboys getting their first break in life.

Other callers to the doors were umbrella menders, picture framers, men carrying a roll of linoleum on their shoulders, cutlers (knives and shears), collectors of boots and shoes for repair, gypsy women who could sell you artificial flowers or tell your fortune, as well as a travelling barber. The gas meter collector was always welcome by reason of the fact that there might be a refund of some coppers. There was a constant stream of beggars, some of whom had their own particular "patrons." However, most remembered of all was the travelling dentist who usually came on a bicycle to visit his clients. Having parked his bike outside, he took off his bag and was admitted to the front kitchen where he duly proceeded with the extractions.

Grattan Crescent, 1936

Constant callers also were the women with their three-wheel wicker barrows who exchanged delph and glassware for rags and old clothes. These were most persuasive ladies indeed who would seldom take no for an answer. Young children out on the street looked forward to the balloon man who from his barrow also had a plentiful supply of paper windmills, coloured streamers and of course the fizz bags against which dire warnings were issued in vain by parents.

Last but not least were the slop collectors among whom there was keen competition, particularly during the "Emergency" years, and who twice a week collected the left-overs and greasy water which sustained many local piggeries in Inchicore and Bluebell. Nearly all of these collectors were men or boys, but there was at least one woman, Bridget from Grattan Crescent, who came around with her pony and small cart and who also sold eggs and chickens.

The post was delivered twice daily, and once on a Saturday, while up to the early '30s there was a Christmas morning delivery. The bin men made two collections per week. The local library was open six days per week.

Chapter Forty-Eight

Blessings, Old Sayings and Customs

Tailor Paddy Kilbride, originally an inner city man who lived just across the canal on Killworth Road, would say "May God give you the health and strength to wear it", when receiving payment for a garment he had made. Locally it was not uncommon to hear "God be with you", "God save you", "God between us and all harm", or "Praise be to the hand of God" and some of these expressions are still to be heard.

Of a quiet man it might be said that "He would not say boo to a sparrow". Of something which was common knowledge you could hear that "The world and Garret Reilly knows about it". A coat that was too big for somebody might draw the comment that "It would fit Finn McCool". Of a discreet person it would be said: "You could tell him/her the killing of a man".

Pure Irish expressions were not too plentiful. The most notable was "They would give you Lanavaille", a corruption of Lán an Mhála – the full of the bag – usually said mockingly of people who were not too generous.

Directly from the Irish as well we had a phrase which has almost faded out by now – "There wasn't a gig out of him", meaning that there was not a move or a word out of him. The original Irish was "Ní raibh giog as".

A person engaged in rough or heavy work was said to be "mullacking" and this has an Irish ring about it. To make a "fufa" was to make a mess of something.

A generous person is still sometimes said to be "flathulach". An over-talkative child might be told to "whist" or "hold your tongue".

Another old expression which had the stamp of the Irish language on it was "Be the here and there" – "Dar seo is siud".

A man in his cups might exclaim in patriotic fervour "Eireann go brath".

You can still hear people who don't look too well being described as "very dawney", but whether this is of Irish origin I do not know.

Brendan Malone's father used to ask him to break a few "tralleens" – small sticks – in order to light the fire.

Mrs Currivan, formerly of Old Bluebell, was telling me recently that when as a child nearly eighty years ago, she was helping her grandfather to "drop" potatoes he said to her "I will have to make you a little 'praisceen'", which he did. This she explained was a little working apron with pockets and this is exactly as it is described in Dineen's *Irish Dictionary.*

It was only in Old Bluebell that I heard that word which was common enough in the inner city up to now, i.e. "fornenst", meaning near. "I saw her coming fornenst the house." This is probably an example of old English.

A bold young girl was described as a "strap", a stupid person was a "dunderhead", a foolish person was a "gobaloonee", while a man of dubious character was a "quare officer".

An Inchicore person going out the road, usually towards County Dublin or Kildare would say that "They were going up the country". In the railway works men who came in from Robinhood or the Tallaght direction were called "hill-siders".

Young boys mitching from school were "on the Gerr" and if when playing street football they let the ball go over a high wall, they would say that the ball had been "canted". A halfpenny was a "make", a penny was a "wing", while tuppence was a "duce". The hero in a film, particularly a Western, was always known to youngsters as "the Chap".

Most of the old words and expressions used in the city were common to our area as well. A person who got a good telling off was said to have got a "gate of going". A policeman was described as a "bobby" or a "rozzer", while the arrested person was said to have been "lagged".

"Me ould Sagossa" was a term of endearment said in a joking fashion, but for pure Inchicore "Dublinese" it would be hard to beat "me and the mott and the mott's mother".

Local Customs

Dressing up for Hallowe'en is the only seasonal custom which has to some extent survived until recently, but now seems to be on the wane. However the games played at children's parties in their homes on that night such as snap-apple or money in the basin are things of the past. The chestnut season in the autumn is still observed by young boys, but the marble playing along the street channels which commenced in March and lasted for a few months is long gone.

"The Wran" on Saint Stephen's morning had been customary for countless generations but went out of fashion in Inchicore about 1943. Here the children, both boys and girls, went from door to door carrying a little holly bush with coloured streamers and reciting their verse:

"The Wran, the Wran the king of all birds
On St Stephen's Day was caught in the furze
Although he was little his family was great
Rise up good lady and give us a trait
Up with the kettle and down with the pan
Give us a penny to bury the wran.

Knock at the door and make some noise
Make some noise, make some noise
Knock at the door and make some noise
For we are the wran boys".

For a good number of years carol singing groups went around in the evening time during the weeks before Christmas, bringing quite a festive atmosphere to the streets and avenues of the district.

Girls played "beds" on the footpaths or skipped to various rhymes. Young boys propelled their hoops (usually the rim of an old bicycle wheel) along with the aid of a little stick. Both boys and girls spun their tops on the road or played "Relieve-ee-o", which usually ended with the immortal cry "All in, all in – the game is broke up". With older boys of course, street football was the most popular.

Not so socially acceptable however were the pitch and toss schools ("heads a penny") patronised by young and not so young men and which sometimes broke up in a bout of fisticuffs.

The late Phil Gough who was so interested in the history of the area told me that in his young days eel fishing was a very popular pastime. He explained how they went "bobbin'" for eels, that is with worms and wool and no hooks. In September when the Liffey was in flood they caught scores of them which they brought home in a bucket of water. Also when dried the skins were sometimes used for binding wrists or ankles following a sprain.

Saint Patrick's Day was the traditional start for hikes to the Dublin Hills. Summer brought swimming in the canal or "down the Liffey". In early autumn, mushrooms were sought in the fields of Ballyfermot and blackberries on the hedgerows of its winding roads. Out further near the "Bush of Balgaddy" holly in abundance was to be found in the weeks before Christmas.

Chapter Forty-Nine

INCHICORE HUMOUR

Before the advent of cinema, radio or television, people had by and large to make their own amusement and it was against this background that local humour developed in the various communities throughout the city. Here are some of the stories peculiar to Inchicore and which by now have almost faded away, but are not totally forgotten.

The porter and general factotum at the Inchicore United Workingmen's Club on Emmet Road for many years was a sturdily built little dwarf who invariably wore a waistcoat with sleeves rolled up, corduroy trousers and a cap on the back of his head. During the Troubles, the club was frequently raided by the Black and Tans. On one such occasion when they arrived in the forenoon he was the only person present and happened to be behind the bar at that moment. As they rushed in with guns drawn, they could only see his head above the counter at which the sergeant in charge roared out — "Get up off your knees before I blow your bloody head off".

Father Sweeney, the well known Oblate preacher and missionary, was also an able administrator and successful fund raiser. The story is told that when a little boy in Ring Street swallowed a halfpenny, his mother who was very distressed, ran into her neighbour's house exclaiming "How are we to get the halfpenny out?" to which the neighbour calmly replied, "We will have to send for Father Sweeney".

Volumes could be filled with the folklore of the railway works but just one tall tale will suffice:

A man who was pilfering used to carry out pieces of metal under his large overcoat. However, he got more greedy as he went along and on the occasion in question he concealed more than he was able to carry. The result was that he fell down on the path as he was almost at the gate of the premises. Fellow workers ran over to assist him to his feet, but he shouted out in a loud voice, "Let only those who know my complaint come near me".

There was one member of a local hard-working family who was rather work-shy all his life. On this occasion a neighbour was surprised to meet him out early in the morning on Tyrconnell Road and asked him what had him out so early. The neighbour was astonished when he told him that he was out looking for work. However, the man then went on to explain that it wasn't for himself but rather "for the missus".

Father "Da" Ryan called on an old woman who owned a little huxter shop and whom he thought might not be attending to her religious duties. After a while he broached the subject to her to which she replied "Listen here Father Ryan, I am neither better nor worse since this time last year and you would be better off calling on those besters who won't pay me what they owe me".

On hearing that a well known blackguard (not an Inchicore man!) had died the night before, a local woman did not appear to have much sympathy for him when she declared that "He will know goat from kid this morning".

There was also the widow woman in the Puck who had taken in some of her in-laws to live with her in her small house and she said that things were so bad that she would be better off "eating chaff".

When asked how he got over Christmas, a North Terrace man said that he fell over it.

In another old story Mr Willie Stumpf, the well known German businessman who established one of the first pork shops in Inchicore in the early part of this century, is mentioned. Incidentally, Mr Stumpf along with his fellow nationals, was interned by the British authorities for the duration of World War I. The story goes that "Scald" McLoughlin was drinking in the "Horse & Jockey" with another ex-soldier when the usual dispute arose as to which of them had done the most fighting during the War. The "Scald" had the last word however, when he told those present that the only German his buddy had ever seen was Mr Stumpf in his shop up the road.

Many years ago Danish butter was put on sale in Ireland but did not prove very popular as it was too strong for the Irish palate. An Inchicore man's wife was giving him this butter on his bread at teatime every evening but in the end he could take no more of it. So when he came home this evening he said to her, "No more of this Danish butter for me – I know the Danes killed Brian Ború but I will be damned if they are going to kill me as well".

An Old Railway Ballad

The subject of this ballad was close to retirement when this particular strike which he joined took place, but fortunately the drivers won their case and so he did not lose his pensions:

Marks Duffy is a sturdy old man,
A sturdy old man is he;
A driver he was in Inchicore
For years and years you see,
But now he's gone, his work is done,
A pension he has got;
But 'tis not of his pension I mean to sing,
Believe me, lads, 'tis not,
For when there was trouble amongst us

Old Duffy was a man
And took his stand with the rest of us –
Deny it he who can.

Chorus:
Drink a health to old Duffy, lads,
And give him a cheer galore,
For he's the man that led the van
In the struggle at Inchicore.

The day we did the strike declare,
We said, "What shall you do?"
He answered, "The question is not fair,
But this I say to you:
I'm growing old and feeble now,
To me a pension's due,
But I'll forfeit all in the good old cause,
And take my place with you."

And for this stand Marks Duffy made
I think he's none the worse –
He has good health and also wealth,
So he doesn't care a curse.
And every time at Jim McCann's
He gets his pint of beer,
The boys all shake him by the hands,
And greet him with a cheer."

Chapter Fifty

Old Street Names, Cottages and Yards

Old Name	Later Name
The Chapel Road	Tyrconnell Road
The Back Road	Inchicore Road
Berry's Lane	Spa Road
Tramway Terrace and Lennox St	Thomas Davis St
Watery Lane	Brookfield Road
The Front Road or Richmond	Emmet Road
Bentley's Lane	Luby Road
Coopers Hollow or The Puck	Tyrone Place
McCann's Yard	Saint James's Place
The High Road	Kilmainham Lane
Brodericks Yard	Myra Cottages
Barnett's Lane	Golden Vale Cottages
Murray's Lane	Richmond Cottages

The last three, all off Emmet Road, were demolished over twenty years ago and have only recently been replaced by new houses, known as Myra Close. Murray's Lane should not be confused with Murray's Cottages, which are still in existence in the Woodfield district.

In the early thirties Darcy's Yard just off the lower part of Tyrconnell Road and quite near the Camac River gave way to new private residences, one of which is "Avondale". Across the road somewhat later Lavin's three small cottages at the entrance to Saint James's Place were taken down.

During the 1937 widening of Grattan Crescent (shown as Cow and Calf Lane on one old deed) a number of shops and old dwellings were demolished. Amongst these were the Brush Yard, consisting of six small cottages and Corporation Cleansing Depot (hence the name) and Egan's Yard of eleven small cottages. The latter at one time had also been the scene of a forge and is today the Black Lion car park. Further around the Crescent near the Conradh na Gaeilge Hall, Saint Joseph's Place, with its five small cottages also went at this time as did "Honey" Munroe's piggery. Later the nearby Larkin's Lane was closed off.

Myra Cottages, off Emmet Road prior to demolition in 1973

During the long overdue clearing of the old dwellings in Goldenbridge in the 1960s, the "Puck" passed away as well as the nearby Byrne's Yard and Gorman's Yard.

The thirteen red brick houses of Albert Place on Inchicore Road had to give way in the 1970s to a major extension of the Rowntree Mackintosh factory.

In Old Kilmainham, Ardiff's Cottages, Faulkner's Cottages and Saw Mill Cottages have gone, but Carrickfoyle Terrace and Lady Lane still remain. The latter was sometimes indicated as Lady's Lane and is possibly one of the oldest street names in the entire district. Shannon Terrace is called after a local family of tanners and is the site of the original Kilmainham Jail. Kearn's Place is called after a local manufacturer.

In Islandbridge the nineteen small dwellings of Woodroffes Cottages which faced each other in a narrow lane opposite the barracks were demolished about thirty years ago. They were built by a publican of that name and were the subject of much complaint in the last century because of their unsanitary condition.

In the "Ranch" the sixteen small sturdy little dwellings known as Saint Mary's Terrace were demolished over twenty years ago to make way for a road widening scheme which never took place! It is only in the last two years that new houses were built on the vacant site and these have been named as part of Sarsfield Road.

Originally every small group of houses with as few even as two or three dwellings were given a name resulting in innumerable local addresses. Many of these were named after the person who had built them or members of their families. With regard to the latter, there are still three remaining name plates, i.e. Madeiline Terrace and Ellen Villa on Emmet Road and Rose Terrace on Tyrconnell Road, to remind us of those bygone times.

The West British influence manifested itself in York Villas, Victoria Terrace, Spencer Terrace, Lennox Street, Abercorn Terrace and Saint George's Villas. Members of "Jack's Army" might be interested to know that there was a Charlton Terrace on Inchicore Road. Indeed another famous sportsman, the Irish-American boxer "Gentleman Jim" Corbett, stayed at number 15 on that terrace with the Gunning family in the summer of 1909 when he visited his mother's old home in Islandbridge as well as the Inchicore Railway Works.

The allocation of patriotic names such as Emmet, Sarsfield, Davis and Grattan in the last quarter of the previous century reflected the growing influence of the nationalist members of Dublin Corporation. At the top of Brookfield Road there was a "Patriotic Terrace" where, appropriately enough, William Partridge one time resided.

Turvey Avenue most likely derives from a family name. Pádraig Mac Ionnraic tells me that one of his ancestors, Edward Turvey, was a shoemaker up to 1761 at Bow Bridge which he noted also was described in the Registry of Deeds as "Bow Bridge or Lough Boy". How long the latter survived in common usage, we do not know but it looks like a corruption of Loch Buí, a yellow pool.

Chapter Fifty-One

OLD PUBS, INNS AND OLD SOCIETIES

THE BLACK LYON 1734

The Black Lion, or as originally known the Black Lyon, is the oldest pub in Inchicore. Mr Eamonn Casey, that authority on the history of Dublin pubs, has told us that he traced a licence for it from 1734 on or close to the present site. When we remember that it was only some years earlier in 1729 that an Act of Parliament gave the go-ahead for a turnpike road along here we can see the attraction for a coaching inn at this location. The importance of the venue was further enhanced with the provision of a forge on the Grattan Crescent side of the inn where the car park is now situated.

Over its lengthy history the Black Lion had many owners, the longest being the Egan family who were there for nearly 100 years. In this century it was owned by McCanns, P. J. McEvoy, Hardy's and finally the present incumbents, the Dillon family. Up to fifty years ago, as was customary then, the proprietors and their families lived at the premises. Many of the staff were also accommodated there with their own quarters.

THE COW AND CALF INN

Another pub which could nearly have been as old as the Black Lion was the Cow and Calf Inn. It too was on the route of a turnpike road, the one to Mullingar established in 1786. It was situated on the site of the Model School near the junction of Sarsfield Road and Grattan Crescent and on ground which belonged to Lord Cloncurry. Beside it was the Cow and Calf Farm which stretched along the side of Grattan Crescent and lower Tyrconnell Road.

There is an interesting reference in the records of the County Dublin Grand Jury to a contract in 1838 for repairing "sixty three perches of the road by the Cow and Calf". It was also mentioned in the contract that "the gravel and stones would be drawn from the pit or quarry on the townland of Inchicore occupied by Mrs. Geraghty".

Following the building of the railway houses the necessity for a school arose and this gave rise to the Model School in 1853 which brought an end to the inn. The last proprietor was a Mr J. Kavanagh and the licence may have been transferred to the new establishment on the other side of Sarsfield Road, "The Great Southern and Western Railway House", later Cleary's and now Murphy's.

The Cow and Calf was unique in being the only local inn which was actually named on old maps, but we shall probably never know the significance of this.

The Foresters Arms

The McCann family, who were both publicans and builders, built this pub and provision shop with spacious living accommodation and an extensive garden alongside it about 1860 at Grattan Crescent. They called it the Foresters Arms because of their association with the society known as the Irish National Foresters. They also built the two houses on Grattan Crescent known as Tyrconnell Villas and were later to acquire the Black Lion across the road in addition to their own pub. With regard to the latter they for some reason changed the name about 1900 from the Foresters' Arms to Tyrconnell House.

One of the principals was James McCann, a nationally minded man who was elected as a councillor for the Inchicore Kilmainham area on Dublin Corporation. An old picture of the Black Lion shows his name in Irish – Seamus MacAnna – on the signboard. Following his death in 1918 Tyrconnell House passed into the possession of the well known Guinan family while the Black Lion was acquired by P. J. McEvoy.

Very recently, the name of Tyrconnell House has been altered by the present owners to the Village Inn.

The Patriots Inn 1793

Another of the very old pubs of the district is that fine three storey premises on the corner of Kilmainham Lane and South Circular Road known today as "The Patriots". It was established by a John Ward in 1793, perhaps in anticipation of the opening of the new jail across the road three years later in 1796. However, being very close to Bully's Acre he already had a substantial funeral trade on his doorstep and, as earlier mentioned, could in addition to the pints provide his customers with the necessary implements for grave digging when required. The pub became known as "The Victoria Tavern" in 1835 following the accession of that lady to the English throne.

Margaret Drummond whom we have already met took over about 1856. During her tenure she availed of the inn licence to provide accommodation for both travellers and those who were visiting relatives and friends incarcerated in the "Big House" across the way. On the strength of this also she got an extension which allowed her to serve liquor from 5.00 a.m.

When the Murrays of Inchicore House acquired the premises in 1898 they changed the name to the "Kilmainham Tavern". They left in the 1920s and moved down to the "Bow Bridge Tavern" instead. Since then there has been a variety of owners and names, amongst these being the "Welcome Inn" with its slogan "Welcome all to Welcome Inn", the "Leaders Inn" and finally "The Patriots Inn". The legend on the artistic signboard says it all:

> "This old pub standeth on sacred ground surrounded by the high walls of Royal Kilmainham Hospital by the ancient cemetery of Bully's Acre and the dungeons of Kilmainham Jail. The Patriots Inn has been closer to the pulse of Irish History than any contemporary pub."

Emmet Road

Emmet Road has a goodly number of licensed premises, something which can be attributed to the presence there of Richmond Barracks for well over a hundred years. Amongst these are Richmond House (McDowells) and Emmet House on the corner of Vincent Street, the latter at one time being also known as the Italian Warehouse. The following advertisement in Saunders' Newsletter of June 1818 could have applied to either of those houses:

PUBLIC HOUSE – TO BE LET

THAT CAPITAL NEW HOUSE AT GOLDENBRIDGE LATELY OCCUPIED IN PUBLIC BUSINESS BY MR. ARTHUR MCCAUL, FOR WHICH IT IS FITTED OUT WITH BAR AND TAP ROOMS FIXTURES COMPLETE.

FROM ITS SITUATION ON A GREAT PUBLIC ROAD AND AT THE ENTRANCE TO RICHMOND BARRACKS IT MUST PROVE A MOST DESIRABLE SITUATION FOR ANY PERSON EMBARKING IN THE PUBLIC AND PROVISION BUSINESS.

PROPOSALS WILL BE RECEIVED BY MESSRS. TREVOR KEOGH & CO., BREWERY, ARDEE ST.

McDowells is one of those rare old Dublin pubs which still maintains the atmosphere and character of the last century.

Other old pubs on the road are the "Horse & Jockey" and the "Glen of Aherlow" which was formerly Mrs Sheridan's "Rose Tavern". Also "Coffey's Lounge", previously McInerneys and "Tom Tavey's", previously Gunn's.

In Vincent Street were two small pubs: "McGrath's", which also operated a side-car business, and the "Golden Bridge Tavern".

In the fifties Brendan Behan from time to time crossed the canal from Crumlin via the iron foot-bridge to meet a few of his old pals in McGraths. On other occasions he ambled on to meet another buddy, Bill Finnegan, in his little barber's shop at Grattan Crescent.

The "Golden Bridge Tavern" was remarkable for the fact that, like some other pubs in the city in the last century, they provided their own metal tokens. These were used when small change was scarce or for use when small bagatelle tables were provided for customers. Pubs using these tokens had their own individual designs and in the case of the "Golden Bridge Tavern" it was a railway engine as we can see from the illustration.

Other Establishments

The "Waterloo Tavern" at Islandbridge was established about 1820 and is today Dillons' "Black & Amber". Two other Islandbridge pubs which were in existence up to about thirty years ago were "Gilligans" (Rose Eager's) and on the other side of the river "The Athlete's Rest". Likewise the very imposing "Doyle's" directly opposite Kilmainham Jail also went about the same time, in this case when Rowntrees' factory was being extended.

The "Half Moon" was a very old pub in Kilmainham, but we do not know its location. The present Carrigans in Old Kilmainham is very old also and probably dates back to the original Kilmainham Jail, which was across the road from it. In 1889 it was bought by P. J. Muldowney, a noted hurler and footballer who was also very active in G.A.A. administration in Dublin city and county. The business was continued by his family until 1977.

Canal Pubs

Kelly's "Black Horse Inn" at the 3rd Lock Bridge was established in 1764, no doubt in anticipation of the pending completion of the Grand Canal. This was one of the pubs which was required by law to make one of its stores available as a morgue in the case of canal drownings and the late Mrs McElroy remembered, as a child, it being so used. Previous owners in the past hundred years or so were McKennas, Woodcocks, Murrays and Moores.

The first licensee of the 7th Lock Pub in 1846 was one Mary Madigan who prior to that apparently operated some form of sheebeen there. In 1852 the premises were bought out by the Grand Canal Company and leased to a Hogan family who also had the responsibility of acting as lock keepers. In 1890 it passed to James Murray, grocer and publican, but became better known as "Mary Theresa's", after his wife's name. During Mr Murray's tenure he succeeded in buying back the title from the Canal Company. Several other occupants such as Bannons and English were to follow and in 1988 the premises were completely rebuilt and modernised. It is now known as Killeen House.

During the years of more restricted drinking hours Inchicore men often walked up the side of the canal to get a drink at this pub and it used to be said that "they were doing the bona fide".

The Many Murrays

The above mentioned James Murray was a member of a family who at one stage simultaneously owned the 7th Lock, the Black Horse and what later became the "Pine Tree" in the "Ranch". One of them also built Murray's Cottages on Sarsfield Road. They were not however connected in any way with the other Murray family who lived in Inchicore House and who also were publicans.

Old Clubs

After the Railway Institute or Dining Hall, the next oldest club in the area is the Inchicore United Workingmen's Club, Emmet Road, which was formed in 1884 to "provide the members with rational recreation and the means of meeting socially". It has been said that it was established by a number of railwaymen who were not happy for some reason with the rules of the Dining Hall. To have built such a fine red-brick building in the heart of the district at that time showed much resourcefulness on the part of those concerned who were probably mostly tradesmen and may have done some of the work themselves.

In 1890 there was an "Inchicore Catholic Club" which seems to have been accommodated in the annexe attached to the Leo Hall. It did not last too long however and the annexe was later used as the infants' section of the old Oblate School.

Inchicore Friendly Society

Back in 1857 there was absolutely no social welfare of any description and self-help was the name of the game. With a view to providing some small amount of financial assistance in the event of sickness or injury a group of railway employees came together in that year and established the Inchicore Friendly Society. Its first registered office and meeting place was not in Inchicore itself but rather in Islandbridge at a room in what was described as the "Wellington Hotel", now the Black and Amber pub. They subsequently moved to the Spa Tavern in Goldenbridge, the Horse and Jockey on Emmet Road, the Forester's Arms at Grattan Crescent and the Great Southern and Western Railway House at Woodfield before finally settling down in 1896 at the Workmen's Club, where they remained until they dissolved in 1961.

One of the trustees in 1912 was John Regan of 28 South Terrace.

The Inchicore Christian Burial Society

This old tontine society was founded in 1877, again at a time when the majority of people had very little income and funeral expenses could cause financial problems. It was originally known as the Darcy Society as its secretary and one of the founding members was a John Darcy who lived in the cottages also known as Darcy's Yard. These as already mentioned were just off the lower part of Tyrconnell Road and it was there that the members came on Sunday mornings to pay their weekly subscription. Today by a coincidence a much larger financial institution, the Trustee Savings Bank, which also had its origins as a "Penny" bank, is situated near this old location.

The officers in 1913 apart from John Darcy were Thomas Callaghan (Ring Street) and Daniel Mahon (Vincent Street) with the patriot Patrick O'Carroll acting as auditor. The registered office was shown as 11 Auburn Cottages which we presume was the official name for Darcy's Yard.

When these cottages were demolished in the early thirties the society continued its business at Mrs Curran's house at Saint James's Place across the road. The members were then paying eight pence per week and received a "divvy" of one pound and six shillings at Christmas. At the time of a bereavement a sum of £5 was paid and also small loans were made at a nominal interest.

Names associated with the society in those years were Tom Clare, Jack White, Tommy Ellis, John Heffernan and Jack Connolly of Phoenix Street as secretary. The latter introduced a policy of higher subscriptions and larger pay-outs and the membership was now between 600 and 700. His son Willie remembers as a young man being one of those who helped to deliver the Christmas bonus in small envelopes in the district.

The society ended in 1964 to be followed one year later by the first local branch of the Credit Union movement.

Chapter Fifty-Two

AR SON NA GAEILGE

In the midst of the economic gloom of the 1950s there were new stirrings in Irish cultural circles with the formation of Comhaltas Ceoltoiri Éireann in 1951 and Gael Linn a few years later. It was in January 1951 that the current Craobh Inse Chór of Conradh na Gaeilge came into existence at Saint Brigid's Child Welfare Centre. This little building to the rear of Saint Michael's Church was originally an annexe of Richmond Barracks and used as a band room in British times.

Conradh na Gaeilge was founded in 1893 and there was a branch in Inchicore from at least 1900. A public meeting to launch it officially was held in the C.B.S. schools in Goldenbridge in November 1900. An early enthusiast was Brother Lannigan of that school but from the previous March Father Ring had provided a room for classes at the Oblate School. Present at the public meeting was Arthur Griffith and many local councillors as well as Willie Rooney, the Gaelic League's dedicated organiser who probably made the arrangements for the meeting.

Other branches came and went over the years at the Emmet Hall, the Leo Hall, Model School, Workmen's Club and a room over "Granny" Moran's shop on Tyrconnell Road. Some of these branches had very notable teachers as outlined by Cissie Egan in her recollections. Another class was conducted by an officer of the newly formed Irish Free State army in 1922 at the little shop beside Larkin's Lane which had previously been the Sinn Féin election rooms. In 1926 a Ceili held by the then Craobh Inse Chór in Parnell Square was the first such function to be broadcast by "2RN", the forerunner of Radio Éireann. Old timer Mick Neill told me that he remembers collecting copies of O'Growney's First Irish Lessons in the city and bringing them to the Workmen's Club in the years before World War I. He also mentioned that for several years they held a Saint Patrick's Night concert at the club and that on Saint John's Night (26th June) they organised a bonfire night on the open ground to the rear of the premises.

RECOLLECTIONS OF MS CISSIE EGAN

"As a young girl I joined with some of my school friends and we went along to the Irish classes which at that time were held in the Inchicore Model School in the early 1930s. Goldenbridge Convent School was our Alma

Mater, and so this was an opportunity for us to see inside the other school and to savour the teaching of Irish by native Irish speakers. It was also for us our first experience of evening classes and an opportunity to escape the drudgery of home exercises at least for one evening each week. And there were boys in the class too!

"The weekly fee was threepence. The schoolroom as I remember it was big with a high ceiling and very long windows. The desks were re-arranged around the fire and the extra floor space was available at the time when we practiced our Irish dancing – not just solo dancing, but real lively set dances. In those years, the school did not boast electricity or gaslight, but this did not hinder our activities. The heating was adequate – the griseach or hot ashes, remained in the huge fireplace after the ordinary school day and this helped to ignite the hard lumpy turf sods which filled the buckets at the fireside. The turf could be bought at twelve sods for a penny from the turf men who came to Inchicore at weekends with their ponies and carts to sell turf, chickens and fresh vegetables. They travelled on Fridays and at dusk they could be seen asleep under their carts on the pathway on the Lucan Road, near Chapelizod. Early on Saturday they recommenced their leisurely journey from Kildare towards the city, selling as they went.

"It was our great privilege as youngsters to go to a house in Woodfield, home of a Miss Jackson, to collect the buckets filled with turf sods and to carry them to the school in good time before the classes would begin. When the fire was well alight we returned again to the same house to bring the oil lamps which provided the lighting in the class room. I can still remember the tall stately figure of Miss Jackson's father as he handed us the lamps, having first ensured that the globes of fine glass were securely in place.

"When the class had assembled and the lessons began, we were in another world. Around the fire there, we might have been in any house in the Gaeltacht. Our teachers were gentle and understanding and the adult native speakers who came to encourage us to speak together, to sing and dance together, were treasures indeed. It is a pity that the passing of time has erased many of their names from my memory, but I still recollect the gentle Siobhán Ní Lionnáin from Ring, the fatherly Seán Ó Conbhuidhe, the writer Seán Ó hOgáin and the young smiling Kerryman Seán Ó Suilleabháin.

"Let me return to the activities of Conradh na Gaeilge in Inchicore. When the winter was past we took our lessons seated under the chestnut tree in the schoolyard. We told stories and recited poetry, while the older committee members and visitors entertained us with stories from the past and introduced us to the delights of Irish Folklore. Before the classes adjourned for the summer holidays we all went together to the annual Siamsa at the Old Bawn, Tallaght. We saved our pennies for this outing and we really enjoyed the simple ham/salad tea provided, and hours of music, dancing and singing.

Others very much involved with this craobh were the secretary Maire Ní Chearúill of Saw Mill Cottage, Mairéad Ní Lanagáin, Seán Ó Ciarúsa and Peadar Ó Máille.

Other Groups

During the Emergency years another group, Aiseirí, kept the flag flying and met at the Kildare Garage on Emmet Road where also the City of Dublin Girls' Pipe Band practiced for many years. This was followed for a few years by Craobh Liam Partridge, again at the Workmen's Club and organised by Citizen Army veteran George Oman of Anner Road and his friend Garda David Power, an Irish speaker from County Waterford. In the mid forties a lively group of mainly Bulfin Estate teenagers, "Cumann Óige na h-Éireann", held weekly ceilithe at the Athletic Union Hall. Then in the late forties Irish classes were held by Macra Fáil, the junior branch of Fianna Fáil, and assisted by Tom Folan, a native speaker from Spiddal.

Craobh Inse Chór (1951)

When the present Craobh Inse Chór came on the scene in 1951 it faced like its predecessors the same difficulty in securing suitable accommodation as there was still a great dearth of halls in the area. They determined to provide some form of premises for themselves but while this was not achieved until 1959 it was a move which gave more continuity to their efforts. In the meantime they had been around all the usual venues including a room in Keogh Square and the use at times of members homes. The site for the new club-hall at Grattan Crescent was secured from Dublin Corporation through the good offices of the then councillor and later Minister for Defence Mr Kevin Boland. Following an extensive canvass of the district by the members the wherewithal was raised through the sale of Gael Linn pools which allowed a generous rate of commission. Large-scale aeriochts were also held mainly at the Civil Service Hurling Ground in Islandbridge. The most ambitious of these outdoor concerts were the ones held under lights at the Camac Glen, 3rd Lock Bridge, in 1963/'64 as part of Inchicore Youth Week, the latter being masterminded by Father Conor Murphy OMI.

Names associated with the early years of the Craobh were George Oman, Seán and Seosamh Ó Broin, Patricia and Dick Cullen, Seán Caomhánach and Séamus Ó Coileain. Some years later the much talented and widely travelled Liam Ó Buacháin was to make an immense contribution to the Craobh also.

The small hall in its early years played host to such well known musicians and entertainers as Niall Toibín, Seán Maguire, Tony MacMahon and the young piper Liam Ó Floinn and Cabaret Gael Linn, several of whose members later formed the nucleus

Feis Inse Chór about 1962 with Presentation Convent Clondalkin Choir, their teacher and Liam Ó Buacháin, Cathaoirleach

of the Chieftains. Other good friends in those times were harpists Treasa Ní Ghairbhí and Cáit Ní Chonchuir, Bean Uí h-Aodha, Seán Óg Ó Tuama, Liam Ó Murchú, Donall Ó Cuill and local man Breandán Ó Dúill. Also in the early years a very successful girl's club was conducted by the talented young women of Réalt na n-Óg.

Another major event was Feis Inse Chór (1959–1971) under the secretaryship of Seán de Cléir, held at various local venues, mainly the C.I.E. Dining Hall and Áras Mhuire. The dancing section attracted entries from all over Ireland while the Irish language debating competition was supported by many of the major Dublin secondary schools. One of the adjudicators here was An t-Athair (later Cardinal) Tomás Ó Fiaich. A Gaeltacht holiday project for adults also proved successful.

A popular event still at the hall is the annual symposium where current affairs are debated by a panel of well-known personalities. Many of our leading politicians and public figures have over the years participated in this forum.

In 1972 the Craobh established Inchicore's first pre-school "An Naíonra" which is still in action. It was this venture which gave rise in 1977 to Gael Scoil Inse Chór, now located at Islandbridge across the road from the site of Saint Maighneann's monastery.

Chapter Fifty-Three

Old Communities

The oldest housing estate in the district is that which was built by the Great Southern and Western Railway Company for its employees. The first houses in the scheme were built in 1846 and consisted of South Terrace, North Terrace and The Square. As the work force increased, additional dwellings were built at West Terrace, Granite Terrace, Abercorn Terrace, Saint Patrick's Terrace and Saint George's Villas. The first houses had concrete washed facades with Gothic doorways while the later terraces were either brownbrick, redbrick or granite. However one and all were known to the old-timers of the district as "The Cottages". The estate was surrounded by a high cut-stone limestone wall which still remains as a feature of the complex and it was behind this wall that the Inchicore Works community came into being. There was a heavy iron gate at the Grattan Crescent entrance but this was removed about thirty years ago. This gate was never closed over in living memory but older residents believed it was customary to do so once a year in earlier times. For some reason one private dwelling was also built in the middle of the railway works itself and this was last occupied by the McClelland family.

The original entrance to the works was at the rear of Abercorn/Saint Patrick's Terrace and here was situated a single storey house known down to modern times as the "Gate Lodge".

As might be expected there was a large minority of people of English background whose forebears had come to Inchicore right from the start of the railways and in this connection names such as Penycook, Fishburn, Clothier, Caswell and Overend come to mind. In relation to the 141 houses built, the amount of ground given over to the scheme was very extensive indeed and allowed for large open spaces as well as long gardens, both front and rear in many cases. Down the years the estate was maintained by the company and their horse drawn wagon collected the bins several times per week. The men in charge also looked after the Works' fire-engine for it was horse drawn as well. There is a story told that on one occasion the Works' fire brigade was called out to help deal with a fire at the railway company's Great Southern Hotel at Parknasilla in County Kerry! The fire-engine was put on a wagon, the horse in a horse-box and the fire crew in a small passenger coach when they all set off for Killarney from where they drove out to Parknasilla.

In modern times Dublin Corporation took over responsibility for the area and later C.I.E. relinquished its interest in the houses. The down side of living in these houses was the fact that they had to be vacated when the employee reached the retirement age or even should he have died before then. In those cases where there was another family member working for the company it was usually possible to have the house transferred to his name. Houses had also to be vacated if the employee was dismissed and this too was a sanction which was threatened if complaints were received regarding anti-social behaviour by a tenant's family.

The upper portion of the estate was known as the "Pond Field" and you would often hear that somebody "lived in the Pond Field". It got its name from the ornamental pond which was close to the Dining Hall and which was fed by that mostly underground streamlet which flowed from Jamestown, Ring Street, the Oblate grounds and Tyrconnell Park. The pond with its swan house was the centre of a very pretty recreational area with seats, shrubs and plants and surrounded by a hedge. Ernest Joynt in his railway recollections makes an interesting reference to it during a harsh winter towards the end of the last century. He wrote:

> "The winter I spent in the foundry was one of the coldest I ever remember and for two or three weeks there was an intense frost. The pond around the Dining Hall was thickly frozen over and was covered by skaters every night moving to and fro under the light of flares placed around the brink of the water."

This pond was filled in during the mid-twenties and the immediate area converted into a sports field still very much in use. Another place near here but closer to the Works was known as "The Plant" from a plantation of trees which can be seen on old maps.

At the lower end of the estate to the rear of South Terrace is a further area known to the present day as the "cowsheds". The walls of the substantial stone building which gives rise to the name still stand and the rings which secured the cows are remembered by the older generation. The late Agatha Roche told me that her grandmother old Mrs Houlihan (formerly Eliza Lee) kept a small dairy there and used to graze the cows in a field near the Bobbin Mill. One wonders if this building was there from the time of the Cow & Calf Farm already mentioned and which previously formed part of this portion of the estate.

The social life of the area centred around the Dining Hall now the Inchicore Sports and Social Club. Here for generations activities such as concerts, entertainments, dances and gymnastics took place and at one time it even boasted its own string orchestra.

The last house on South Terrace, number 30, which was larger than the rest, was originally occupied by a clerk of works. One person holding that position who lived there with his family was Kieran Holohan, a Laois man coming from a long line of stone-masons. He was also chairman of the management committee of the Railway Institute (Dining Hall) as well as playing an active role in the life of the community. An old photograph shows him as a man of commanding appearance. In the course of a newspaper obituary of 1895 it was stated that Mr Holohan was also "a devoted and silent worker in the national cause dating back as far as 1867".

Anyone who lived on South Terrace always remembered the hundreds of men who walked up and down to the Works in all weathers and particularly the "flypast" of the cyclists which took up to twenty minutes each evening at 5.15 p.m. Then at any hour of the day or night individual firemen and drivers could be seen with their distinctive wicker baskets under their arm as they went to join their trains.

The Model Schools

The Model School is the oldest school in the district and also one of the oldest in Ireland. It was built in 1853 on part of the railway companies ground to cater for the influx of children from the new housing estate. The site had previously been occupied by the old Cow & Calf Inn. Always a national school it had three separate departments for boys, girls and infants. At the turn of the century the then headmaster Barney Flanagan lived in the last house in North Terrace and was the only non-railway employee known to have occupied one of the railway houses.

Over its long history the school had many well known figures both on the staff and amongst its pupils. One of these was the distinguished dramatist, T. C. Murray who was headmaster of the boys' school until his retirement in 1932. Another headmaster was Elias – better known as "Bunty" – Maguire a prize-winning singer at the Feis Ceoil and father of the acclaimed violinist Hugh Maguire. It was Mr Maguire who trained the school choir which broadcast from the old 2RN station in 1937 and then went on to produce a seventy-eight record on the Parlaphone label which was something of a feat at that time. The late Mick Kavanagh, who was secretary of Inchicore Harriers for many years, remembered going as a member of the forty strong choir to the studio at the G.P.O. on a special tram which had been hired for the occasion. The records which featured Adeste Fidelis and Óro Mo Bhaidín were distributed by Duffy's of Thomas Street and sold at 2/6 each. Mick also remembered that "Bunty" got the boys to sell the records locally with a small commission for themselves and they carried them around in their schoolbags which made them very weighty indeed.

A later headmaster was Mr George Brown of "Inchicore Hibernians" fame who had a very long service at the school. At one stage he set up a night school there which was of great benefit to the young people of the area. Another staff member for a short period was the Irish poet Caoimhín Ó Conghaile.

Amongst the well known pupils was the poet Thomas Kinsella then residing at Phoenix Street and who received all his primary education at the Model. Another pupil was the renowned handballer Tom Soye who was Irish champion for seven consecutive years.

A piece of the boys' playground was acquired by Dublin Corporation in 1934 for the purpose of widening Grattan Crescent and with it went seven chestnut trees but one fine specimen still remains. This was the yard where at lunch time some future stars such as Jimmy O'Neill, Dessie Byrne, Jimmy Cummins, Michael Gaff, Theo Foley and Jimmy Mullen practiced their early football skills.

THE RANCH

"The Ranch", a small community of houses adjoining Sarsfield Road while at some remove from modern built-up Inchicore could be said to have been located in the area of the original Inchicore townland. It consisted of Saint Mary's Terrace (demolished about twenty five years ago), Saint Mary's Avenue, First Avenue, Phoenix Street, Liffey Street and Park Street. How "The Ranch" got its name is not known, but it has been suggested that drovers on their way to the Dublin market rested their cattle overnight in the fields nearby.

Saint Mary's Terrace bordering Sarsfield Road and possibly dating to 1856 was the oldest part of this community. The area then being on the verge of the broad tillage and cattle lands of Ballyfermot it may have been built for farm labourers or for some of the workers of the newly established railway works just across the fields.

As mentioned in an earlier chapter a little toll house and turnpike gate once stood near the Ranch corner. Before bringing the turnpike roads in County Dublin to an end a public inquiry was held in 1854. One of those giving evidence was a George Godfrey Place who stated that he held 400/500 acres "beyond the gate". He went on to say that he also had some houses there and "the parties very often object

Saint Mary's Terrace (The Ranch) 1937. Keyber Pass entrance to railway works on the right

to the turnpike and many refuse to take the houses in view of the tolls". It is just possible that the houses mentioned were those of Saint Mary's Terrace. Shortly after this inquiry the turnpike roads were brought to an end but the toll house survived to within living memory and in fact was used for small social get-togethers as late as the 1920s.

The fourteen one-storey little houses on this terrace with a couple of steps going up to them and small gardens were different from the other houses insofar that each of them had separate accommodation for two families but with a common hall door. Here on summer Sundays senior citizens often brought out chairs to watch the world go by, to see the first motor cars passing or the side-cars on the way to Lucan or the Strawberry Beds. An old rhyme began: "The gig broke down at Palmerstown and the jarvey lost his whip". Also on fine days men from the Works sat opposite on the low wall of Rice's field to eat their lunch and to quaff it down with a jug of porter from the nearby Moore's.

Some of my forebears were "Ranchers" as the residents of this area are still called. One of them, my great grandfather Patrick Byrne, described as a labourer, was born near Clondalkin (the family burial place was the ancient Kilbride cemetery) and had come in to seek employment in the newly opened Railway Works. He married an Elizabeth Byrne whose folk had come from Lucan seeking railway employment also.

Here, by way of digression, I put forward the view that the name Byrne is so widespread in West County Dublin and indeed in the city that not all of the clan moved or were moved to County Wicklow following the Anglo-Norman invasion. The other alternative is that a large number of them later managed to return from that county.

Patrick and Elizabeth eventually settled down at number one Saint Mary's Terrace directly opposite the "Khyber Pass" entrance to the railway. Some of their family later went to live in the railway houses and the next occupants of number one for some years were to be Elizabeth's relatives. When the latter moved on to the new housing scheme in the "Bungalow" they were replaced by some of my mother's folks who occupied both sides of the house. Here like so many other "Ranchers" they kept railway boarders, mainly firemen and drivers, while at the end of the long garden to the rear they had a dairy and several cows.

During their tenure in the pre-radio era Sunday afternoon gramophone recitals and musical evenings were a feature and some of Dublin's foremost singers sung in that small dwelling.

Members of the Banim family who lived in the Ranch had a herbal cure for the treatment of jaundice. Another well known resident was Matty Geoghegan who played professional football with Belfast Celtic. Also remembered is the boy soprano James Pearson who sang with the Model School choir.

One of the oldest shops in Inchicore was Flemings of First Avenue which up to recently had been in business for 100 years. One of the many people who come to mind with Seamus Fleming as a young boy was Jack ("Faireye") Fogarty, who was an expert shot when out hunting for rabbits or pigeons. Another was the well known "Hector" McDonnell who went to his reward only a few years ago.

It was in the large wooden hut at Saint Mary's Avenue that the flamboyant Labour T.D. Sean Dunne held his weekly clinic, although that word would not have been known then.

Quite a number of Ranchers, both men and women, were involved in the 1916 Rising and War of Independence and names like Lucy Fleming, Myra Geoghegan, Mick White, Mick Neill, Martin Kavanagh are remembered as well as Citizen Army members such as Ned Keogh and the Bradleys. As elsewhere, it had those who were aggressively pro-British, and some of these on one occasion encouraged a raiding party of soldiers to dig up a certain garden, which they did but without any result.

In the pre-1916 days another lady insisted regularly on loudly playing "God Save the King" on a gramophone just beside her window until finally it was smashed in.

In conclusion it can be said that most of the old "Ranchers" or their forebears had a rural background. Again like all the other local communities they had a great loyalty to the church and thought nothing of the considerable distance they had to walk to the various religious services.

The Bungalow

For decades there had been a grave housing shortage, not only in the area but also throughout the city. The local councillors had been pressing this matter for years and as a result Dublin Corporation finally purchased 12 acres of ground from the Oblate Fathers in April 1902 with a view to building 350 small two storey houses. However this was to be a long drawn out process with the houses eventually being built in three phases.

A Corporation report stated that "the ground contains ample space to provide a scheme of dwellings capable of meeting the fullest demands for proper housing accommodation for the artisan and workingman population in the Inchicore and Kilmainham districts." The purchase price of £4,000 was described as fair and reasonable and the money was used by the fathers to pay off the remaining debt on the church. They could have obtained a higher price from private developers but preferred to see the ground being used for working-class dwellings.

It was a few years before the work got under way, but only 110 houses were built and were not ready for occupation until 1907. The houses in question were at Ring Street, O'Donoghue Street and part of Nash Street. The weekly rent of the larger "parlour" house was 6/- and the smaller size 3/-. The latter were to be reserved strictly for those in receipt of a labourer's wages.

It was agreed in 1908 to build a further 110 houses but this phase was not completed until August 1913. It was more than a year later before the final complement of houses was commenced, the outbreak of the Great War having caused a further delay. These last houses were occupied late in 1916.

Mostly wide streets were provided as well as a spacious green in the centre. This was the first large scale housing development in Inchicore since the building of the railway houses. It was officially known as "The Oblate Site" but soon became popularly known as "The Bungalow". It is said that when the work originally commenced there was only one small house on the site, a bungalow in fact, and hence the name by which it is still known.

Before the scheme was fully completed a minor "border" problem was settled amicably. The boundary between Dublin City and County at that time ran in an irregular fashion close to the north side of Jamestown Road. Some of the land on the county side was owned by Mr Alec Strain and it adjoined the "Bungalow" site which was totally within the city boundary and in order to provide more ground for future housing the Corporation swapped a piece of the city land for a portion of Mr Strain's county land. This also involved some diversion of the direction of the little stream which flowed through Jamestown and under Ring Street. Later Mr Strain built a row of houses on his adjusted holding on Jamestown Road.

Colourful Characters

The area had its share of colourful characters and every second person seemed to have a nickname. Well remembered still is "Father" Hartnett who on meeting an old pal whom he hadn't seen for a long time would say "Kneel down my son and I will give you my blessing". Also remembered is "Pharaoh" Bourke, Molly Reilly and "Madam" Monks. Young ladies came from far and near to the "Madam's" house in Ring Street to have their fortunes told and usually got a slice of cake and a cup of tea while waiting their turn. On occasion when the humour took her she might get them all up in the small room and put them through a figure of the Haymaker's Jig.

As elsewhere in Dublin those early residents had to make a good deal of their own amusement. The principal place for house dancing was Mrs Murphy's of Railway Avenue which had an extension to the rear and where the floor was treated with candle grease for the benefit of the dancers. The sandwiches and refreshments had to be made next door and brought in later during the session. In the summer two local musicians Jack and Andy Tighe were to the fore in organising children's outdoor concerts and "gig" races around the Green for which the winner got a prize of one penny! They also gave recitals for the adults on the footpath outside their own house at New Road. Jack was also a tap dancer with several appearances at the Olympia Theatre to his credit.

There were many other talented residents, notably the tenor Frank Coleman who sang in the Theatre Royal and who was only one of a very musical family.

In a less mobile society than now there was much inter-marrying within the community and it was often said that in Inchicore you wouldn't know where you were talking. This brings to mind that the branches of one extended family were distinguished from each other by being known as either the "Fair" Goughs or the "Dark" Goughs.

Stephen O'Donoghue

As already mentioned two of the streets were named after Father Ring O.M.I. and Councillor Partridge, while Nash Street honoured the much respected Church of Ireland clergyman, the Reverend G. D. Nash, who ministered at Saint Jude's. The origin of O'Donoghue Street however has always been a problem with some maintaining that he had been an Oblate priest. It was Simon Quigley who put forward the view that he was a Fenian and this has proved to be correct. His full name was Stephen O'Donoghue and he was one of three men killed at the "Battle of Tallaght" during the Fenian rising of 1867. He was from Booterstown and we do not know what, if any, his connection was with Inchicore. However his name was previously mentioned in the district back in the last century when that organisation known as the Irish National Foresters called their local group "Branch Stephen O'Donoghue". Councillor James McCann who was probably attached to the foresters as he called his pub "The Forester's Arms" may have put forward the name at a Corporation meeting but we still do not know if O'Donoghue had an actual association with the area.

The late Mrs Annie McElroy told me she remembered the Foresters parading through the district on Saint Patrick's Day in their distinctive regalia accompanied by their pipe-band and carrying banners with long tassels attached – to keep the national spirit alive as she said.

Peadar Kearney

In Inchicore during the War of Independence the largest number of activists came from the Bungalow, notwithstanding that like the rest of the district there was also a very vocal pro-British minority. As well as individuals whole families such as the O'Connors, Doyles, McElroys and O'Neills were involved with the independence movement. It was here also that people such as Nellie Bushell, Willoughby Scott and Captain Jim Donnelly lived and towards the end of the Civil War Peadar Kearney came to reside here as well.

It was Peadar Kearney, a northside man, who wrote the words of the national anthem *The Soldier's Song*. In 1923 he came with his family to 25 O'Donoghue Street where he remained until his death in December 1942. From an early age he had been involved with the national movement and took part in the Rising. Like Nellie Bushell he was an employee of the Abbey Theatre. He was a prolific song and ballad writer and apart from the national anthem his best-known song was *Down by the Glenside.*

For the ten years prior to Peadar's death his nephew Séamus de Búrca visited him every week at his O'Donoghue Street home and usually found him with a book in his hand for he was an inveterate reader. Of one of these visits to his uncle Séamus wrote:

> "On this summer's day it is a pleasure to sit here at the open door with the sun streaming in, the trees of the Oblate Fathers' ground bending beneath their weight of foliage. Occasionally the chiming of the church-tower clock warns us that time is passing as we listen fascinated by the high-pitched voice painting word pictures. Not until the Angelus chimes out do we notice that time has slipped forward."

Peadar Kearney was fifty-nine years of age at the time of his death.

Chapter Fifty-Four

Beyond the 3rd Lock Bridge

The City Bounds

Up to 1938 it could said that Dublin city effectively ended at the 3rd Lock Bridge. A circular hitching rail outside the Black Horse public house was a reminder of the bygone days of horse transport not yet quite over.

On the right hand side there were no houses at all until nearly a mile up the road Dowlings' beautiful residence "Cremorne" at Bluebell was reached. Today this is the site of the Church of Our Lady of the Wayside. The fields of Dowlings farm which produced a wide variety of crops extended all along the side of the road. Here on a summer's day men could be seen making the hay. This brings to mind that at the beginning of this century farmers in this district sometimes went down to the Fountain in James's Street to hire additional seasonal labourers.

Just beyond the bridge on the left hand side was a shop called "Mountain View", while down in the Camac glen was Magee's white-washed round shaped dwelling in the Austrian style. A little further on, a footbridge across the river provided a shortcut to Crumlin. The only house on this side of the road was Warrens until two cottages were reached just before Prescotts dye works with its high chimney. In 1919 the latter was taken over by the Lambe Brothers from County Armagh who established the successful Fruitfield Jams there which provided much employment for the next fifty years. The Lambe family took up residence in the handsome dwelling nearby called "Naisetra" which was recently under threat but has been saved by the concerted effort of the local community. The name as is generally known is artesian spelt backwards, the original owner following this profession. There is in fact a well in the grounds of the house. The next dwelling was the Georgian "Landsdowne House" occupied by Alderman Murty O'Beirne of Dublin Corporation and his family. This house was later used as a laboratory by Roadstone before its demolition. The gate lodge at the entrance to Landsdowne Valley, originally a pretty passway across to Drimnagh, followed.

Another landmark on the Clondalkin side of Bluebell was Portlester House, the home of the patriotic Flood sisters. A few hundred yards further up the road opposite the Old Mill House and near the two cottages known as Avonbeg, a forge was situated up to 1920. Also it was at this point that the little Coolfan crossed under the road to join the Camac, but before doing so formed a wayside pond where ducks paddled about and passing horses were watered.

The 3rd Lock Bridge was one of the venues where the South County Dublin Harriers met during the winter season. What excitement as they gathered, and then with bugle blowing and hounds baying the huntsmen cantered up the avenue of Jamestown House. An account of a particular meet on 6th January 1937 tells how they then headed across the wide wooden bridge known as the "dancing bridge" above the railway works before galloping through the fields of Ballyfermot. Having passed Stone House they checked in at Rafters farm "Árd na Gréine", now the parochial house and after that it was on to Blackditch, Neilstown, Balgaddy and Old Esker.

SOUTH COUNTY DUBLIN HARRIERS

(formerly Hillside Harrier Drag Hunt)

MEET

MARCH, 1929

Saturday, 2nd	...	3rd Lock, Inchicore
Saturday, 9th	...	Point-to-Point
Wednesday, 13th	...	Rathfarnham
Saturday, 16th	...	Rathcoole
Wednesday, 20th	...	Templeogue Bridge
Saturday, 23rd	...	Crumlin Village
Wednesday, 27th	...	Dundrum
Saturday, 30th	...	Kingswood

At 2 o'clock

Old Bluebell

The district of Bluebell takes its name from an inn known as the "Blue Bell" which was on the south side of the Old Naas Road just before the gate lodge of Landsdowne Valley was reached. Some of the structure of the inn remained as part of Landsdowne House which later occupied the site. The sign board and name of the last proprietor of the inn, William Burke, remained for years after its closure and was remembered by people into this century. Later there was a further little pub for a number of years owned by Mrs Ward right at the entrance to Bluebell cemetery, but nothing remains of this now.

A short distance away on the same side of the road as the "Blue Bell" was a second old inn known as the "Red Lyon." The earliest reference to these two inns was in 1757 when they were mentioned in rentals payable to the Earl of Shelbourne who at that time owned Drimnagh Castle and surrounding lands. It is most likely however that they were both in existence before that date. Another inn mentioned in these rentals was the "Slip & Hales", but we do not know its location.

The Old Naas Road, apart from being narrow, was very dangerous due to acute bends and a dip where it crossed over the Camac by means of a little three-arch bridge. As far back as 1798 in the days of coach travel the need to do something about this hazardous stretch was realised. An Act of Parliament was passed at that time ordering the members of the turnpike commission to have a new road at least sixty feet wide built from a spot known as the Sandy Banks "through the lands at the rere of the Red Lyon and Blue Bell Inns". However this project was never carried out and it was not until the late 1940s that the by-pass was built more or less on the line of that proposed in 1798!

The Bluebell story goes back much further than the inn as is evidenced by the little ruin within the older portion of the local cemetery. This is the remains of a medieval oratory associated with the Anglo-Norman presence in the neighbourhood of Drimnagh Castle and was officially known as the Parish Church of Drimna. There is a reference to it in a Saint Patrick's Cathedral document of 1547 and on the Down Survey Map of 1654 it is clearly shown as "The Old Chapple".

I would put forward the theory that the neighbouring place name of Killeen (in Irish An Chillín meaning "the little church") originally referred to a previous Celtic oratory on the same site as the ruin. One way or the other, it is most likely, given the presence of the river and mills and the choice of a nearby location for Drimnagh Castle, that there was always a settlement of people even from earliest times in the area which has come to be known as Bluebell. The presence of the pre-historic tumulus only a short distance away near the Long Mile Road lends further weight to this view.

A visitor to Bluebell in 1890 found that much of the ruin was thickly covered by ivy and commented that the west end was of unusual height in relation to ground level dimensions. He also noted the oblong window at this end high above the rudely arched doorway and surmised that there may have been a gallery there originally.

This oratory ruin along with the much older granite shaft in Bully's Acre are the only two ancient monuments in the whole area.

In the old part of the cemetery the earliest tombstone was dated from 1736, but this burial place would go back much further to the days of the oratory and even before then. A number of the large old tombstones survive still but are illegible. The following is an excerpt from one of them which was recorded many years ago:

Alas she has gone that good neighbour
Who always paid the poor for labour
Nor drove the beggar from her door
But gentle was to rich and poor
God let her have a blessed seat
And let her offspring all be great.

In 1903 the cemetery was extended, but in recent years has been closed except for those with rights there. Many of the older generation of Inchicore and Bluebell folk lie here in what is a quiet and peaceful setting close to the Camac river.

Bluebell was noted for its several woollen mills on the Crooked River. One of these was owned by Robert Wall, described in 1882 as a wool, shawl and frieze manufacturer. This Wall family had their private residence at Tyrconnell Road, Inchicore. The other mill was owned by Samuel E. Hill of Camac House and was referred to by Malachy Horan of Killinarden who was born in 1847:

> "A couple of fleeces of wool would get you the makings of a suit. There were many at it but Hill of Bluebell made the best stuff, the frieze. He charged 3 pence the pound for making yarn from your own wool. We brought the cloth home and it was there the suits were made by a travelling tailor."

Malachy's opinion was borne out at the Dublin International Exhibition of 1865 where the adjudicators declared that this mill had displayed an excellent assortment of friezes "remarkable for their finish and strength".

When this mill closed it became the Nugget Boot Polish Company.

The Granny Bush

Both the one storey houses with their large gardens on the side of the Old Naas Road and their counterparts to the rear in Bluebell Lane were built about 1910. All of these replaced much older small cottages. Canal Terrace dates from before 1900 and is still known as the Land League cottages. It was here that the jolly Michael O'Neill who was full of the lore of Old Bluebell lived until his death some years ago. He

Ploughman Jem Maher at Bluebell, about 1941

remembered the older women going to Mass on Sundays in their black shawls and button boots. He also remembered them on fine summer evenings sitting on a stone under what was known as the "Granny Bush" in Bluebell Lane and here they knitted and sewed or put patches on trousers as they chatted away.

After all those years Michael still recalled as a small boy the appetising smell of rashers and eggs being fried by crew members on the passing canal boats. Other memories were of six little cottages in the lane "stacked together like loaves of bread". The last one of these was unoccupied and here locals used to gather for house dances with hens and chickens looking in the back window. Games played in his youth were pitch and quotes, the latter being a flat stone, and "Filly Folks Tail". The one and a half ton tombstones laid flat to deter the grave snatchers he referred to as "Kenappers".

Michael enjoyed his many years with the Bluebell Fife & Drum Band and their many outings when porter was only two pence a pint.

Also in Bluebell Lane was Riverside House, better known as Maggie Murphy's. This formidable lady and her sister managed a small dairy holding here and it was no bother to either of them to buy and sell their cattle in the market. Another holding nearby was "Millrose", owned by the well known Hanlon family.

One of Michael's neighbours, the ever young Josie Hunt, remembers her mother leaving out the sheets on the grass for bleaching, particularly on a frosty night. She also has faint memories of some of the wake games which were beginning to die out

The Nugget Boot Polish Company, Bluebell, formerly a woolen mills

in her young days. These involved forfeits when, for example, a person might be asked on a wet and windy night to go out and pull a head of cabbage. Also should someone fall asleep during the wake the others would blacken his or her face with soot.

Another memory is of Bluebell people, both men and women, going down the canal to attend the 6.30 a.m. Mass each morning during a mission or retreat in the Oblates. They were fasting of course and then after Mass they went up the canal again to snatch a hasty breakfast before reporting for work at 8.00 a.m.

In 1929 a spacious housing estate known as Camac Park was provided by the Soldiers' and Sailors' Trust for ex-British army men and their families on a site which was previously called the Nine Acres.

Old Bluebell was always well known as an industrious and thrifty community where many earned their livelihood in the local mills or the Inchicore railway works or with local farmers. Incomes were very often supplemented by the cultivation of large vegetable gardens and sometimes by pig and poultry rearing.

In days gone by the community spirit was best exemplified by the local band and football teams. The Bluebell Wolfe Tone Fife and Drum Band was in existence from at least 1891 when it played at the Parnell meeting in Inchicore. Like so many other such bands in County Dublin it only came to an end in the 1960s despite the valiant efforts of people like the late Mick Walsh to keep it going. By then also time had begun to catch up with Old Bluebell as new housing and industrial estates were built nearby. That the old spirit still carried on was shown once more by the building of a fine community centre in 1980 for which both old and new residents worked in harmony.

Chapter Fifty-Five

The Crooked River

The little Camac River which flows through Inchicore and Kilmainham has its source in the Dublin hills near Ballinascorney, or as the Cromwellian surveyors of 1654 put it:

> "The little Cammock descends from the mountains by many small rills dispensing its streams in many parts of the west of this barony."

It takes many twists and turns as it makes its way through Brittas, Crooksling, Saggart, Baldonnell, Corkagh, Clondalkin, Killeen, Bluebell, Drimnagh, Inchicore and Kilmainham before entering the Liffey under Heuston Station. At least one old Inchicore man used to refer to it as the crooked river, and how correct he was! – for its original Irish name An Chamog signifies curved or crooked. As previously mentioned the earliest reference to the river was in 1326 in the *Register of Kilmainham*. Here it was stated that a portion of land had been given to one Peter Ludlow, a carpenter, on condition that he maintained all the timberwork at a mill on the Camoke. Other anglicised forms of the name used later were Le Camocke, Cammock, Commock and finally Camac, by which it is still known.

The Camac's flow of water was supplemented by the diversion of another stream through an artificial channel not too far from its source and also by several other natural streams which joined it on its seventeen mile journey down to the Liffey. One of these small streams is the now almost forgotten Coolfan, which flows down through Newlands, Ballymount and Robinhood before crossing under the Naas Road to merge with the Camac less than a mile from Blue Bell. The Irish form of the name is An Caol Fionn, meaning the narrow clear stream.

A stone building known as the "Old Mill House" under which the Coolfan actually flowed was situated almost on the verge of the north side of the Naas Road and not far from where the two rivers met. It was last occupied before road widening as a dwelling and shop by the Shelley family.

The Camac then flows in a wide circle through the Blue Bell district and crosses under the old Naas Road and the dual carriageway before passing near to Drimnagh Castle and entering what became known as the Landsdowne Valley. This name derived from the Landsdowne family, who acquired the castle in the last century. In ancient times however this was Cromghlinn or the winding glen, which became anglicised as Crumlin, a name that eventually drifted southwards to its present location. Our river flowed down this glen and then under Golden Bridge, before heading for Kilmainham, Bow Bridge and the Liffey.

River Camac near Turvey Avenue

The Many Mills

There can hardly have been a more productive little river than the Camac in any part of Ireland. Its waters, from earliest times to within living memory, turned many a mill wheel providing power for an amazing range of enterprises, of which there were nearly thirty along its course. Originally these were water mills used for grinding corn, particularly at monasteries such as Kilmainham and Clondalkin. When the Hospitallers took over at Kilmainham they made more extensive use of the water power as we have seen from the reference to a Fulling Mill in the *Extent*. Fulling is the art of cleaning, thickening and softening the woven fabric. Kilmainham Mills at this same location changed hands many times over the years and is still in operation today although water power is no longer used. Many however will remember the very large mill-wheel which was still turning up to about forty years ago.

Another popular use of the river was for woollen mills, of which there were two at Bluebell and one at Inchicore Road. The latter, known as the Hibernian Mills, was pretty extensive and had been established by the Willans, a Welsh family, in the early nineteenth century. At this location there had been a previous mill for many centuries being referred to as the Upper Mill in a document of 1630.

> "A parcel of pasture and meadow on each side of the river Commock near the west end of Kilmainham bounded by the road south and the new water course of the Upper Mill on the north."

The Willans also built a row of houses for their employees as well as the Congregational Church across the road. They themselves lived in "Susan Vale" a house which is still occupied.

Over the years mills were sometimes put to a series of different uses and this one changed from woollens to flour and finally became the Metropolitan Laundry early in the present century. Also in this century one of the Bluebell woollen mills became the Nugget Boot Polish Company while the flour mills at Mount Brown later produced paper.

From the late eighteenth century paper making became widespread in Dublin and as mentioned earlier the Camac supported six paper mills in all, including Golden Bridge. From the time of the invention of the steam engine not all mills relied totally on water power and some of them alternated the two sources of power, water of course being the cheaper.

The diversity of the use to which the Camac water was put is further illustrated by the several gunpowder mills at Corkagh near Clondalkin, the linseed oil mills at Fairview also near Clondalkin, the printing works known as the Holly Brook Mills just above the 3rd Lock Bridge and the electricity generated at the Metropolitan Laundry.

The Holly Brook Mill owned by the Warrens, an old Dublin printing family, was down in the glen of the Camac river below their dwelling, Holly Brook House, which stood on the side of the Naas Road. This printing works which specialised in the printing and binding of religious books went out of business about 1912. One member of the family, Father Patrick Warren, was later Parish Priest of Chapelizod. Another branch of the family also had a printing establishment in Old Kilmainham.

The Camac's last contribution to local mills before it joined the Liffey was at the rere of Saint Patrick's Hospital, from where a millrace dating to at least 1673 was taken off and which crossed Steeven's Lane to what is now Guinness property.

On the negative side, much hardship was caused in years gone by to the residents of the mud-walled cottages of Turvey Avenue by flooding and also to other small houses near the river in Old Kilmainham. During the great rainstorm of 8th December 1955 people had to be evacuated and some were accommodated in the Parochial Hall in James's Street.

Egan's Pond

All of the mills required a holding pond nearby as well as a millrace. One of these ponds, two and a half acres in extent, was at Grattan Crescent and on a higher level than the Camac. It was fed by a channel of water taken from that river at a weir to the rear of Tyrconnell Road near the cinema. A millrace then continued from the pond to the mill/laundry on Inchicore Road and further still to the Kilmainham Mill, passing on its way the massive wall of the jail.

This pond was known to older residents as Egan's Pond and we can only assume that it had some association with the family of that name who were the proprietors of the nearby Black Lion for well over 100 years. In its own way, it was a picturesque nature reserve where swans and ducks nested amongst the reeds year after year. Unfortunately when the laundry went out of business the pond was neglected and it deteriorated into a swamp. A new owner had it filled with large quantities of heavy rubble from the historic Wood Quay site, something which for a time attracted the attention of amateur archaeologists armed with metal detectors. Finally, after years of agitation by the local residents' association, Dublin Corporation took it over as a public park. Perhaps in years to come if some Wood Quay artifacts should surface here future historians may conclude that this was the site of the elusive longphort! For the record, further rubble from Wood Quay was dumped at the back of the "Ranch" to form a foundation for the new motorway.

Chapter Fifty-Six

The Latter Decades

The Latter Decades

In Ireland generally the 1950s and early 1960s were a time of continuing unemployment and massive emigration. Nevertheless the traditional local industries which provided a considerable amount of work, perhaps more for women than for men, kept going still. A six-week rail strike at Inchicore in 1950 brought the long established National Union of Railwaymen to an end in this country.

A revolutionary change took place at the Inchicore Railway Works in the early 1950s with the change-over from steam to diesel engines. A whole way of life at the Works was coming to an end and many of the old skills were no longer required. It was the end also for the famous running shed, the massive coal tower and coal bank. Although the change was necessary it resulted, along with the continuing competition from road transport, in a steady decline in the workforce. Unfortunately nobody at the time had the foresight to diversify into other enterprises.

It was in those years that the Inchicore Hibernian's Gaelic Football Club under the guidance of Mr George Brown, principal of the Model School, was coming to the fore and in 1958 they won the County Dublin Junior Championship.

A Visit to Old Kilmainham

"The old water-mill was working when we visited Kilmainham. I must confess that I too was thrilled as I watched the big wheel splashing in the turbid millrace. I recalled George Elliot's picturesque phraseology when in *The Mill on the Floss* she wrote of 'the unresting wheel sending out its diamond jets of water.'"

"It was certainly difficult to imagine that behind the group of charming well-kept cottages the traffic was rushing along heedless of the fact that here a few yards away life ran as serenely as it did in mediaeval days.

"Sandra (an American visitor) was also fascinated by the fact that here in this quiet corner of the city time apparently stood still. This was one place where Dublin remained unchanged.

"We were brought back to reality when we found ourselves surrounded by a group of chubby, good-looking children, 'Eh, mister', said one bright lad, 'come on and I'll show you Shakespeare's house.'

> "We followed him into the courtyard. The big house with the four floors, the beautifully proportioned windows, the delightful door and the quaint figure of the dreamer certainly gave us a thrill. I cannot recall seeing anything like it anywhere in Dublin. It is now set in flats and certainly it is remarkably well kept considering its age."
>
> – John McCaffrey in *The Irish Press*
> November 1952

The Shakespeare House described above was officially Riversdale House which originally had a large garden in front of it and was situated at 40 Old Kilmainham. It dated from at least 1725 and as earlier mentioned it was for a long number of years the residence of the lawyer Sir Simon Bradstreet in the eighteenth century. In 1912 when overgrowing ivy was being taken down from the front of the house a statue of William Shakespeare over the entrance door was discovered which closely resembled the Westminster Abbey statue in honour of the poet. By 1965 the house was in decay and it was pulled down but unfortunately the statue also went with it.

Another equally old house which stood on the other side of the road known as "Ashmount" survived until 1993.

Railway workers on Tyrconnell Road during the Oblate Father's centenary celebrations, 1956

Oblate Centenary

The Oblate Fathers' Centenary in 1956 was marked with an elaborate programme of events and a guard of honour of sodality men wearing their blue sashes lined both sides of Tyrconnell Road when President Seán T. Ó Ceallaigh arrived for the Commemorative Mass. The organising committee also published the scholarly and valuable centenary number *Across a Century.*

The Saint Vincent's Youth Club

From 1958 to 1981 Saint Vincent's Youth Club catered for the disadvantaged young people of Keogh Square and later Saint Michael's Estate. As well as a wide range of sporting activities the Club assisted the youth to secure employment and where necessary provided reading and writing classes. The parents were involved by means of a back-up committee which later became the Keogh Square Residents' Association. For over seventeen years holidays were provided for both boys and girls at venues in many parts of Ireland. In 1975 the Club undertook a summer project, one of the first in Dublin City, and in 1976 was instrumental in building a youth centre at Emmet Road which in 1981 became the Saint Michael's Parish Community Centre.

Another major achievement was the publication for many years of the monthly community magazine *The Link* which not only covered Inchicore but Bluebell as well and at one stage sold over 1,000 copies per month. The file of this publication should provide future social historians with a mine of information.

Funeral of William T. Cosgrave

The state funeral of William T. Cosgrave, first President of the Irish Free State, took place to Goldenbridge Cemetery on 18th November 1965. The very large attendance was headed by President Éamonn de Valera and Taoiseach Seán Lemass. It was a day of torrential rain as the gun-carriage bearing the coffin and the cortege drove up Saint Vincent's Street to the cemetery where following the graveside prayers military honours were rendered.

Amongst the clergy present was Father James Moran O.M.I., superior of House of Retreat, who had served at the Glencree establishment when Mr Cosgrave spent some time there disguised as a clerical student during the War of Independence.

A Lively Scene

During the post-War period Inchicore was being gradually surrounded by great new housing estates at Drimnagh, Walkinstown and Ballyfermot and it was to these that many of the young newly married people went to live, although Walkinstown was considered to be a "bit of a foreigner". Locally, additional housing was provided at Bulfin Gardens, Jamestown Avenue and Oblate Drive.

The area presented a lively scene, what with the constant flow of workers coming and going either on foot or on bicycle, the many factory hooters, each with its own distinctive wail rending the air four times a day and the great variety of door to door deliveries. Then throughout the night the distant thud-thud of canal boat engines and the nearer puff-puff of railway steam-engines could be heard. Also the district was teeming with a young population to be seen playing their games after school on footpaths, streets and waste ground. Summer holidays were limited to five or six weeks and a mid-term break was unheard of. While the population could be broadly described as working class there was also a strong business community. Nearly all of the latter, such as grocers, publicans, bank managers and butchers, lived with their families beside or over their premises. There were also doctors, pharmacists, teachers, policemen and even T.D.s living in the area.

All churches were packed on Sundays as well as for the numerous novenas and missions. Last Mass was at twelve noon, before and after which it was customary for the menfolk to tarry in conversation on the footpath outside. Monthly sodalities for men, women, boys and girls were all strongly supported. Best remembered of the Easter ceremonies was the office of Tenebrae at the Oblate Church when the whole

Bus assembly works at Spa Road, 1941

community of about thirty priests in white surplices chanted the divine office in Latin. The church was in darkness save for the lighted candles on a high stand which were gradually extinguished. The ceremony came to an end in dramatic fashion as the priests one after another closed their heavy missals with a loud impact. Good Friday was a solemn day with even Radio Éireann off the air and all shops in the area closed during the Stations of the Cross at 3.00 p.m.

Economic Progress

The 50th anniversary of the 1916 Rising was celebrated enthusiastically in 1966 and Kilmainham Gaol was re-opened again, this time as a museum. It had been restored by the Herculean efforts of voluntary workers from all over the city who spent years on the project, which to them had been a labour of love. Some of the local people who were involved with the work of the Restoration Committee were Patricia Valentine, John Sammon and Paddy McWeeney. In the weeks which followed its opening long queues of visitors formed, some of which stretched down as far as the Library.

In the latter half of the 1960s the state commenced to move into an era of greater prosperity and employment for the first time since self-government. Soon the sight of people with large brown paper parcels tied with string and waiting for tram or bus on a Monday morning to take them in to "uncle's", as the pawn shop in James's Street was known, would be but a memory. However further economic recessions were to follow in the 1980s before eventually the present "Celtic Tiger" emerged.

Community Activities

For some reason the 1970s were a high point of unpaid voluntary activities, not only among the youth clubs and other groups, but also the newly formed resident associations. The latter included Bulfin Estate, who built their own centre, Keogh Square, Oblate Site, Tyrconnell, CIE Estate and GIWME, which covered Grattan Crescent, Inchicore Road, Woodfield and Emmet Road. Together these associations formed the Federation of Inchicore Resident Associations. The Federation organised two or three annual community weeks for the entire area with a wide-ranging programme of events for young and old. Its most important achievement was the Health Centre on Emmet Road which was only provided by the powers that be after a lengthy and tenacious campaign. It can also take credit for the all-weather pitch at Saint Michael's Estate and the eventual conversion of the "Swamp" at Grattan Crescent into a public park. Over the years most, but not all, of these residents associations and the Federation itself fell by the wayside but of late some of them are coming to life again.

It was also in this decade that John Gleeson and myself with the backing of Tim Dawson and Frank Murphy, both of the Old Dublin Society, launched the Inchicore and District Local Historical Society. The society, which had the use of the Conradh Hall, lasted for over ten years and during that time held regular lectures and pleasant outings to places of historical interest in city and county. Also, the contacts made in those years were to be of much benefit later on during the preparation of this publication.

The Harry McCaffrey and Margaret Kane Irish dancing schools catered for hundreds of pupils. The Saint Cecilia Accordion Band under Johnny Mitchell and supported by a very interested parents' committee provided a musical outlet for many more. For further variety still, Father Horan OMI introduced basketball to the area. Also the local Catholic Boy Scouts and Girl Guides had their origins in these years as well.

Changing Times

In 1972 in an attempt to bring about a ceasefire in the six counties, Dr John O'Connell T.D. arranged a secret meeting at his residence, "Beaconsfield", on Inchicore Road between the then leaders of the Provisional IRA and Mr Harold Wilson, former British Prime Minister. Nothing came of these talks.

In this decade, notwithstanding the increased prosperity, the old ways were giving ground to the new technology. It was against this background that many of

The heart of Inchicore in the early fifties

the traditional industries in the area, such as Brassingtons' Saw Mills, the Metropolitan and Dunlops' Laundries, the Nugget Boot Polish Company, Lambs Jams and the Spa Road Coach Works came to an end while Rowntrees limited their operations to distribution. Since then some compensation has been gained through the new industrial estates at Goldenbridge and Jamestown and the development of lesser enterprises at Old Kilmainham.

Keogh Square, which had by now deteriorated, was demolished and replaced by the high rise flats known as Saint Michael's Estate in 1970 and the last remaining housing blackspots in the district were also removed. Sadly it has to be recorded that these belated improvements were not followed up by any major initiatives such as major resource centres to improve the lot of the underprivileged, particularly the youth, and inevitably this neglect brought social problems in its train. Credit of course, has to be given to the voluntary groups who continued to provide services to the best of their ability as well as those Sisters who chose to live in the flats.

In 1986 only the spire of Saint Jude's Church on Inchicore Road was saved despite the efforts of the Inchicore/Kilmainham Heritage Group to have the entire building preserved.

In 1556 as earlier related the Northern chief Shane O'Neill made his submission to an English Viceroy at Kilmainham. At this same venue on 6th November 1994, a protective cordon of Irish soldiers having taken up position that morning, an Irish Taoiseach, Mr Albert Reynolds, met an English Prime Minister, Mr John Major, for a summit meeting in the ongoing saga of Anglo-Irish relations.

In the last few years there has been a big increase in the number of small industries in the area and in the building of apartments on every available site. There is also an increasing young population.

Inchicore/Bluebell/Islandbridge and part of Kilmainham along with Rialto have been designated as a Partnership Area and, more recently, Dublin Corporation has published an Action Plan. Hopes are high that these welcome moves, together with an increasing pride in both our heritage and environment, will herald a new beginning for this old locality as a new millennium beckons.

Ní neart go chur le chéile.

Acknowledgements

For their kind assistance, co-operation and courtesy, I wish to thank the Trustees and staff of the National Library of Ireland, the staffs of the National Museum, Royal Irish Academy, Royal Society of Antiquaries of Ireland, National Archives, Trinity College, Irish Manuscripts Commission, Department of Arts, Heritage, Gaeltacht and the Islands, Roinn Bhéaloideas Éireann, U.C.D., An Coimisiúin Logainmneacha, Dublin City & County Archives, Gilbert Library, Kilmainham Jail, Royal Hospital Kilmainham, Inchicore Library, Military Archives, Gárda Síochána Archives, Iarnród Éireann, Bus Éireann, Railway Record Society, Conradh na Gaeilge, Dublin Cemeteries Committee and members of The Old Dublin Society, who since their foundation in 1934 have built up a treasure-house of information on the city and its environs.

In particular, I wish to thank Mr Fergal Tobin for his invaluable advice and assistance and likewise Dr Howard Clarke, Dr Dáithí Ó h-Ógáin, Dr Noel Kissane, Dr Seán Ó Cearnaigh, Dr W. Nolan, Dr F. Darcy, Professor F. X. Martin O.S.A., Fr W. McGonagle O.M.I., Fr Michael O'Connor O.M.I., Canon J. Crawford, Mícheál Ó Siochrú, Pádraig Ó Snodaigh, Eugene A. Coyle, Geraldine Stout, Raghnall Ó Floinn, Piarais and Diarmuid O'Connor, Seán Dwyer, Kathleen Collins, Rory O'Farrell, Charlotte Brooks, Patrick Cooke, Curator Kilmainham Jail, Níamh O'Sullivan, Catherine Marshall, Curator, Royal Hospital, Deirdre Uí Eineacháin, Síobhán de h-Óir, Colette Ellison, Síobhán O'Rafferty, Eilís Ní Bhrádaigh, Margaret Clancy, Eugene Field, William Dick, Peter Rigney, Hugh Geraghty, Cyril McIntyre, Seán Kennedy, Patrick Healy, Archivists Mary Clarke, Pauline Duffy, Caitríona Crowe and Gregory O'Connor, Comdt P. Young, Comdt V. Lang, Richard Flatman, Diarmuid Breathnach, Seán MacMathúna, Bláthnaid Uí Bhrádaigh, Lar Joye, Aoife O'Shea, Tony Roach, Eamonn Casey, Gráinne Doran, Paula Howard, George McCullough, General Manager Glasnevin Cemetery, Michael Donohue, Caretaker Goldenbridge Cemetery, Joseph Morton, Kilmainham Courthouse and Martin Arthur our local librarian.

I am also indebted to the late Professor T. P. Ó Néill, Éamonn de h-Óir, Pearse Doyle and Tomás Scott. Ar Dheis Láimh Dé go raibh siad uilig.

Likewise much credit is due to Mr P. J. Cantwell, Manager, Trustee Savings Bank, Dr William Boles and Mr James Doody, Manufacturing Manager, Inchicore Works, all of whom helped in a variety of ways.

I am extremely grateful to the Heritage Council as the main sponsors of the work and also to the Trustee Savings Bank and Iarnród Éireann for additional funding.

I was indeed blessed with such competent and willing people as Marie Dunne, Jean O'Hanlon and Shirley and David Kerr who over the years undertook the arduous task of typing, retyping and word-processing from my not exactly copperplate hand. I also wish to thank Lynda Burke who undertook the proof-reading and Séamus Ó Maitiú for kindly reading the finished manuscript.

In the earlier stages Christopher Keogh assisted with the research for as long as he was in a position to do so and was very successful in what he undertook. Robert O'Regan next came to my assistance for several years. Not only did Bob follow up the numerous references which I gave him, but he also used his own initiative to unearth other items which I might never have come across. To both these fellow Inchicore men I express my gratitude.

Neither must I overlook our "Village Barber" Thomas Fagan for his continuous interest and help in so many ways.

It is obvious that no local history would be complete without the reminiscences and recollections of its senior citizens both past and present. In conclusion therefore, I am happy to thank and to list to the best of my ability all such persons as well as others who helped in any way:

John Byrne
Margaret Byrne
Gertrude Byrne
Mick Byrne
Elizabeth Byrne
Pat Byrne
Anthony Byrne
Daniel Behan
William Booker
Maura Brady
Battie Brennan
Kathleen Brophy
Jim Clarke
Michael Conaghan Ald.
Willie Connolly
John Connor
Benny Connolly
Dan Conroy
Dick Cullen
Lily Cullen
Elizabeth Currivan
Danny Darcy
Helen Darcy
Tim Dawson
Maureen Dempsey
Richard Dowling
Comdt Seán Dowling
John Doyle
Joseph Dunne
Michael Dwyer
Arthur Farrell
Deirdre Farrell
John Gogarty
Paddy Guilfoyle
William Goggins
Benny Gough
Phil Gough
Tommy Hillick
Willie Hillick
Peggy Hope
Masie Houlihan
Josie Hunt
Peggy Jennings
Mick Kavanagh
Seán Kavanagh
Mary Kelly
June Kelly
Frank Kelly
John Kennedy
Jim Mitchell T.D.
Edward King
Dermot Larkin
Eleanor Larkin
Lily Mackin
Tom Maher
Brendan Malone
Jim Malone
Tom McCann
Annie McElroy
Eoin Mac Daithi
Ray McGovern
Rita McGowan
Pádraig Mac Ionraic
Tommy McLoughlin
Phil Mooney
Frances Moran
Frank Murphy
Seán Murphy
Bernard Neary
Pat O'Callaghan
Pádraig Ó Cearbhaill
Mary O'Connell
Gerard O'Connell
Michael O'Flanagan
Pádraig Ó Laoghaire
Liam O'Meara
Michael O'Neill
Gerard O'Reilly
Mick O'Reilly
Joseph Owens
Philip Preston
Margaret Quigley
Seán Quigley
Simon Quigley
Anne Reynolds
Theresa Reynolds
Phil Robinson
Nellie Ryan
Paddy Ryan
Val Scott
Fr Ml. Swords
Thomas A. Tighe
Thomas C. Tighe
Séamus Ware
Joseph Williams
Ethel Woodful

Morgan Frazer
Seamus Fleming
Margaret Forrestal
Seamus Farmer
Dolores Owens
Joe Mooney
Kitty Phillips
Anthony Power
Patrick Myler
Rita Woodful
George Wilson
Frank Matthews
Rev. Arthur Hughes

Seosamh Ó Broin
Meitheamh 1999

Bibliography

Abbreviations:

D.H.R.	–	Dublin Historical Record
R.I.A.	–	Royal Irish Academy
N.L.I.	–	National Library of Ireland
N.A.	–	National Archives
J.R.S.A.I.	–	Journal of the Royal Society of Antiquaries of Ireland

Chapter 1

Antiquities & Place Names of South County Dublin, Liam Price (D.H.R. Vol II)

Patterns in the Past: Co. Dublin 5000 BC to AD 1000, Geraldine Stout and Matthew Stout (Dublin City & County edited by Galen & Whelan)

The Excavation of a Composite Tumulus at Drimnagh, H.E. Kilbride-Jones (J.R.S.A.I 1939)

Traditions of Drimnagh, Liam Ua Broin (J.R.S.A.I 1942)

Sketches, Notes & Diaries (1759 - 1830), Austin Cooper, N.L.I.

The Illustrated Archaeology of Ireland (Edited by Michael Ryan)

Roadways in Ancient Ireland, Colm O'Lochlainn (Feil-Scribhinn Eoin Mhic Neill)

Life of Maighneann in Silva Gadelica (1-XXX1), Standish H. O'Grady

The Martyrology of Aengus (Whittley Stokes)

Translation of verse by Dr. Daithí Ó h-Ogáin

Dublin & the Four Masters, B. MacGiolla Phádraig M.A. (D.H.R. Vol VI)

Ireland AD 800 to AD 1600, Fr. John Ryan S.J.

Early Christian Ireland, Dr. Maire & Dr. Liam de Paor including final quotation

Chapter 2

The Bloodied Eagle, Dr. Howard B. Clarke (Irish Sword XVIII)

Norse Dublin, Edward Curtis M.A., D. Litt (D.H.R. Vol IV)

Scandanavian Objects found at Islandbridge / Kilmainham, S. Coffey & E.C.R. Armstrong (R.I.A., 1910)

Norse Antiquities in Ireland, Johannes Boe, Oslo, Vol. 3

A Neglected Viking Burial (C.S. Briggs, M. Guido & A. Walsh)

On the Scandanavian Antiquities lately discovered at Islandbridge, W.R. Wilde (R.I.A., 1866)

The Topographical Development of Scandanavian Dublin, John Bradley (Dublin City and County, Galen & Whelan)

The Vikings in Ireland, Dr. Liam S. Gogan (Irish Times 22/10/1934)

Irish Independent Report (13/2/1933)

Irish Press Reports 19/4/1934 & 16/10/1934

The Danes & Norsemen in England, Scotland and Ireland, J.J.A. Worsaae 1852

Lewis Topographical Dictionary 1837 (Finds at Bully's Acre)

A Re-consideration of the Location/Context of the Viking Burials at Kilmainham/Islandbridge, Elizabeth O'Brien (Dublin and Beyond The Pale)

Chapters 3–7

Medieval Dublin, The Making of a Metropolis, Editor Dr. Howard B. Clarke
The Hospitallers of Kilmainham and their Guests, Charles McNeill (J.R.S.A.I 1924)
The Knights Hospitallers of St. John of Jerusalem at Kilmainham, Dr. G. Lennox Barrow (D.H.R. Vol 28)
A History of Medieval Ireland, A.J. Othway-Ruthven
Ireland in the Middle Ages, Dr. Seán Duffy
Irish Monastic Possessions, Newport White (Irish Mss. Commission) re "Extent of Kilmainham".
The Reformation in Dublin, Fr. Myles Ronan, re "Extent of Kilmainham".
The Bell of Kilmainham, E. Percival Wright (J.R.S.A.I 1900)
Irish Medieval Tiles, Eames & Fanning (R.I.A. 1988)
The Fisheries of the River Liffey, A.E.J. Went (J.R.S.A.I 1953/54)
The Liffey in Dublin, J.W. de Courcy
History of the City of Dublin, Warburton Whitelaw & Walsh
Lazar Houses of St. Laurence & St. Stephen in Dublin, Rev. Myles Ronan
The Custom of Riding the Franchise of the City of Dublin, Paul Ferguson (Sinsear 1979)
An Leabhar Branach, Seán MacAirt (Dublin Institute for Advanced Studies)
The Revolt of Silken Thomas, Laurence McCorristine
Calendar of Patent Rolls, Elizabeth (1576–1602)
Calendar of State Papers, Elizabeth (1598–1599)

Chapters 8–9

Patent Roll 9, James I, Part 2
The Depositions, Trinity College Dublin MSS. 809 & 810
Court of Outlaws, Anal. Hib. XXIII (1966) & Kilmainham
The History of a Settlement Older than Dublin (Colm Kenny)
Hell or Connaught, Peter Beresford Ellis
The Civil Survey, Co. of Dublin Vol VII, Robert C. Simington
An Ghaeilge i mBaile Átha Cliath, Dr. Liam Mac Mathúna
Some Inhabitants of the Baronies of Newcastle and Uppercross, edited by Richard M. Flatman (Irish Genealogist, Vol. VIII & V112)
Heart Money Rolls for Co. Dublin (Kildare Archaeological Society Journal)
The Royal Hospital Kilmainham, Coy. Sgt. E. Tobin (An Cosantoir)
The Royal Hospital, Childers & Stewart
History of The Royal Hospital, Rev. N. Burton
The Hospitals of Kilmainham, Laurence O'Dea (D.H.R. 1965)
The Charter of the Royal Hospital, Public Records Office
Bully's Acre & Royal Hospital Kilmainham Graveyards, Seán Murphy
The Journal of John Stevens, Edited by Robert H. Murray
Oakbeams of R.H.K., P. Ó Néill (Anois 7/9/1991)
Map N.L.I.

Chapters 10–12

The Annesley Case, Earnán P. de Blaghd (D.H.R. 1962)
The Annesley Case, Howells State Trials (Vol. 17)
Horses, Lords and Racing Men, Dr. Fergus A. D'Arcy
Exshaws Magazine 6/8/1747 (K. Races)
Sleaters Gazetteer Dec 1763
Natural History of County Dublin (1772), Dr. Rutty

Islandbridge Barracks, Comdt. P.D. O'Donnell (An Cosantoir)
Kilcullen Road Company, Directors Journal 1787 (National Library)
Kilcullen Turn Pike, Joseph Lecky (J.R.S.A.I Vol 113)
Mullingar Road Company Minute Book (Dublin Co. Council)
Traditions of Drimnagh, Liam Ua Broin (J.R.S.A.I 1942)
St. Catherines Bells, Walter Meyler
Early History of the Grand Canal, Henry Phillips (D.H.R. Vol 1)
The Grand Canal, Henry Phillips (Kildare Archaeological Journal)
The Grand Canal of Ireland, Ruth Delaney
The Grand Canal at Inchicore & Kilmainham (Inchicore & Kilmainham Development Project)

Chapters 13–14

Bully's Acre & Royal Hospital Kilmainham Graveyards, Sean Murphy
The Royal Hospital, Childers & Stewart
A History of Co. Dublin, Frances E. Ball.
Hibernian Journal 7/4/1780 (Body Snatching)
St. Catherines Bells, Walter Meyler
Freemans Journal, 9/10/1787
Dublin Hanged, P.J. Henry
History of Clonmel, W.P. Burke
Bucks and Bruisers (Ref. to "Bully" Egan), J.C. Reid
Co. Dublin Elections, Eugene A. Coyle (D.H.R. 1991)
Sir Ed Newenham, Eugene A. Coyle (D.H.R. 1993)
Kilmainham a Settlement Older than Dublin (Colm Kenny)
Anal. Hib. 1966 (Court of Outlaws)
Prisons in England & Ireland 1784 (Howard)
Hibernian Magazine 19/3/1786, 20/3/1786, 28/3/1786 and Garda Review August 1960
Kilmainham Jail, A.J. Nowlan (D.H.R. 1958)
Kilmainham Jail, Freida Kelly
Botany Bay, Con Costello
Sleators Gazette 4/11/68 (Execution at Gallows Hill)
Hibernian Journal 26/2/72 (Highwaymen)
Irish Priests in Penal Times, W.P. Burke

Chapter 15

The Personnel of the Dublin Society of United Irishmen, R.W. McDowell (Irish Historical Studies Vol 2 1940)
The Lives and Times of the United Irishmen, Dr. R.R. Madden
Antrim and Down in 1798, Dr. R.R. Madden
A History of the Augustinians in Dublin, Fr. T.C. Butler, OSA
A History of the Catholic Church in Australia, Cardinal Moran, re Fr. J. Harold
Newcastle Lyons
A Parish of the Pale (Geography Publications) re Fr. J. Harold
When they followed Henry Joy, Michael O'Flanagan
Brother Luke Cullen, MS9760, N.L.I.
The Prison Journal of Anne Devlin, Edited by John Finnegan
The Unfortunate Mr. Robert Emmet, Leon Ó Broin
The Emmet Insurrection, J.W. Hammond (D.H.R. Vol IX)
Cloncurry MSS 5657/8/9, N.L.I.

Personal Recollections, Lord Cloncurry
The Year of Liberty, Thomas Packenham (re Fox & Geese incident)

Chapters 16–18

Regency Rogue (Dan Donnelly), Patrick Myler
Act of George 3 (1818) Enclosure of Commons (T.C.D.)
The Gorgeous Mask, Edited by D. Dickson (Trinity History Workshop) re road relief works.
The Travellers New Guide through Ireland 1815 (John Cummins)
History of Richmond Barracks, George Campbell, former teacher St. Michaels C.B.S.
Dublin Military Barracks, Comdt. P.D. O'Donnell (D.H.R. 1971)
Crown & Castle, Edward Bryan
Irish Papermaking & Excise Duty, Professor T.P. O'Neill
Paper Making in the British Isles, A.H. Shorten
Progress in Irish Printing, H. Ewen (Alex Thom 1936)
History of Corkagh and the Camac, J.R.W. Dick
St. Catherines Bells, Walter Meyler
History of Dublin Catholic Cemeteries, William Fitzpatrick
Glasnevin Cemetery Records, courtesy Mr. George McCullough, General Manager
Freemans Journal, October 1829
A History of the Catholic Church in Australia (containing wording on Fr. Harold's tombstone), Cardinal Moran
The impact of the Great Famine, Pat Cooke (Old Inchicore & Kilmainham Journal No. 3)
Thoms Directory 1850

Chapters 19–21

The Great Southern & Western Railway, Kevin Murray & D.B. McNeill (Irish Railway Record Society)
Dublin Transport, Kevin Murray (Victorian Dublin 1980)
Iompair Éireann, Cyril McIntyre (Inniú, Sept. 1973)
The Works, Greg Ryan
The Engineer (5/9/1879)
The Railway Magazine
Link Magazine 1953 (C.I.E.)
On The Move, Micheál Ó Riain
Across a Century 1956 (Oblate Centenary Record)
Father W.M.J. Ring O.M.I. by Móna Ní Thuairisg
Programme of 1923 Oblate Fete courtesy of Rev. Fr. W. McGonagle O.M.I. contains information re Fr. Cooke and the Railway Works which is not in "Across a Century" (Oblate Centenary record)
A History of the Augustinian Friars in Dublin, Fr. T.C Butler O.S.A.
The Lourdes Messenger 1902 re Brother Costigan, O.M.I.
The Irish Builder 1868 (Dublin Townships)
Dublin Corporation Archives (Dublin Townships)
Dublin, The Deposed Capital, Mary E. Daly
District Map, Frank Matthews & Seamus Farmer

Chapters 22–28

The Phoenix Park Murders, Tom Coyle
Twenty Five Years, Catherine Tynan
Mr. E. Joynt's Journal

Pre-Trial statements, Pages 63, 64, 190, 191, 199, 200 N.L.I.
Tipperary's G.A.A. Story, Canon Fogarty
Catch & Kick, Eoghan Corry
"Sport", Freemans Journal
D.M.P. Records 523W/9662, National Archives
Liffey Gaels, Brother D.J. Vaughan
Jamestown Races, Freemans Journal
Parnell, Freemans Journal & Irish Times reports
Inchicore House, W.A. Henderson (Evening Herald, October 1919)
Irish Names of Places, Patrick Joyce
Logainmneacha B.Á.C., Éamonn de h-Óir (Studia Hibernica 1975)
Traditions of Clondalkin, Liam Ua Broin (J.R.S.A.I 1944)
Ballyfermot Castle, E.R. Dix (Irish Builder Vol. 40 1898)
Sir Roland FitzEustace, Lord of Portlester, Rory O'Farrell
Irish Quarterly Review 1858 (Goldenbridge reformatory)
Goldenbridge The View From Valperiso, Theresa Durkin
Irish Christian Advocate (14/8/1885)
Story of a Soldiers Life, Lord Wolseley
The Life of Lord Wolseley, Maurice & Arthurs
The Dublin "She Barracks", Anthony Kinsella (The Irish Sword 1992)

Chapters 29–32

The Engineers strike at Inchicore Railway Works, Hugh Geraghty and Peter Rigney (Saothar)
Dublin Corporation Archives (Housing Committee)
Ernest Joynt Memoirs
St. Judes Centenary Record, 1964
The Irish Worker 1913 (July)
History of the Irish Citizen Army, R.M. Fox
"Feachtas na gCairteacha", Seán Mac Mathúna (Feasta, Samhain 1979)
Have You Heard of William Partridge?, Hugh Geraghty (Liberty, April 1978)
The Mallin Family, Seosamh Ó Mealláin (Inniú 1966)

Chapters 33–36

Reminiscences of an Irish Volunteer, Peadar Doyle (United Ireland Magazine Oct. 1935)
Francis Ledwidge, Alice Curtayne
Francis Ledwidge, The Poems Complete, Liam O'Meara
Irish Times Rebellion Handbook 1916
Under the Starry Plough, Frank Robbins
Cuimhní Chinn, Liam Ó Briain
The Defence of the South Dublin Union, Major J.V. Joyce (an t-Oglach)
Richmond Barracks, George Campbell
With the Marrowbone Lane Garrison, Capt. T. Young (an t-Oglach)
Capuchin Annual 1942
Intelligence Notes, B. MacGiolla Choille
A Chronicle of Jails, Darell Figgis
Joseph Doyle Remembers (article by Thomas Fox, Evening Herald 7/9/1964)
Seán T. – Reminiscences of former President Seán T. Ó Ceallaigh.
Alan L. Ramsay. From Ballsbridge to South Dublin Union, A. Kinsella (D.H.R. XLVIII, 1945)

Chapters 37–43

O'Connor family papers
Peadar Doyle family papers
George Dwyer papers
Edward Bennett papers
Mick Morrissey article (Irish Press 12/10/53)
Nellie Bushell, S. Scully (D.H.R. 1988)
Nellie Bushell, T. Finnegan (Evening Herald 12/4/63)
Nellie Bushell, May Craig Abbey Memories
The Dublin Brigade Handbook
War by the Irish, John McCann
Dublin's Fighting Story (Published by The Kerryman)
Seán Treacy, Desmond Ryan
On Another Man's Wound, Ernie O'Malley
The Works, Greg Ryan
Ernest Joynt Journal and Railway Recollections (in more detail in Locomotive Magazine 1933)
The Last Post (National Graves Association)
History of the Irish Army, Lt. Col. J. Duggan
Constance de Markievicz, Jacqueline Van Voris (1967)
Prison Letters of Countess Markievicz, Esther Roper
Conversations with Comdt. Sean Dowling, O/C 4th Batt., Michael Dwyer, Michael O'Neill, Paddy Ryan, Phil Robinson (nephew of Capt. J. Donnelly), Mrs. A. McElroy, Mrs. O'Connell & Mrs. Cullen

Chapters 44–56

Father John O'Sullivan (Intercom newsletter)
Garda Siochana Archives, Dublin Castle
Across a Century (Oblate Fathers)
Catholic Standard 14/2/1941
St. Patrick's Athletic Records
Roadstone 21 Years (Tom Roche Senior)
Irish National War Memorial Committee
The "Wran" Verses (courtesy Rita Woodfull)
Old Railway Verses (courtesy Pat Byrne)
Dublin's Pubs, Eamonn Casey
Grand Jury Presentations (Dublin Co. Council)
Records of Registrar, Friendly Societies (National Archives)
An Claidheamh Solais, 3/11/1900 (Public Meeting)
Dublin Corporation Archives (Reports of Housing Committee)
Memorials of the Dead
Austin Cooper (Sketches, Notes & Diaries)
Dublin Tavern Tokens, Arthur E.J. Went (D.H.R. Vol. 21)
Lourdes Messenger July 1973 (The Model School, George Brown)
Malachy Horan Remembers, Dr. George A. Little
Peadar Kearney, Seamus de Burca (D.H.R. 1974)
Some Rentals of the Earl of Shelbourne's estates, Thomas Kelly (D.H.R. ii)
South County Dublin Harriers, James E. Norton
Dublin International Exhibition, Nellie O'Cleirigh (D.H.R. 1994)

Iompair Éireann, Cyril McIntyre (Inniú, Sept. 1973)
Irish Book Lover, Vol. XV re Shakespeare House
Old Inchicore & Kilmainham Journal No 2 (Peter Keenahan) re Shakespeare House

Also

A History of Co. Dublin (John D'Alton)
A History of Co. Dublin (Frances E. Ball)
The Neighbourhood of Dublin (W. Joyce)
Sources for Local Studies (Dr. W. Nolan)
Wilson's Directory
Pettigrew & Oulton's Directory
Thom's Directory
Reminiscences of Frank Kelly

Photo Credits, courtesy of:

National Museum, pages 2, 8, 9, 11, 12, 14, 187, 196, 212
Department of Arts, Culture, Gaeltacht and the Islands, pages 1, 7, 45
National Library, pages 42, 55, 100, 121
Iarnród Éireann, pages 105, 130, 209, 294
Kilmainham Jail, page 213
National Portrait Gallery, page 50
Evening Herald, page 156
Oblate Fathers, pages 111, 112, 114, 240
John Kennedy, page 108, 229
W.A. Camwell, cover photo
Cyril McIntyre, page 296
Seamus Robinson, page 159
Dr. W. Boles, pages 59, 65, 160, 161, 253, 298
Patrick Healy, pages 235, 236, 262
Liam Dillon, page 161
Tommy Kelly, page 63
The Cant family, page 139
Deirdre Farrell, pages 250, 277
Seán Quigley, page 245
William R. Dick, page 287
John Byrne, page 113
Michael O'Neill, page 286
Edward King, page 3
Tim Dawson, pages 20, 80
Frank Murphy, pages 143, 290
John Nesbitt, page 89
Shay Whelan, page 181
Rita McGowan, page 147
Ethel Woodful, page 234
Popperfoto, pages 188, 189
Thomas Fagan, pages 19, 241
Joseph Guilfoyle, page 176
Pearse Doyle, page 183
Mary Foley, page 247
Diarmuid O'Connor, page 210
W. Goggins, page 220